*New Perspectives in German Studies*

**General Editors:** Professor Michael Butler, Head of Department of German Studies, University of Birmingham and Professor William Paterson, Director of the Institute of German Studies, University of Birmingham

Over the last twenty years the concept of German studies has undergone major transformation. The traditional mixture of language and literary studies, related very closely to the discipline as practised in German universities, has expanded to embrace history, politics, economics and cultural studies. The conventional boundaries between all these disciplines have become increasingly blurred, a process which has been accelerated markedly since German unification in 1989/90.

**New Perspectives in German Studies**, developed in conjunction with the Institute for German Studies at the University of Birmingham, has been designed to respond precisely to this trend of the interdisciplinary approach to the study of German and to cater for the growing interest in Germany in the context of European integration. The books in this series will focus on the modern period, from 1750 to the present day.

*Titles include:*

Michael Butler and Robert Evans (*editors*)
THE CHALLENGE OF GERMAN CULTURE
Essays Presented to Wilfried van der Will

Michael Butler, Malcolm Pender and Joy Charnley (*editors*)
THE MAKING OF MODERN SWITZERLAND 1848–1998

Jonathan Grix
THE ROLE OF THE MASSES IN THE COLLAPSE OF THE GDR

New Perspectives in German Studies
Series Standing Order ISBN 0-333-92430-4 hardcover
Series Standing Order ISBN 0-333-92434-7 paperback
(*outside North America only*)

You can receive future titles in this series as they are published by placing a standing order. Please contact your bookseller or, in case of difficulty, write to us at the address below with your name and address, the title of the series and the ISBN quoted above.

Customer Services Department, Macmillan Distribution Ltd, Houndmills, Basingstoke, Hampshire RG21 6XS, England

Wilfried van der Will

# The Challenge of German Culture

## Essays Presented to Wilfried van der Will

Edited by

**Michael Butler**
*Professor of Modern German Literature*
*University of Birmingham*

and

**Robert Evans**
*Lecturer in German*
*University of Birmingham*

First published 2000 by
PALGRAVE
Houndmills, Basingstoke, Hampshire RG21 6XS and
175 Fifth Avenue, New York, N.Y. 10010
Companies and representatives throughout the world

PALGRAVE is the new global academic imprint of
St. Martin's Press LLC Scholarly and Reference Division and
Palgrave Publishers Ltd (formerly Macmillan Press Ltd).

ISBN 0–333–80090–7

This book is printed on paper suitable for recycling and
made from fully managed and sustained forest sources.

A catalogue record for this book is available
from the British Library.

Library of Congress Cataloging-in-Publication Data
The challenge of German culture / essays presented to Wilfried van der Will
/ edited by Michael Butler and Robert Evans.
     p. cm. — (New perspectives in German studies)
   Includes bibliographical references and index.
   ISBN 0–333–80090–7
     1. German literature—History and criticism. 2. German studies.
   I. Butler, Michael, 1935– II. Evans, Robert, 1964– III. Series.

   PT36.B88 C43 2000
   830.9—dc21
                                                        00–041509

10   9   8   7   6   5   4   3   2
09   08   07   06   05   04   03   02

Printed and bound in Great Britain by
Antony Rowe Ltd, Chippenham, Wiltshire

# Contents

# Wilfried van der Will

Wilfried van der Will first came to Birmingham over forty years ago to study as an Occasional Student for two terms during his career as an undergraduate at Cologne University, which also included a semester at the University of Vienna. Having passed his *Abitur* in 1955 at the grammar school in St Tönis near Krefeld, he was awarded a prestigious scholarship by the Studienstiftung des deutschen Volkes to read German, English, Philosophy and Sociology at Cologne. The arrival in Birmingham of this precocious talent did not escape the eagle eye of Roy Pascal, who promptly invited him to take up a Lektorship in the German Department once he had completed his degree.

Returning to Cologne, Wilfried finished his PhD (on Gerhart Hauptmann), immediately followed by the First State Examination, to the profound irritation of his German professors who were compelled by etiquette to address him as 'Herr Doktor' throughout his viva. A year as a Colloquial Assistant in the Victorian splendour of the Arts Faculty in Edmond Street in central Birmingham with colleagues of the calibre of Roy Pascal, Siegbert Prawer, Richard Hinton Thomas, Bill Lockwood and Bernard Standring – the doyenne of the Department, Caroline Cunningham, who was to become a close friend, was already ensconced on the Edgbaston Campus – was an ideal training in the arcane mysteries of British university life. Not surprisingly, Wilfried was offered an Assistant Lectureship the following year and his fate was sealed: there followed promotion to a full Lectureship in 1964, a Senior Lectureship in 1982, a Readership in Modern German Studies in 1988 and a Personal Chair in 1990.

Such bare facts hardly do justice to a career which has had a decisive impact on German Studies in his adopted country. One of the first exponents of multidisciplinarity, drawing on social, political, literary and art history, Wilfried van der Will has published a string of books, each of which punctuates the broad stages of development that have taken place over the last thirty years in British German Studies. His first brief monograph, *Pikaro heute* (1967), drew attention to a persistent cultural theme in the work of Thomas Mann, Döblin, Brecht and Grass and exerted an influence far beyond its modest size. At a time when scholarship in German Studies was still predominantly an affair of the solitary researcher,

Wilfried proceeded to anticipate by over a decade the move towards more collaborative work in the profession with his partnership first with Richard Hinton Thomas, then with his own PhD student Rob Burns, and most recently with Brandon Taylor and Eva Kolinsky.

These books invariably opened up fresh approaches and fresh fields of enquiry. The van der Will and Hinton Thomas volume, *The German Novel and the Affluent Society* (1968) – together with a German version substantially reworked and enlarged by Wilfried, *Der deutsche Roman und die Wohlstandsgesellschaft* (1969) – swiftly established itself as a classic study of the post-war German novel. Like all first-class research, it grew directly out of teaching – in this case the highly innovative MA in Contemporary German Language, Literature and Society which the Birmingham Department ran from 1966 to 1969 and which drew on sociological theory to illuminate literary texts. The same methodological innovation marks Wilfried's major collaborative work with Rob Burns, in particular the two volumes on the 'Arbeiterkulturbewegung' in the Weimar Republic and the equally pioneering *Protest and Democracy in West Germany* (1982). In many ways, Wilfried's wide-ranging cultural interests are summed up in the two edited volumes, *The Nazification of Art* (1990, with Brandon Taylor) and *The Cambridge Companion to Modern German Culture* (1998, with Eva Kolinsky). Bringing together scholars from a variety of disciplines, these books underline the advantages to be gained from broadening the discipline's range and embracing the creative tensions of interdisciplinarity.

The Birmingham Department's success in winning a fierce competition to found a DAAD-supported 'centre of excellence' in German Studies, the brainchild of the then German Ambassador, Hermann von Richthofen, was due in no small measure to Wilfried's energetic input into the Department's and University's concept for the Institute for German Studies, which opened its doors in 1994 under the Directorship of Willie Paterson. It was a natural decision to second Wilfried for the first three years as Deputy Director to help launch the new postgraduate Institute with its emphasis on contemporary German politics, economics, history and cultural studies within the European context. With its insistence on a high competence in the German language as a bedrock skill, the IGS complements the Department's work and has enormously enriched teaching and research in German Studies at Birmingham.

It is precisely in the area of 'Europe' that the Birmingham German Department has been fortunate in having such a committed European as Wilfried van der Will on its staff for the last forty years. He has ensured that German Studies at Birmingham have remained constantly open to innovation and experiment. German literature and language, philosophy, history and politics are Wilfried's predominant interests and his profession of them has enthused generations of undergraduates and postgraduates, a considerable number of whom have gone on themselves to successful university careers. These scholarly pursuits are the expression of a temperament peculiar, perhaps, to the Rhineland: an undogmatic belief in historical materialism is leavened by a refreshing streak of hedonism; high intellectual seriousness, although driven by an almost Protestant work-ethic, still bears the traces of a Catholic childhood visible perhaps only to the trained eye. Such a complex and paradoxical amalgam has kept his Birmingham colleagues constantly on their cultural toes. A happy marriage and a daughter who is firmly bent on matching her father's vitality add up to a career that anyone could envy. But envy is not the word. The only adequate response to Wilfried's contribution to the University of Birmingham in particular, and to German Studies in general, is to recall the words of Goethe's Ottilie in *Die Wahlverwandtschaften*: 'Gegen große Vorzüge eines andern gibt es kein Rettungsmittel als die Liebe.' In an analogous spirit of collegial affection we present these essays to Wilfried to mark his 65th birthday and his official retirement.

*Michael Butler*
*September, 2000*

# Notes on the Contributors

KEITH BULLIVANT: Professor of German, Department of Germanic and Slavic Studies, University of Florida, Gainesville, USA.

ROB BURNS: Professor of German Studies, Department of German Studies, University of Warwick.

MICHAEL BUTLER: Professor of Modern German Literature and Head of the Department of German Studies, University of Birmingham.

BILL DODD: Reader in German, Department of German Studies, University of Birmingham.

MANFRED DURZAK: Professor of Modern German Literature, University of Paderborn, Germany.

ROBERT EVANS: Lecturer in German, Department of German Studies, University of Birmingham.

JONATHAN GRIX: Assistant Director, Institute for German Studies, University of Birmingham.

NIGEL HARRIS: Senior Lecturer in German, Department of German Studies, University of Birmingham.

DAVID HILL: Senior Lecturer in German, Department of German Studies, University of Birmingham.

CHARLIE JEFFERY: Professor of German Politics and Deputy Director, Institute for German Studies, University of Birmingham.

MARTIN KANE: Reader in Modern German Studies, School of European and Modern Language Studies, University of Kent at Canterbury.

JOHN KLAPPER: Senior Lecturer in German, Department of German Studies, University of Birmingham.

EVA KOLINSKY: Research Professor in German History, University of Wolverhampton.

GÜNTER MINNERUP: Lecturer in German, Department of German Studies, University of Birmingham.

**WILLIAM E. PATERSON:** Professor and Director of the Institute for German Studies, University of Birmingham.

**RICHARD SHEPPARD:** Titular Professor of German and Fellow of Magdalen College, Oxford.

**RONALD SPEIRS:** Professor of German, Department of German Studies, University of Birmingham.

**MARTIN SWALES:** Professor of German, Department of German, University College London.

**RUTH WHITTLE:** Lecturer in German, Department of German Studies, University of Birmingham.

# 1

# Hadubrand's 'Frageversäumnis' in the *Hildebrandslied*

*Robert Evans*

## I

The Old High German *Hildebrandslied* needs little introduction. Comprising sixty-eight lines, some of them incomplete, of alliterative verse, the poem represents the only surviving fragment of a Germanic heroic lay from the Old High German period.[1] A narrator recounts how two warriors, Hildebrand and Hadubrand, face each other in single combat as the champions of their respective armies. In accordance with warrior custom, Hildebrand, the older man, asks his opponent about the latter's parentage. Hadubrand's answer, however, causes Hildebrand to realize that the man he is about to engage in mortal combat is none other than his own son, the infant whom he had abandoned some thirty years earlier when fleeing into exile with Dietrich, his feudal lord, in order to escape from their deadly enemy Otacher. Hildebrand tries to persuade Hadubrand of this fact and attempts a reconciliation, but Hadubrand will have none of it, claiming that his father is dead and rejecting Hildebrand's approaches as treacherous. Hildebrand must now decide whether he should unilaterally refuse to fight and thereby betray his lord and army, suffering in consequence a very public loss of honour, or join battle with his own son. Reluctantly he adopts the latter course. The fighting is being described in all its savagery when the text abruptly breaks off, giving no indication as to the outcome of the encounter.

One puzzling question raised by the *Hildebrandslied* appears to have been largely neglected by previous commentators: namely, why is it that Hadubrand makes no attempt to test the veracity of Hildebrand's claim to be his long-lost father?[2] Hadubrand could surely establish once and for all whether there is any truth in the older man's words by asking him a simple question (or questions) about his mother, Hildebrand's wife, a question which the stranger standing in front of him could only be expected to answer convincingly if he really were Hadubrand's father.[3] Even if we make the (arguably unwarranted) assumption that Hadubrand's mother died shortly after his father fled with Dietrich and whilst Hadubrand himself was still a small child,[4] there must be *something* which those who brought Hadubrand up had told him about his mother which he could now use to test whether Hildebrand's claim has any substance or not.[5] Yet Hadubrand does not seek to question Hildebrand in this way. Is this simply because he places no credence in Hildebrand's claim and hence sees no need to question him about it? Or does he perhaps refrain from questioning Hildebrand because he thinks that there might be some truth in the latter's claim and would rather not know for certain whether his adversary is indeed his long-lost father? This essay will examine the possible reasons why Hadubrand does not ask Hildebrand a question which could definitively establish for him whether the latter is his father or not. It will seek to explain Hadubrand's 'Frageversäumnis'.[6]

## II

Let us begin by exploring what grounds Hadubrand might have for believing that Hildebrand could be his father. First, it is plain that Hildebrand is old enough to be so. We know from the text that Hildebrand had sired a child before fleeing with Dietrich,

> 'her furlaet in lante luttila sitten
> prut in bure, barn unwahsan,
> arbeo laosa: her raet ostar hina.' (ll. 20–2)

> ('In his homeland he left sitting in his house
> his young wife and ungrown child, bereft of
> any inheritance. He rode off to the east.')

and that he has subsequently been in exile for thirty years:

'ih wallota sumaro enti wintro sehstic ur lante,' (l. 50)

('For sixty summers and winters I have been
wandering outside of my homeland.')

Moreover, that Hildebrand looks his age seems to be supported by the
fact that Hadubrand both calls him an 'alter Hun' (l. 39) and then refers
specifically to his advanced age a couple of lines later:

'pist also gialtet man, so du ewin inwit fortos.' (l. 41)

('You have reached such a great age by continually
having engaged in treachery.')

In other words, it is hard to imagine that Hadubrand does not realize
that the man standing in front of him is, if nothing else, at least the right
sort of age to be his father.

Second, Hildebrand's claim to be Hadubrand's father is arguably given
some substance by the fact that not only is Hildebrand still active as a
warrior at his advanced age, but he is also apparently the champion of
his army. Hadubrand clearly believes his father to have been an
outstanding warrior. This is demonstrated by the glowing terms in which
he describes him:

'her was Otachre ummet tirri,
degano dechisto miti Deotrichhe.
her was eo folches at ente: imo was eo fehta ti leop:
chud was her ... chonnem mannum.' (ll. 25–8)

('He was exceedingly hostile towards Otacher,
the most loyal of warriors to Dietrich. He was
always at the forefront of the army; fighting was
always very dear to him. He was known to brave
men.')

Encapsulated within these four lines we can see all the essential attributes
of a successful Germanic warrior in the Dark Ages: hostility towards one's
enemies (l. 25), loyalty to one's own leader (l. 26), bravery and a love of
fighting (l. 27), renown amongst one's peers (l. 28). Hadubrand must
realize, when Hildebrand first claims to be a close relative,

> 'wettu irmingot [quad Hiltibrant] obana ab hevane,
> dat du neo dana halt mit sus sippan man
> dinc ni gileitos ...' (ll. 30–2)

> ('I call almighty God from Heaven above', said
> Hildebrand, 'to witness that you have never
> engaged such a close kinsman in single combat.')

not only that his opponent is approximately the right age to be his father, but also that this man, still fighting and seemingly still the champion of his army at such an advanced age,[7] is likely to have had an exceptionally distinguished and successful military career. Hence he must possess the very same qualities which Hadubrand has attributed to his own long-lost father in lines 25–8.

Third, there is geographical evidence which might seem to Hadubrand to support Hildebrand's claim to be his father. In both line 18 ('forn her ostar giweit') and line 22 ('her raet ostar hina') we are told by Hadubrand that Hildebrand fled east with Dietrich. When Hildebrand comes to fight his son, he appears to be wearing Hunnish armour and/or trappings:

> want her do ar arme wuntane bauga,
> cheisuringu gitan, so imo se der chuning gap,
> Huneo truhtin: 'dat ih dir it nu bi huldi gibu.' (ll. 33–5)[8]

> (He then unwound from his arm spiral rings made
> of imperial gold which the king, the lord of the
> Huns, had given him: 'I now give you this as a
> token of friendship.')

This fact is not lost on Hadubrand, who refers to his opponent as an 'alter Hun' (l. 39).[9] If Hadubrand can recognize Hildebrand's equipment as being that of a Hun, then he clearly has some knowledge of who the Huns are and therefore where they come from. In other words, Hadubrand is highly likely to have known that the Huns, amongst whom his adversary has clearly spent time, came from the east,[10] the same direction in which his father and Dietrich had last been seen heading some thirty years previously.

A fourth reason for arguing that Hadubrand may suspect that there is some truth in Hildebrand's claim concerns the apparent difference in tone between Hadubrand's statement in line 29 that he does not think that his father is still alive, 'ni waniu ih iu lib habbe ...'

('I do not think that he is still alive.')

and his unequivocal assertion in line 44, namely after Hildebrand has claimed kinship (l. 31) and has offered Hadubrand his arm-rings as a token of friendship (ll. 33–5), that his father is dead:

'tot ist Hiltibrant, Heribrantes suno.'

('Hildebrand, son of Heribrand, is dead.')

Whilst Hadubrand's statement in line 44 makes it clear that he has understood Hildebrand's claim to be a 'sippan man' (l. 31) as a claim to be his father,[11] there also seems to be a case here for arguing that the change in Hadubrand's tone from one of supposition in line 29 to one of certainty in line 44 may reflect an inner crisis brought on by the realization that the man standing before him could indeed be his long-lost father. In other words, line 44 may represent the culmination of a desperate and panic-stricken attempt on Hadubrand's part (beginning with the ostensible rejection of Hildebrand's peace-offering in lines 37–8 and followed by an accusation of treachery against the older man in lines 39–41) to convince himself, in the light of the doubts raised in his mind by Hildebrand's claims, that his father really is dead, and that this opponent, with whom he believes he has no choice but to do battle, must therefore be a treacherous liar whom he can kill with a clear conscience.[12]

## III

The arguments marshalled hitherto suggest that Hadubrand may refrain from questioning Hildebrand and thereby testing the veracity of the latter's claim to be his long-lost father because he is afraid that this claim may be true. It is now time to examine the case for arguing that Hadubrand does not try to establish whether there is any truth in Hildebrand's claim because he simply does not believe it and therefore does not see any need to investigate it any further.

First, it must be remembered that, at the time of his encounter with Hildebrand, Hadubrand has seemingly believed for some time that his father is dead. We are not told for precisely how long he has believed this, only that he was informed of his father's death by seafarers:

'dat sagetun mi seolidante
westar ubar wentilseo, dat inan wic furnam:' (ll. 42–3)

('Seafarers travelling westwards across the
Mediterranean told me that a battle took him away.')

Although Hadubrand has been told of his father's death by strangers and not by his own people (the 'usere liuti' of line 15, who had told him of his father's character and subsequent flight), there are two good reasons why he should believe their reports to be true. The seafarers have not just told Hadubrand that his father is dead, but they have also told him *how* his father died (that is, in battle), something which would surely have lent credence to their claims that Hildebrand was dead. Furthermore, Hadubrand states that the seafarers were sailing *westwards* across the Mediterranean, that is to say they were coming from the east, the direction in which Hildebrand had earlier fled. Given, therefore, that the seafarers were coming from the direction in which Hildebrand was last seen heading (albeit some years earlier), it does not seem unreasonable for Hadubrand to accept that they could well have come across people who had known Hildebrand and who knew of his fate. If Hadubrand has these good reasons for accepting what the seafarers had told him as the truth and if their version of events has remained unchallenged throughout the intervening period, why should Hadubrand *not* reject Hildebrand's claim to be a 'sippan man' (that is, his father) as a total and outrageous fabrication?

This interpretation, however, requires an explanation for Hadubrand's change of tone in line 44 as against line 29. If Hadubrand is already firmly convinced in line 29 that his father is dead, then why does he use the verb *wānen* and seemingly introduce an element of doubt about this fact? Why does he not simply state that his father *is* dead as he subsequently does in line 44? The most plausible explanation for Hadubrand's behaviour seems to lie in a change in his attitude towards his opponent, a change which takes place as a direct result of Hildebrand's claim to be a 'sippan man' (l. 31) and his offer of arm-rings as a token of friendship (ll. 33–5). Throughout his speech in answer to Hildebrand's questions about his parentage (ll. 15–29), Hadubrand is both polite and forthcoming, quite happily supplying the older man with all the relevant information.[13] His use of *wānen* can be seen as an indication of his courtesy. Rather than simply concluding his speech with an abrupt and unequivocal 'my father is dead', he 'hedges' using *wānen* in order to be more polite, even though he has no doubts that his father is indeed dead.[14] In short, Hadubrand behaves throughout his speech in lines 15–29 in a professional manner and one befitting his status as the champion of his army. The same cannot, however, be said of Hildebrand in lines 30–5, and it is arguably Hildebrand's words and actions in these six lines which bring about the change in Hadubrand's attitude towards his opponent. If Hadubrand is firmly convinced that his father is dead, then he can only regard Hildebrand's claim to be his father as both preposterous and, perhaps even more damagingly, as a cynical misuse of the information he has so politely, readily and professionally supplied.[15] As if this were not enough for Hadubrand, his opponent then proceeds to offend still further against the warrior's professional code of conduct by making a peace-offering to a man with whom he is about to engage in mortal combat.[16] Under these circumstances it is hardly surprising that Hadubrand abandons his earlier politeness and rejects Hildebrand's words as lies and his actions as treachery:[17]

'mit geru scal man geba infahan,
ort widar orte ...
du bist dir alter Hun, ummet spaher,
spenis mih mit dinem wortun, wili mih dinu speru werpan.
pist also gialtet man, so du ewin inwit fortos.' (ll. 37–41)[18]

('One should receive such a gift with the lance,
point against point. You old Hun, you are exceedingly
cunning. You entice me with your words, but you want
to hurl your spear at me. You have reached such a great
age by continually having engaged in treachery.')

Second, the fact that Hildebrand proffers his son arm-rings as a peace-offering may in itself serve to support the view that Hadubrand does not believe a word of the older man's claims. It has been argued earlier that if Hadubrand suspects there might be some truth in Hildebrand's claim to be his father, his grounds for not seeking to question Hildebrand and establish once and for all whether or not it is true may be that he would rather fight whilst clinging to the belief that the man before him might not be his father, than face the prospect of having to fight in the certain knowledge of his adversary's true identity. This argument is only valid, however, if it is impossible for Hadubrand to back out of the combat; that is, if his loyalty to his leader and his army, combined with his warrior's pride and sense of honour, exclude the possibility of him refusing to fight. Whether Hadubrand does have any scope for refusing to fight is something which we shall probably never know, but Hildebrand, for his part, does seem to have some scope for doing so – hence his peace-offering to Hadubrand in lines 33–5. Hildebrand manifestly feels that he can refuse to fight such a close kinsman without compromising his loyalty or honour, but only on one very important condition, namely that his opponent does likewise. In other words, a bilateral refusal to fight appears in Hildebrand's eyes to be permissible, whereas a unilateral refusal on his part does not. That this is so can be seen in Hildebrand's comments after his peace-offering has been rejected and he has resigned himself to proceeding with the combat:

> 'der si doh nu argosto [quad Hiltibrant] ostarliuto,
> der dir nu wiges warne, nu dih es so wel lustit,' (ll. 58–9)

> ('May he now be the most cowardly of the eastern
> people', said Hildebrand, 'who would refuse you combat,
> now that you are so eager for it.')

If Hildebrand perceives it to be legitimate to agree, under certain circumstances (such as his opponent being a kinsman), to a bilateral refusal to engage in combat without any damage to his reputation, then it is reasonable to assume that Hadubrand – like his opponent, a Germanic warrior and the champion of his lord's army – might think similarly. Moreover, it could be argued that Hildebrand might not have troubled to make such a public peace-offering[19] if he did not think that Hadubrand, like himself, had some room for manoeuvre in the matter of whether to fight or not. If Hadubrand does indeed have some scope for refusing to fight, albeit bilaterally, his failure even to attempt to establish whether or not Hildebrand is his father would seem to suggest that he simply does not believe a word of what Hildebrand says.

A third piece of evidence in support of the view that Hadubrand simply does not believe his opponent's claim to be his father can be found in lines 58–9. Hildebrand, effectively now resigned to the prospect of having to do battle with his own son, says that only the most cowardly eastern warrior would deny Hadubrand the combat now that he is so eager for it. This last comment may be highly significant. In stating 'nu dih es (= wiges) so wel lustit' (l. 59), Hildebrand is concluding that Hadubrand, far from simply not being prepared to pull out of the combat, positively *wants* it to take place (hence the use of the verb *lusten*[20]). After standing face to face with Hadubrand, hearing what he has to say and observing his reactions to all that has been said to him, Hildebrand, who is, after all, in the best position to judge such things, seemingly does not detect even the slightest sign of doubt in Hadubrand. Either Hadubrand has a quite exceptional talent for concealing his true feelings, or else he simply has no doubts because he does not believe that Hildebrand can possibly be his father.

## IV

What, then, can be concluded about the reasons behind Hadubrand's 'Frageversäumnis' in the *Hildebrandslied*? Does he refrain from testing the veracity of Hildebrand's claim to be his father because he is afraid that it may be true and would rather cling to the hope that the man before him, whom he must shortly engage in mortal combat, might not be his father? Or does he simply not believe Hildebrand's claim in the first place and thus sees no need to investigate it any further? Although it has been shown that a case can be made from the text for both inter-pretations, the latter appears ultimately to be far more plausible. The crucial issue here seems to be that any argument in support of the alternative viewpoint has to be based on the assumption that Hadubrand's words and behaviour throughout the text are not to be taken at face value. It requires that Hadubrand's dismissal of Hildebrand's claim as lies, his rejection of the latter's peace-offering as treachery and the insults which he heaps upon the older man in the process (ll. 37–44), should not be seen as a reflection of his utter contempt for Hildebrand's words and actions, but should instead be regarded as a desperate attempt on Hadubrand's part to remove the seeds of doubt which Hildebrand's words have planted in his mind. Such an interpretation of Hadubrand's words and behaviour, however, seems rather far-fetched for a number of reasons. Although it can be argued, for example, that Hildebrand may strike Hadubrand as being the right age to be the latter's father and that he is returning from the same direction in which Hadubrand knows his father to have fled many years earlier, Hadubrand, as we have seen, has very good grounds for believing his father to be dead. Moreover, Hadubrand's change of tone between line 29 and line 44 in all probability reflects not a panic-stricken attempt to overcome his doubts and convince himself that his adversary is not his father, but rather an indignant reaction to what he perceives to be dishonourable behaviour on Hildebrand's part. Finally, it is plain that Hildebrand himself appears by line 59 to have detected not the slightest indication of doubt in the younger man's words and actions (and

Hildebrand must surely have been looking and hoping for just such an indication), but has instead concluded that Hadubrand is as keen as ever to go ahead with the combat. In other words, Hildebrand, after observing Hadubrand at close quarters and listening to all he has to say, reluctantly comes to the conclusion that Hadubrand's words and actions can indeed only be taken at face value.

In summary, it seems to me that Hadubrand's 'Frageversäumnis' in the *Hildebrandslied* almost certainly stems from the fact that he simply never believes that there can be any truth in Hildebrand's claim to be his father and so sees no need to investigate this claim any further. The most obvious explanation appears, on this occasion at least, also to be the correct one.

## Notes

1. All line references are to the text as it appears in W. Braune and E. Ebbinghaus (eds), *Althochdeutsches Lesebuch* (17th edition, Tübingen, 1994), pp. 84–5. The translations are my own.
2. Hildebrand claims to be Hadubrand's father on two occasions in the text. The first occurs in line 31 when he tells Hadubrand that he (Hadubrand) has never engaged in combat against such a close kinsman ('sus sippan man'), and the second is in line 53 when Hildebrand refers to Hadubrand as his own dear child ('suasat chind'). Some commentators point out that on the first occasion Hildebrand does not state openly that he is Hadubrand's father, but claims only to be a kinsman – see for example B. Murdoch, *Old High German Literature* (Boston, 1983), p. 61. In this essay, however, I will show that, despite Hildebrand's apparent 'hedging', Hadubrand is in no doubt whatsoever that the older man is claiming to be his father at this point.
3. Given Hildebrand's (presumably exaggerated) claim that he knows all humanity ('chud ist mir al irmindeot', l. 13), Hadubrand would, to be on the safe side, probably need to ask him something more detailed than merely his (Hadubrand's) mother's name.
4. Neither the name nor the fate of Hadubrand's mother is revealed in the text. The only reference to her (l. 21) is as the young wife ('prut in bure') whom Hildebrand left behind when he fled with Dietrich. The grounds for thinking that she may have died while Hadubrand was still small are to be found in lines 15–17 when Hadubrand states that he was told who his father was by the old and the wise amongst his own people ('usere liuti, alte anti frote'). It is arguably unlikely that Hadubrand would have been given such information by anyone other than his mother if she were still alive.
5. Given that Hadubrand's people have clearly told him so much about his father (ll. 15–29), it seems inconceivable that they would not also have given him a certain amount of information about his mother.
6. The term 'Frageversäumnis', meaning 'failure to ask a question', has been used by some commentators in connection with Wolfram von Eschenbach's *Parzival*, especially with regard to the eponymous hero's failure, upon his

first visit to the Grail Castle, to ask his uncle Anfortas what ails him and so put an end to the latter's suffering (*Parzival*, 255, esp. ll. 17–19).

7. It is difficult to know what the average male life expectancy was in Europe around AD 500, but there can be no doubt that Hildebrand has exceeded it.

8. We are not told, however, whether the army of which Hildebrand is now the champion is itself Hunnish. H. Kuhn ('Hildebrand, Dietrich von Bern und die Nibelungen' in his *Text und Theorie*, Stuttgart, 1969, p. 131) believes that Hildebrand is still Dietrich's vassal and that the encounter with Hadubrand represents, in the legend of Dietrich von Bern, a stage in Dietrich's return from exile (perhaps with a Hunnish contingent in his army). Kuhn does not, on the other hand, think it likely that Hadubrand is fighting for Otacher – 'Kein Hörer wird leicht daraus ableiten, daß Hadubrand als Mann, gar als Vorkämpfer Odoakers auftritt' (p. 31).

9. Hadubrand may, of course, intend this remark as an insult – see note 18 below.

10. The Huns originated from Asia, but swept westwards during the fourth and fifth centuries AD, overrunning much of central and eastern Europe.

11. On this issue see F. Norman, *Three Essays on the 'Hildebrandslied'*, ed. A.T. Hatto (London, 1973), p. 20 and p. 45. Murdoch (*op. cit.*, p. 61) believes that Hildebrand possibly refrains from stating openly that he is Hadubrand's father in line 31 because he has been inhibited by Hadubrand's earlier remark (l. 22) that he and his mother were left 'arbeo laosa', namely without any inheritance, when his father fled with Dietrich. This possibility cannot be discounted, but it relies upon Hadubrand's 'arbeo laosa' either being intended as a criticism of his father or, if not, on it at least being regarded as such by Hildebrand. In the light of the praise which Hadubrand subsequently heaps upon his long-lost father (ll. 25–8), however, both of these interpretations of the remark appear unlikely.

12. I find it difficult to accept J. Knight Bostock's suggestion (*A Handbook on Old High German Literature*, 2nd edition revised by K.C. King and D.R. McLintock, Oxford, 1976, p. 53) that there is no significant change in Hadubrand's tone between line 29 and line 44. Bostock argues that Old High German *wānen*, 'to think, believe', implies greater conviction and certainty than its New High German derivative *wähnen*, 'to believe (mistakenly)'. Whilst there may be some validity in this argument, a wealth of historical and etymological evidence suggests that the Old High German verb meant 'to think, suppose, presume' and nothing more definite than that (that is, *wānen* still allowed for a degree of doubt) – see for example J. Splett, *Althochdeutsches Wörterbuch* (Berlin, 1993), I (2), p. 1059.

13. See Norman (*op. cit.*, p. 44).

14. I find implausible Gutenbrunner's explanation of line 29 as 'Die Vaterliebe hindert Hadubrand, schon an dieser Stelle zu sagen: "tot ist Hiltibrant"' – see S. Gutenbrunner, *Von Hildebrand und Hadubrand* (Heidelberg, 1976), pp. 99–100.

15. See Bostock (*op. cit.*, p. 51).

16. Norman (*op. cit.*, p. 20 and p. 45) argues that Hildebrand's invocation of the Almighty (l. 30) to bear witness to his claim to be a 'sippan man' further enrages Hadubrand in that the latter considers it blasphemous of Hildebrand

to invoke God in support of what he (Hadubrand) believes to be an outrageously false claim.

17. Hadubrand presumably thinks that Hildebrand is resorting to such measures because the latter recognizes that he has met in the younger man an opponent whom he cannot defeat by fair means.

18. Most commentators take Hadubrand's reference to Hildebrand as an 'alter Hun' at face value; that is, they are of the opinion that Hadubrand genuinely believes Hildebrand to be a Hun (see for example, Bostock (*op. cit.*, p. 51); Murdoch (*op. cit.*, p. 55); Norman (*op. cit.*, p. 45, note 4); W. Schröder, 'Hadubrands tragische Blindheit und der Schluß des *Hildebrandsliedes*', *Deutsche Vierteljahrsschrift für Literaturwissenschaft und Geistesgeschichte*, 37 (1963), pp. 481–97, esp. p. 481). This interpretation assumes, however, that Hildebrand's physical features, which the younger man can presumably see quite clearly (hence his references to Hildebrand's advanced age, ll. 39 and 41), seem to Hadubrand to be consistent with those of a Hun. Given that the Huns, unlike the Germani, do not appear to have been fair-skinned (see O. Maenchen-Helfen, *The World of the Huns*, California, 1973, pp. 360–4), such an assumption may not be justified. Furthermore, both A.T. Hatto ('On the Excellence of the *Hildebrandslied*', *Modern Language Review*, 68 (1973), pp. 820–38, esp. p. 835) and D.R. McLintock ('The Politics of the *Hildebrandslied*', *New German Studies*, 2 (1974), pp. 61–81, esp. p. 64) make the point that the Huns were widely distrusted and regarded as treacherous, so there may be grounds for thinking that Hadubrand is not using 'alter Hun' as a purely factual description of Hildebrand, but as a term of abuse, knowing full well from his opponent's physical features that this man is *not* a Hun.

19. Hildebrand's peace-offering is 'public' in that the encounter with Hadubrand seems to be taking place in the 'no-man's-land' between their armies ('untar heriun tuem', l. 3). It is hard to imagine that the armies would not have been looking on and have been able to observe Hildebrand's actions from a distance.

20. The Old High German verb *lusten*, 'to desire', is being used impersonally here, taking the accusative of the person desiring and the genitive of the thing desired.

# 2
# Willehalm and Puzzât, Guillelme and Baucent: The Hero and His Horse in Wolfram's *Willehalm* and in the *Bataille d'Aliscans*

*Nigel Harris*

## I

At the end of Book I of Wolfram von Eschenbach's *Willehalm*, the eponymous hero flees into the mountains surrounding the field of Alischanz, thereby escaping certain death at the hands of a huge Saracen army. The beginning of Book II describes him looking down on the field and seeing that it remains covered 'mit heidenschefte unbezalt,/ als ob ûf einer grôzen walt/ niht wan baniere blüeten' (58,5–7; 'with countless heathens, as though in a huge forest there were nothing blossoming but banners', p. 43);[1] and then, apparently out of the blue, he turns to his horse, Puzzât, and addresses him in the following terms:

> 'ouwê', sprach er, 'Puzzât,
> kundestû nû geben rât,
> war ich kêren möhte!
> wie mir dîn kraft getöhte
> waere wir an disen stunden
> gesunt und âne wunden,
> wolden mich die heiden jagen,

13

ez möhte etslîches mâc beklagen!
nû sî wir bêde unvarende
und ich die vreude sparende.
dû maht des wesen sicher:
wicken, habern, kicher,
gersten unde lindez heu,
daz ich dich dâ bî wol gevreu,
ob wir wider ze Oransche komen,
hânt mir'z die heiden niht benomen.
ich enhân trôstes mêr wan dich:
dîn snelheit müeze troesten mich.' (58,21 – 59,8)

('Alas', he said, 'Puzzât, if only you could advise me which way to turn!
How could I use your strength if we were now fit and free from
wounds! Then, if the heathens took it into their heads to chase me,
some of their kinsmen would have cause to regret it. Now both of us
are lame, and I am bereft of joy. You can be sure of one thing: if we
get back to Orange, provided that the heathens have not taken it away
from me, I shall make you happy with vetch and oats, peas, barley
and sweet hay. Now I have no solace but you. May your speed bring
me consolation.' (p. 43))

This brief scene, which contrasts starkly with the warlike activity
surrounding it, continues with a vivid description of the profusely
perspiring Puzzât, followed by an account of Willehalm wiping the sweat
from his horse's back and the latter in consequence regaining his
strength:

sîn hâr was im brûn gevar,
von wîzem schûme drûfe gar
als ez eins winders waere besnît.
der vürste nam sîn kursît,
einen pfelle, brâht von Trîant:
swaz er sweizes ûf dem orse vant,
den kund er drabe wol strîchen.
dô begunde im müede entwîchen:
ez dreste und grâzte,
von dem kunreiz ez sich mâzte
vil unkrefte, die ez truoc. (59,9–19)

(The horse's coat was brown, and covered all over with white foam, as if it had a winter's snow upon it. The noble Willehalm took his cloak, a piece of silk from Triant, and expertly he wiped all the sweat from the horse's back. Then Puzzât's weariness began to leave him: he snuffled and snorted, and thanks to Willehalm's care he recovered from the tremendous weariness which had come over him. (p. 43))

This is Puzzât's most extended appearance in the poem, but not his only one. In 37,10–13, he is named, along with Willehalm's sword Schoiûse, and we are told that Willehalm has performed 'manic rîterlîchiu getât' ('many deeds of chivalry', p. 33) on his back. Towards the end of Book I he is described as bearing the wounded Margrave away from Alischanz (56,10f.), wading in so doing through human blood ('sîn ors durh mannen bluot gewet', 56,14). A little later, he is accorded passing mentions in the scene in which Willehalm encounters his mortally wounded nephew Vivianz (61,19; 70,9f.; 71,17–19), and in his ensuing combats first with fifteen heathen kings and then with Tenebruns and Arofel (72,29; 77,14–17); but in 82,9, the narrator tells us, without offering any details, that he is badly wounded ('sêre wunt'). Having acquired Arofel's outstanding horse Volatîn, Willehalm now no longer needs Puzzât; but he sympathetically removes the latter's harness, 'daz ez sich hungers werte' ('so that he might find food for himself', 82,11; p. 54). In practice, however, the faithful steed decides to follow Willehalm wherever he goes ('mit im ez dan doch kêrte':/ swâ sîn herre vor im reit,/ die selben slâ ez niht vermeit', 82,12–14) – a loyal impulse which in fact works to Willehalm's disadvantage, in that it causes him shortly afterwards to be recognized by a group of Saracen knights (84,20 – 85,15). In the ensuing combat with them, Puzzât is killed, and Willehalm laments his loss ('Puzzât lac tôt,/ sîn ors: daz begund er klagen', 88,22f.).

## II

Neither Puzzât nor the close relationship he enjoys with his master is Wolfram's own invention. Rather, they are based on material found in Wolfram's principal source, the late twelfth-century *chanson de geste* known as the *Bataille d'Aliscans*. In this work, Puzzât's counterpart Baucent is first mentioned when he is addressed as follows by Willehalm's equivalent Guillelme:[2]

'Civaus', fait il, 'molt par estes laseç,
Se vos fuiseç qatre jorn soiorneç,
Ja me refusse as Sarrasins mellez,
Si m'en veniasse, car a mor sui navreç.[3]
Mais or voy bien, aider no me poeç,
Se dex m'aÿ, n'en doi estre blasmeç,
Car tot jorn molt bien serviç m'aveç.
Petit fu hoi, ne fuiseç galopeç,
De vos servise vos rent merci et greç.
S'estre poeç a Orence meneç,
N'i seroit sele devant dui mois paseç,
N'i manegerois d'orge, ne soit vaneç,
Dos fois et troys o les bacins cureç,
E li foraies iert jentis foinç de preç,
Trestot exliç e dex seixons fenés,
Ne beüsieç s'a vasiaus ne doreç;
Lo jor seroix catre foiç coreez
E dex ce[r]s pailes mult bien envelupeç.
Se en Spagne ies des paians meneç,
Si m'aït dex, mult en seroie ireç.' (581–99)

('My horse', he says, 'you are very tired. If you had rested for four days, I would have done battle with the Saracens again and would have avenged myself, for I am wounded to the death. But I now see very well that you cannot help me. May God help me, I am not to blame for it,[4] because you have always served me very well. There has hardly been a moment when I have not ridden you, and I give you grateful thanks for your service. If you could be taken back to Orange, no saddle would be placed on you there for two months; there you would only eat barley that had been sifted and cleaned three times in the basin; the forage would be excellent meadow-hay, all selected and cut in season; you would only drink out of a golden vessel; and you would be groomed four times a day and well covered in rich cloths. If you are taken to Spain by the heathens, God help me, I shall be very angry.')

As in *Willehalm*, the horse makes an immediate, and indeed remarkable response:

Bauçan l'entend si a fronchié dex neç
Aysi l'entend cum s'il fust hom seneç.
La teste drice si a des piez grateç,

Reprent s'aleine si est bien recovrez.
Ensi honist cum s'il fust lués geteç,
Fors de la stable et de novel ferez. (600–5)

(Baucent understands him and snorts through his nostrils – he understands him like a wise man. He holds his head up and paws [the ground] with his hooves; he gets his breath back and is fully recovered. He whinnies as if he had just been pushed out of the stable and been newly shod.)

In the *Aliscans*, there are in all four occasions on which Guillelme talks to Baucent. Two of these are merely short 'pep talks' before the combats with the fifteen kings and with Danebrus and Arïofles respectively: in 1083–5 Guillelme tells his mount that if he can carry him through, he will be well rewarded for this service ('mult vos cuit bien cest servise merir');[5] and in 1239–41 he thanks and encourages Baucent with the words 'mult le m'aveç ben fait', and expresses pleasure that he remains in good heart ('de bon hait'). The fourth, however, is more substantial. Finding himself a second time looking down over countless hordes of Saracens, Guillelme again turns to Baucent for companionship. He dismounts, rubs the horse's flanks and sides, kisses him most tenderly ('lo baise por molt grant amisteç', 722) and asks him what he will do ('qe la fareç?', 723). He then remarks that Baucent's flanks are wet with blood and perspiration ('mol voy vos flanç sanglant et tresüez', 724), and expresses sympathy both with his tiredness (725) and with his wounds ('forment me poise qant si iestes navréç', 727). Finally he reminds Baucent of his dependence on him, with the words 'se tu recroiç, a ma fin sui torneç' (728 – 'if you give way, it's the end of me'). Baucent's response then proceeds along similar lines to that recorded in 600–5. Again he both hears and understands Guillelme ('Bauçant l'oÿ si l'intendi aseç'), snorts ('ha fronché del nez', 730) and raises his head ('dreçe la testa', 731), and this time he also pricks up his ears ('dreçe l'oreile', 730). All in all, he is soon thoroughly reinvigorated ('revigoreç', 731).

Baucent, like Puzzât, also makes a series of fleeting appearances in the episodes in which Guillelme meets the dying Vivïen (807f., 1017, 1030f., 1063) and then kills the fifteen kings (1120, 1140); but he is severely injured by two of these kings, one of whom wounds him in the crop and the other in the side (1203). This almost causes Baucent's entrails to fall out ('li boel a poi n'en sont volé', 1204), but he miraculously survives, because God does not want him to die ('dex ne plait', 1206). Thereafter we are given regular reminders of Baucent's parlous state of health.

Shortly before the combat with Arïofles, Guillelme remarks that he can feel Baucent bleeding to death beneath him (1326f.); during the combat itself he can only move very slowly (1356); and after it, he is described as very weary (1535). This leads Guillelme to remove his equipment, so that he might not be captured by Saracens and be able to move more easily (1535–9). Nevertheless, Baucent still follows him (1547, 1561), thereby facilitating Guillelme's identification by his adversaries (1578, 1627). Soon afterwards Baucent is encircled by heathen soldiers and cut to pieces ('tot le detrencent', 1647). Guillelme mourns for him intensely ('Aÿ, Baucent, com vos avoy aimé!/ Ja mais meylor n'en aurai recovré,/ Molt sui por vos dolent e bosiné', 1685–7) ('Alas Baucent, how I loved you! I will never find a better. On your account I am very sad and bereft'); and, in his speech to Baudus immediately afterwards, he vows, at some peril to himself, to avenge the horse's death (1702–4).

It is surely already obvious that the relationship between the hero and his horse is presented in a largely similar way in *Willehalm* and in the *Aliscans*. In both works, they experience many things together and enjoy a close relationship; the two passages quoted at length above share several common motifs, such as the knight's recognition of his mount's weariness, his promise of appetizing fodder at Orange, and the horse's eventual recovery; moreover, the outlines of Puzzât's career and that of Baucent are essentially the same. Nevertheless, there are also several important differences between the two versions, which to my knowledge have never been studied before, but which arguably reveal much not only about the narrative techniques and priorities of the two poets, but also about their basic view of animals and the way they relate to humans. The remainder of this essay will briefly investigate some of these differences, dealing first with questions of literary technique and then with issues of animality and humanity.

## III

The most obvious difference between the presentation of Baucent and that of Puzzât is, of course, that the former is treated at considerably greater length. Not only does Guillelme address his mount on four occasions as against Willehalm's one, but the *Aliscans* also devotes much more attention to the horse's response to these words, and relates the circumstances of the latter stages of his career in markedly greater detail. *Willehalm* contains, for example, far fewer references to Puzzât's injuries and their consequences, and omits altogether to tell us how or at whose hands he is both initially wounded and later killed. Wolfram, then, simply omits much detail, presumably on the grounds that it is not germane to his primary narrative and thematic concerns. He also, however, conflates material from two originally discrete scenes to form one new one. The exchange between Willehalm and Puzzât quoted at the beginning of this essay is self-evidently based primarily on their duologue in *Aliscans* 581–605; but it also incorporates elements from their other substantial conversation, in *Aliscans* 720–31. These include the knight's statement of his dependence on his horse (728; 59,7f.), the motif of the latter's sweat (724; 59,9–15), and perhaps also the rubbing down of his sides (721; 59,14f.). Changes such as these are not only entirely characteristic of Wolfram's narrative technique,[6] but are also symptomatic of the kind of difference one would expect to obtain between a paratactically and paradigmatically structured *chanson de geste*, on the one hand, and a much more obviously syntagmatic, romance-influenced *opus mixtum*, on the other.

With regard to the additions that Wolfram has made to the Baucent material in the *Aliscans*, perhaps the most notable from the point of view of literary technique are his provision of introductory and background information concerning Puzzât, and his use of passages of vivid description. In 37,11–13, as we have seen, Willehalm's horse is specifically named as Puzzât, 'dâ manic rîterlîchiu getât/ ûf wart begangen'. Later, certain of these 'deeds of chivalry' are detailed by the heathens who observe the wounded, riderless Puzzât following in Willehalm's tracks: 'That horse was ridden by the man who killed Pinel and also slew our comrades Arfiklant and Turkant. It was the same horse which carried the man who killed Turpiun, the mighty King of Falturmie' (85,1–7; p. 55). These passages imply strongly that Wolfram felt it desirable to familiarize an audience otherwise ignorant of the *chanson de geste* tradition with certain basic information concerning it.[7] The French poet, by contrast, apparently sees no need to introduce Baucent in advance of his first conversation with Guillelme, nor to provide any details of events preceding those of the *Aliscans* itself. For him, it is perfectly legitimate to begin his narrative *in medias res*, given that it constituted merely a part of an extended cycle of *chansons* concerning Guillelme with which his audience is likely to have been familiar.

Wolfram's gift for original and graphic description is demonstrated in our current context by his account, in 56,14, of Puzzât wading through 'mannen bluot' on the battlefield and, perhaps especially, by his reference to the horse's sweat-drenched brown coat as 'covered all over with white foam, as if it had a winter's snow upon it' (59,9–11; p. 43). This latter description is of interest also in that he has changed Baucent's colour somewhat by comparison with the *Aliscans*. The French horse, according to Desireç's rather curious description in 1584, is 'sor baucent rofin', reddish sorrel with white spots.[8] Wolfram's contrasting reference to Puzzât's *brown* coat may have been made simply to enhance the persuasiveness of his snow image, or indeed to form a contrast with 'the brilliant reds and greens and golds of the battlefield';[9] but it may well also represent a simple misunderstanding of the French source. Wolfram's French was, after all, far from perfect – as indeed becomes plain also in line 59,6, in which he changes Guillelme's conjecture that Baucent *himself* might be taken by the heathen (*Aliscans* 598) into a suggestion that the horse's *fodder* might have been plundered.

## IV

Discussion of the arguably differing perspectives on animals and their dealings with humans suggested by the two works can begin with the simple assertion that the *Aliscans* poet finds horses more intrinsically interesting than does Wolfram. He chronicles Baucent's actions, reactions, vicissitudes and eventual fate in far greater detail than does the German author, and also, particularly through his emphasis on the horse's sufferings and savage murder, seems much more concerned to elicit the audience's sympathy for him. Nor is Baucent a unique case. Wolfram's Arofel, for example, devotes only two lines (81,2f.) to praising his horse Volatîn, whereas the *Aliscans'* Arïofles delivers a detailed and impassioned eulogy of Volatile's many merits which occupies no less than thirty (1486–1515).

A further difference between the two works is that the *Aliscans* presents a relationship between man and beast which is considerably more intimate and affectionate than is its equivalent in *Willehalm*. Not that the relationship between Willehalm and Puzzât is anything but close: Willehalm speaks to his horse with gentleness, offers him fine foods as a reward, sensitively wipes away his perspiration, and is later considerate enough both to remove the wounded Puzzât's saddle and to mourn his death; moreover, Puzzât in turn is highly responsive to his master's solicitude, a quality which becomes particularly apparent when he instinctively follows after him in section 82. The relationship between Guillelme and Baucent, however, is closer still. It is symptomatic that Willehalm's address to Puzzât contains several references to his own circumstances and feelings (see 58,21–4, 29f.), whereas Guillelme's words to Baucent concentrate much more squarely on the horse's condition; moreover, Guillelme, unlike Willehalm, repeatedly expresses not just sympathy for but also gratitude towards Baucent, and he promises him not only food, but rest, regular grooming and even a golden bowl to drink from. Furthermore, the brief episode in the *Aliscans* in which Guillelme dismounts and kisses his horse 'por molt grant amisteç' has no equivalent in *Willehalm*, and nor has the motif of Guillelme feeling so strongly about Baucent's death that he wishes to avenge it. In short, Guillelme loves his horse (1685) a little more than Willehalm does.

This greater level of intimacy is made possible by the third and perhaps most significant difference between the two texts' presentation of the interaction between hero and horse, namely that it is much closer to being a relationship between equals. Baucent is, quite simply, more human than Puzzât. As we have seen, Guillelme speaks to him as if he were human; at times the narrator also, for example when telling us that God has decreed to spare him, or when relating the circumstances of his death and Guillelme's reaction to it, speaks of him almost as if he were a knight; and, most strikingly of all, Baucent's own responses to Guillelme's words betoken a level of understanding analagous to that of a person. The physical manifestations of these responses are, it is true, quintessentially equine (snorting, whinnying, and so on); but the cognitive processes which underlie them palpably transcend the conventionally animalistic. 'Aysi l'entend cum s'il fust hom seneç', the narrator tells us in *Aliscans* 601 – he understands Guillelme's words as if he were a wise man; and he recovers his strength not, as does Puzzât, in response to his master wiping away his sweat, but in response to these words alone.

Puzzât, by contrast, is presented in much less anthropomorphic terms. He is capable of responding to sensitive gestures on Willehalm's part, and of demonstrating the obedient loyalty of a domesticated animal; but at no point does his behaviour approximate to that of a human being. It is therefore perhaps significant that the very first words Willehalm speaks to him in 58,21–3 already thematize Puzzât's inability to help him as a human would, namely by offering advice; and it is striking also that several passages speak of Willehalm's horse not as if he were human, but rather in the same context and same way as of his sword Schoiûse (37,10–13; 77,14–17; 85,25–7).

## V

By comparison with the author of his source, then, Wolfram evinces rather less interest in horses for their own sake, implicitly plays down the level of friendship they can enjoy with humans, and appears more concerned to preserve a clear distinction between humanity and animality. These differences of approach are no doubt attributable in large measure to differing interests and expectations on the part of their audiences. Whilst we have no indications as to the precise composition of his audience, it seems reasonable to assume that the *Aliscans* poet will have been writing for people who were both interested in and personally familiar with horses, and who furthermore will have expected him to regale them with stories of at least one 'cheval remarquable, jouant un rôle important dans un ou plusieurs épisodes'.[10] As Jean Bichon has demonstrated, the presence of a horse capable of remarkable feats and/or an exceptionally close relationship with its rider had become almost a 'trait obligé' in *chansons de geste* of this period.[11] Conversely, Wolfram's rather later, almost certainly more courtly audience will have had no such expectations, and indeed are likely to have found their sensibilities somewhat offended by the very close and demonstrative relationship between hero and almost-human horse depicted in the *Aliscans*. That Wolfram did indeed seek to accommodate his narrative at least to some degree to the likely tastes, interests and knowledge levels of a mixed courtly audience is moreover suggested in his Puzzât episodes not only by the omission of any reference to the horse's damaged entrails and gory death, but also by the additional information he gives concerning Willehalm's cloak ('a piece of silk from Triant', 59,12f.; p. 43) and his reason for not carrying Vivianz's body on Puzzât's back: 'I may not place too great a load on Puzzât, if I am to meet the onslaughts of the heathens, for then I shall be able to manoeuvre better in combat with them' (71,16–18; p. 49). The *Aliscans* audience would probably not have been interested in the first of these two pieces of information, and would not have needed to be told the second.

Quite apart from considerations of audience expectation, however, it is perhaps not unduly far-fetched to postulate that the differences we have observed in the two authors' presentation of the relationship between man and horse may be rooted in significantly different conceptions on their part of the qualitative distinction to be drawn between humans and animals. In a recent book Joyce E. Salisbury has surveyed a variety of developments over the course of the twelfth century which suggest that 'the paradigm of the separation of the species was breaking down' and that 'the lines that separated humans from animals were becoming very narrow indeed'.[12] Arguably, the *Aliscans*, which probably dates from the 1180s, has been considerably influenced by this trend. Not only is Baucent at times quasi-human, but, conversely, heathen knights are often referred to as behaving like animals: Arïofles for example snorts like a boar ('come sengler froncha', 1384), and the Saracens are several times said to 'glatir' or 'husler cum chals' – to bark or howl like dogs (81, 4906, 5543, 5592). In *Willehalm*, however, matters are different. Puzzât is emphatically *not* human, and, as I have indicated elsewhere, Wolfram also either omits or relativizes most of the passages in the *Aliscans* which tend towards the dehumanization of the heathens.[13] In his eyes, there clearly still exists an essential, qualitative difference between humanity and animality. Such a distinction is, of course, firmly in line with patristic and medieval theological orthodoxy; and it is of fundamental importance for what are arguably the central themes of *Willehalm* – the kinship with God which humans alone can enjoy as a consequence of Christ's assumption of humanity (1,16–22), and the common human dignity which is shared by both Christians and heathens (306,25 – 307,30, and *passim*). The *Aliscans* poet is fascinated by the idea of a horse understanding words 'cum s'il fust hom seneç' (601); Wolfram (405,17) is more concerned that human beings should *not* be treated 'alsam ein vihe'.

## Notes

1. Quotations from *Willehalm* are taken from the edition by Joachim Heinzle (Altdeutsche Textbibliothek, 108 (Tübingen, 1994)); English translations from the version by Marion E. Gibbs and Sidney M. Johnson (Harmondsworth, 1984).
2. Quotations from the *Aliscans* are taken from Günter Holtus (ed.), *La versione franco-italiana della 'Bataille d'Aliscans': Codex Marcianus fr. VIII [=252]*, Beihefte zur Zeitschrift für romanische Philologie, 205 (Tübingen, 1985; hereafter referred to as 'Holtus'). This edition is based on a manuscript of the *chanson* demonstrably closer (though not identical) to the source used by Wolfram than are the versions used for other editions (including the frequently used 'kritische Ausgabe' of Erich Wienbeck, Wilhelm Hartnacke and Paul Rasch (Halle, 1910; hereafter referred to as 'WHR') and the recent 'Classiques français du Moyen Age' edition of Claude Régnier (CFMA 110–11, Paris, 1990)). The best discussion of the *Aliscans* manuscripts and their relationship to *Willehalm* remains that of Susan Almira Bacon, *The Source of Wolfram's 'Willehalm'*, Sprache und Dichtung, 4 (Tübingen, 1910). The English translations from Holtus are my own; but I am very grateful to my colleague Dr Les Brook, of the Birmingham French Department, for checking them for me and suggesting some emendations.
3. WHR and Régnier (*op. cit.*), here read 'a tort' (WHR 507), unjustly, which is perhaps more appropriate than Holtus's 'a mor'.
4. One would perhaps expect the subject of the verb 'to be' in this phrase to be in the second person; but 'doi' (Holtus 586) is incontrovertibly a first-person form.

5. This passage is more extensive in the other editions. In them, Guillelme specifically asks Baucent to get him over the crest of a hill, expresses confidence in his ability, with God's help, to defeat his opponents, and elicits the by now predictable response of listening, understanding and whinnying (see WHR 990–1001).

6. See for example Marion E. Gibbs, *Narrative Art in Wolfram's 'Willehalm'*, Göppinger Arbeiten zur Germanistik, 159 (Göppingen, 1976), pp. 53–107.

7. Nothing can be known for certain about the precise nature of Wolfram's contemporary audience, but there is strong circumstantial evidence to suggest a link with the court of Landgrave Hermann von Thüringen near Eisenach, a significant centre of literary patronage in the early thirteenth century, but one which is unlikely to have been familiar, except via Wolfram, with the 'Guillaume cycle' of *chansons de geste*. See John Greenfield and Lydia Miklautsch, *Der 'Willehalm' Wolframs von Eschenbach. Eine Einführung* (Berlin/New York, 1998), pp. 5–19.

8. As this formulation in the *Aliscans* suggests, but as Wolfram seems not to have realized, 'baucent' is essentially an adjective, referring to a horse with 'white spots on a coloured ground' (R.H.C. Davis, *The Medieval Warhorse* (London, 1989), p. 137). It is, however, also used as a horse's name in several other *chansons de geste* – see Friedrich Bangert, *Die Tiere im altfranzösischen Epos*, Ausgaben und Abhandlungen aus dem Gebiete der romanischen Philologie, 34 (Marburg, 1885), pp. 24f., 33f.

9. Gibbs, *op. cit.*, p. 197.

10. Jean Bichon, *L'Animal dans la littérature française au XIIe et au XIIIe siècle* (Lille, 1973), p. 323.

11. Bichon provides an exemplary survey of this convention (*op. cit.*, pp. 323–67).

12. Joyce E. Salisbury, *The Beast Within. Animals in the Middle Ages* (New York/London, 1994), p. 2; p. 104.

13. Nigel Harris, 'Animal, Vegetable, Mineral. Some Observations on the Presentation and Function of Natural Phenomena in *Willehalm* and in the Old French *Aliscans*', in Martin H. Jones and Timothy McFarland (eds) *Wolfram's 'Willehalm'* (forthcoming).

# 3
# Bürger and 'das schwankende Wort *Volk*'

*David Hill*

Much of Wilfried van der Will's work revolves around two related issues which have played a prominent role in twentieth-century Germany: the relationship between the mass of the people and the political structures of society, and the relationship between the arts and their audiences. His analysis of the shifting focuses of political power in the West Germany of the 1980s examines the process by which different social groupings claimed to represent the 'people' against the established corridors of power. As the events of 1989–90 have reminded us – the development from 'Wir sind das Volk' to 'Wir sind ein Volk', the victory, so to speak, of *Volkswagen* over the *Volkspolizei* – the term *Volk* is one that continues to be central to German culture, but one that is contentious and problematic. And the term *Volk* is contentious because the identity of the thing the term refers to in both its main semantic dimensions is problematic: it raises, on the one hand, questions of national identity, on the other, questions of democratic sovereignty. The history of Germany has ensured that both of these matters are central to what it is to be German today. Both of them were raised particularly sharply during the 1920s and 1930s, and the other main strand of Wilfried van der Will's work, the analysis of proletarian culture in the Germany of that period, deals with their consequences in the realm of cultural politics, and is concerned with a series of attempts to find forms of artistic production which were appropriate not merely to the intelligentsia, the traditional guardians of art, but to the mass of the people.

Both of these issues, which seem so closely connected to the crises of advanced capitalism in the Germany of the twentieth century, were contentious and problematic, too, at the time when they first gained their importance, when capitalism was beginning to set foot in Germany in the eighteenth century. It was the writers of the *Sturm und Drang*, Herder and Bürger, Goethe and Lenz, who in the early to mid 1770s advanced the idea of the *Volk* in order to define both their ideal audience and the basis of their aesthetic. But by the end of the 1770s, with Goethe and Herder in Weimar, Lenz in the care of his friends and relatives, and Klinger about to move to Russia, the *Sturm und Drang* was on the wane and the term *Volk* seemed to be losing much of its polemical force. Herder expressed increasing doubts about the association of true folksong with the lower classes of society, and also about the modern authors who imitated the popular style.[1]

Histories of literature generally mark the end of this first phase in the revival of interest in folk-poetry not by Herder's doubts but by Schiller's absolute repudiation of Bürger's notion of *Volkspoesie* in his essay 'Über Bürgers Gedichte', which first appeared in the *Allgemeine Literatur-Zeitung* in January 1791. Bürger had persisted in maintaining his adherence – at least in name – to his ideals of *Volkspoesie* and *Popularität* as late as 1789, in the preface to the second edition of his poems, when he had declared: 'Popularität eines poetischen Werkes ist das Siegel seiner Vollkommenheit.'[2] Schiller's response was more than a review of this publication, it was an opportunity for him finally to demolish the view of the *Volk* held by the *Sturm und Drang*, and indeed the aesthetic principles of the *Sturm und Drang*, and at the same time to distance himself from the excesses of his youth and establish criteria which legitimated his mature, Classical style of writing.

Schiller's primary and fundamental objection was that Bürger's claim to be a 'Volksdichter' (*SW*, 13) rests on 'das schwankende Wort "Volk"',[3] and he himself distinguishes two possible meanings of the word. Is this a *Volksdichter* who restricts himself to addressing the *Volk*, in the sense of 'der große Haufen'? Or is the *Volksdichter* a person who strives to create a poetry which will transcend social divisions and address the needs of the *Volk*, in the sense of the whole people? From these two definitions of the word *Volk* Schiller derives two alternative sets of aesthetic principles:

Ein Volksdichter für unsre Zeiten hätte also bloß zwischen dem *Allerleichtesten* und dem *Allerschwersten* die Wahl: entweder sich ausschließend der Fassungskraft des großen Haufens zu bequemen und auf den Beifall der gebildeten Klasse Verzicht zu tun – oder den ungeheuren Abstand, der zwischen beiden sich befindet, durch die Größe seiner Kunst aufzuheben und beide Zwecke vereinigt zu verfolgen. (*NA*, XXII, 248)

The first route is that of Bürger, whom Schiller, with a side-swipe at Bürger's chaotic domestic arrangements, accuses of sensuality and a lack of 'Idealisierkunst'; the second is that of the true poet, 'der, eingeweiht in die Mysterien des Schönen, Edeln und Wahren, zu dem Volke bildend herniedersteigt, aber auch in der vertrautsten Gemeinschaft mit demselben nie seine himmlische Abkunft verleugnet' (*NA*, XXII, 250). Schiller here accuses Bürger of neglecting the 'absoluten, innern Wert' a poem must have and pandering to the 'Kinderverstand des Volks', the term being used here again by Schiller to refer in some sense to the lower classes, not those who are the '*Auswahl* der Nation' but the '*Masse* derselben'. Moreover, Bürger's poems are, according to Schiller, in practice further divisive in that they are addressed to different sections, 'Volksklassen', within the 'Volk' (*NA*, XXII, 248–50).

Schiller's observation on the meanings of the word *Volk* is confirmed by the entry in Johann Christoph Adelung's dictionary. The article 'Volk' which first appeared in 1780 remained almost unchanged in the editions of 1798 and 1811.[4] Adelung broadly distinguishes two main groups of usage, in the first of which the word only normally appears in the singular, whereas in the second it can be used in either the singular or the plural. In the first range of meanings it refers to a sub-group of a larger unit and in the social sense relevant to the present context is defined in the first instance as 'die untern Classen der Glieder einer Nation oder eines Volkes in der folgenden zweyten Hauptbedeutung' (1613).[5] In this second 'Hauptbedeutung' it is approximately equivalent to the newly introduced word 'Nation':

Ein aus mehrern Menschen bestehendes Ganze, doch nur in engerm Verstande, eine Menge Menschen, welche einen gemeinschaftlichen Stammvater erkennen, und durch ein gemeinschaftliche Sprache verbunden sind. (1613)

The historic role that Schiller's argument played in marking a stage in his own development has tended to obscure the fact that it is the culmination of a debate that had been raging for some twenty years. Schiller's observation that Bürger in his legitimation of the *Volksdichter* slithers between these two meanings of *Volk*, the social and the national, had been made some thirteen years earlier in an anonymous review of

*Aus Daniel Wunderlichs Buch*, Bürger's first formal statement of his aesthetic principles. This review had appeared in the autumn of 1778 in the *Neue Bibliothek der schönen Wissenschaften und der freyen Künste*, written by Johann Karl (or Carl) Wezel, who, like Adelung, was associated with the Leipzig Enlightenment:

Was ist Volkspoesie? – Entweder solche, die alle Individuen eines Volks, ihr Stand, die Kultur ihres Kopfs und ihres Herzens mag noch so verschieden seyn, gleich stark interessirt, vergnügt, und also von allen verstanden und empfunden wird: oder solche, die nur die weniger polirten, ungelehrten und geringen Klassen ergötzt.[6]

Wezel, like Schiller, argues that Bürger is unclear about the two meanings of the term *Volk*, which can refer either to the whole of a society or to the members of particular (lower) classes within a society. Like Schiller, he sees the difficulty of creating a truly national *Volkspoesie* in the first sense of *Volk* because the needs and abilities of society have fragmented since the harmonious Greek civilization of Homer's day and have produced a *Volk* in the second sense of the term, an uneducated mass of people that no longer shares a common culture with the educated. *Volkspoesie* is for Wezel only possible, at least at the moment, in the sense of a literature of the lower classes, such as popular hymns, 'die Gassenhauer der Handwerkspurschen'[7] or the collection of songs *Eyn feyner kleyner Almanach*, which – ironically enough – had been published by Nicolai at least in part in order to criticize *Aus Daniel Wunderlichs Buch* and the middle-class sentimentality about primitive peasant life that Bürger was encouraging.[8]

How could Bürger defend himself and explain his use of the term *Volk*? No adequate answer to this question is to be found in Bürger's actual responses to these criticisms. Indeed, there is no record of his reaction to Wezel's criticism,[9] and he was, as he later admitted, too hurt by Schiller's review to answer it adequately. His formal response, 'Vorläufige Antikritik und Anzeige', his poem 'Der Vogel Urselbst' and various epigrams all express outrage, but equally an inability to come to terms with Schiller's argument, and it is significant that he began reworking some of his poetry in order to try and accommodate Schiller's objections at the same time as protesting against them. Bürger was overwhelmed at a personal level because the treachery and humiliation of Schiller's review seemed to reinforce the very public disaster of his marriage to Elise Hahn. Perhaps it seemed like the end of a career. And perhaps the shifts in German culture provoked by the French Revolution and represented by Kant made Bürger suspect that there was something outdated about his ideal of *Popularität.* The real meaning to him of the term *Volk* must be sought at a time when he was less plagued by doubt, nearer the beginnings of his creative life, when he was part of the cultural explosion that was the *Sturm und Drang.*

Bürger's formulations in the 'Herzensausguß über Volks-Poesie' in *Aus Daniel Wunderlichs Buch* of 1776 suggest in the first instance an inclusive understanding of the term *Volk* to mean the whole of society, even including the rulers. For example, he lists the social groups from whom the poet may learn the art of folk-poetry:

> Von der Muse der Romanze und Ballade ganz allein mag unser Volk noch einmal die allgemeine Lieblingsepopee aller Stände, von Pharao an, bis zum Sohn der Magd hinter der Mühle hoffen! ... Unter unsern Bauren, Hirten, Jägern, Bergleuten, Handwerksburschen, Kesselführern, Hechelträgern, Bootsknechten, Fuhrleuten, Trutscheln, Tirolern und Tirolerinnen, kursieret wirklich eine erstaunliche Menge von Liedern. (*SW*, 692f.)

And the poet who gets to know 'das Volk im ganzen', he says, will be able to write poetry that delights not only 'den verfeinerten Weisen' but also 'den rohen Bewohner des Waldes, die Dame am Putztische, wie die Tochter der Natur hinter dem Spinnrocken und auf der Bleiche' (*SW*, 689). These examples show that Bürger, when referring to the *Volk*, was thinking here in the first instance of a rural community, albeit one with extensive communications and trade. This corresponds to the intimate personal knowledge he had of the lower classes through his work as a rural magistrate.[10] At the same time this ideal of primitive community was evidently remote enough from the reality of eighteenth-century German life for Bürger to need rhetorical devices in order to make it plausible. The reference to the pharaoh suggests the archetypical idyll of the Old Testament idealized by the *Sturm und Drang*, and here extends the concept of *Volk* so far as to include the ruler. More generally in this piece, Bürger uses the enthusiastic rhetoric of the supposed poet-cobbler Daniel Wunderlich and thereby evokes the world of Hans Sachs. He is thus able to appeal to a Germany of the past which was socially more integrated. Thus it was too, in the past, that the *Iliad*, the *Orlando furioso* and *The Faerie Queene* existed as popular literature in their respective societies (*SW*, 692). He thereby acknowledges the distance of contemporary reality from this idea of a communitarian *Volk* sharing a common culture. But whereas Nicolai found that distance ridiculous,

Bürger thought it might be bridged by drawing on the vitality of the *Volkslieder* that 'ein deutscher Percy' (*SW*, 693) would perhaps collect. What to the Enlightenment tradition of Wezel, Adelung and Schiller appeared as the muddying of semantic categories was for Bürger an attempt to reveal the hidden secret of the language, namely that there was an essentially German identity which since the loss of community in the modern world might be discerned in the traditions of those undamaged by education and privilege. It was, he argued, only the *Volksdichter*, close to the heart of the German soul, who could adequately translate Homer.[11]

Bürger's formulations at this time reveal the influence of Herder's essay *Auszug aus einem Briefwechsel über Oßian und die Lieder alter Völker*, published in 1773, which played an essential part in ensuring that the concept of the *Volk* came to occupy a central role in eighteenth-century aesthetics. Herder's essay played a decisive role in confirming Bürger in his intellectual development,[12] but Bürger's approach to folk-poetry was rather different from Herder's. Bürger showed little interest in the historical and anthropological dimensions of the idea and focused on the notion of regenerating German poetry by drawing on the directness and vitality of folk-poetry. What they were both engaged in was a revaluation of the term *Volk*, undoing the negative connotations it had acquired. Herder, with his fundamentally historical approach, was conscious that the meaning of the term had changed with the decline of Athenian democracy: 'selbst das Volk ist nicht mehr dasselbe. Dort war dieser Name ehrwürdig: er begriff alle Bürger, Rath und Priester ausgenommen: jetzo ist er gemeiniglich so viel as Pöbel und Canaille.'[13] Herder therefore sees a decline in the status of the word *Volk* accompanying the hierarchization of modern society. By contrast he imagines a true *Volk* comprising all members of society: 'Nur Ein Stand exsistirt im Staate, *Volk* (nicht Pöbel;) zu ihm gehört der König sowohl als der Bauer.'[14]

This ideal of *Volk* envisaged by Herder approaches the second main meaning defined by Adelung, the sense of '*a people*'. Adelung too supported attempts to counter the negative connotations the term *Volk* in its first sense had tended to acquire, but for him this must be effected by revalidating the first meaning, not by obscuring the boundaries between meanings:

Einige neuere Schriftsteller haben dieses Wort in der Bedeutung des größten, aber untersten Theiles einer Nation oder bürgerlichen Gesellschaft wieder zu adeln gesucht, und es ist zu wünschen, daß solches allgemeinen Beyfall finde, indem es an einem Worte fehlet, den größten, aber unverdienter Weise verächtlichsten Theil des Staates mit einem edlen und unverfänglichen Worte zu bezeichnen.[15]

The fact that Adelung includes this comment in a dictionary shows the extent to which the meanings of the word were being contended at the time. His intervention is couched characteristically in the moral discourse of the Enlightenment, which finds that the negative connotations are undeserved ('unverdient'). Herder and Bürger, on the other hand, both attempt to draw together the two meanings of the term *Volk* which Schiller, Wezel and Adelung want to keep separate. They do so by arguing that the essence of the *Volk*, in the sense of society as a whole (Adelung's second meaning), was to be found in the *Volk* in the sense of the lower classes (Adelung's first meaning). As Koepke puts it: 'In diesem Zusammenhang wird deutlich, daß Herder unter "Volk" die große Masse der Menschen einer Gesellschaft meint, die eine Gemeinschaft zu bilden versucht, und deren Geist sich vor allem in den unteren Schichten findet.'[16]

For both Herder and Bürger *Volk* is not a scientific term denoting an aggregation of individuals sharing particular objective socio-economic or political features. It implies the organic integrity of a community, and because it is only within this framework that human beings can fully realize themselves, the term *Volk* also has moral and political connotations. Central to this integrity is the fact that the *Volk* have not been spoiled by the alienation and reification due to intellectualism, what Herder called 'Schattenbegriffe, Halbideen und symbolischen Letternverstand,' or 'Künsteleien, sklavische Erwartungen, furchtsam schleichende Politik und verwirrende Prämeditation'.[17] Bürger's arguments similarly revolve around returning literature to social groups that have been excluded by their lack of education, and he justified his translation of Homer as a 'Poesie, die nicht für den Gelehrten allein sondern fürs ganze Volk sein soll' (*SW*, 654).

The argument he deploys in the 'Herzensausguß über Volks-Poesie' is not in fact directed primarily against an Enlightenment aesthetic, despite criticism of the trivialized, sanitized pastiches of folk-poetry favoured by 'die nackigen Poetenknaben' such as Gleim (*SW*, 692). His defence of folk-poetry revolves around, and repeatedly returns to, a criticism of an over-intellectualized style of writing, and although no names are mentioned, Bürger makes it clear that it is Klopstock and his followers who are accused of speaking a 'Göttersprache' (*SW*, 689) that is inaccessible to 'das Menschengeschlecht im ganzen' (*SW*, 688). His appeal to them uses the same metaphor of vertical separation that Schiller was later to use against him with opposite intent: 'Steiget herab von [den] Gipfeln eurer wolkigen Hochgelahrtheit, und verlanget nicht, daß wir vielen, die wir auf Erden wohnen, zu euch wenigen hinaufklimmen sollen' (*SW*, 692). Bürger was therefore distancing himself from a tradition with which he himself had important personal and ideological connections, but he evidently felt that their means of expression – for example, Klopstock's adoption of classical metres and his exaggeratedly elevated diction – created an articifial distance between the poet and the reality of rural experience in Germany. In particular, it seems likely that Bürger felt Klopstock had failed to overcome social fragmentation in his elitist, backward-looking utopia, *Die deutsche Gelehrtenrepublik* of 1774, in which the *Volk* consisted of a distinct stratum of society containing individuals without the ability to rise into a *Zunft*.[18] Even further from the heart of society is a marginal group, the *Pöbel*, who have no educational potential and are debarred from political activity.[19] What is particularly noteworthy is that Klopstock feels it necessary to emphasize the illegitimacy of attempts by the *Pöbel* to challenge its exclusion from the *Volk*:

> Man hat ihm zu seiner Beruhigung verschiedne andre Benennungen angeboten, als: *Das geringe Volk, der große Haufen, der gemeine Mann*; aber er hat damit nie zufrieden sein, sondern immer: *Das große Volk* heißen wollen ...[20]

This formulation shows how contentious the term *Pöbel* was. Herder, for example, generally used it ironically in order to characterize the arrogance of the upper classes towards the most exploited members of society,[21] and Lenz claimed the *Pöbel* as part of his audience.[22] Bürger does not specifically mention the *Pöbel* in the 'Herzensausguß über Volks-Poesie', but it is clear from the preface to the first edition of his collected poems, which appeared two years later, that he had no intention of excluding them from the *Volk*, which he qualifies with the parenthetical comment, 'worunter ich mitnichten den Pöbel allein verstehe' (*SW*, 717).[23] The word 'allein' may suggest a certain defensiveness on Bürger's part, linked to the negative connotations of the word ('der Begriff der bürgerlichen so wohl als sittlichen Niedrigkeit') identified by Adelung[24] and reinforced by Klopstock, but Bürger's concept of *Volk* is both more inclusive and more emphatically positive than Klopstock's and does not at this stage exclude the *Pöbel*.

Although statements like these about the nature of his audience and, correspondingly, the nature of poetry have a programmatic quality, Bürger was not interested in extensive theoretical elaborations, and the examples we have are relatively few and are apodictic in character. Some were published posthumously and cannot be dated, so it is not easy to reconstruct a detailed account of his development between the two editions of his poems in 1778 and 1789. Nevertheless, although the 1789 edition continues to express allegiance in principle to the ideals of *Volkspoesie* and *Popularität*, there is a significant shift in the content of the term *Volk*: 'In den Begriff des Volkes aber müssen nur diejenigen Merkmale aufgenommen werden, worin ungefähr alle, aber doch die ansehnlichsten Klassen überein kommen' (*SW*, 14). Even if this reservation is taken as referring not to social classes but to individual differences in standards of taste, it indicates that Bürger no longer regards the *Volk* as a seamless totality. There is an even more fundamental revision to his earlier inclusive definitions of *Volk* when he defines his poetic ideal: 'der Geist der Popularität, das ist der Anschaulichkeit und des Lebens für unser gebildetes Volk, – Volk! Nicht Pöbel!' (*SW*, 13f.). The word 'gebildet' points to a significant modification which explains the exclusion of the *Pöbel*. The formulation in *Von der Popularität der Poesie*[25] is more forceful and states in a rather circular and therefore essentialist way that the *Pöbel* cannot possibly share in the common culture of the *Volk*: 'Unter Volk verstehe ich nicht Pöbel. Wenn man verlangt, daß jemand eine leserliche Hand schreibe, so ist wohl nicht die Meinung, daß ihn auch der lesen soll, der überall weder lesen, noch schreiben kann' (*SW*, 730).

Bürger may well have been affected by the criticisms of Nicolai and the increasing doubts of Herder about the existence of a *Volk* with a culture transcending social divisions: 'da wir noch eigentlich kein Volk, keine gemeinschaftliche lebendige Sprache haben, so haben wir noch weniger eine Nationaldichtkunst'.[26] Bürger places less emphasis than Herder on the oral nature of a tradition of folk-poetry, and the formulations he chooses imply that it is specifically lack of education and illiteracy that are responsible for the exclusion of the *Pöbel*. Both editions of Bürger's poems were sold by subscription, and the lists of subscribers, although imperfect indicators of who read the poems, show a clear predominance of the great and the good: both open with several ruling monarchs (*SW*, 1043–71; 1079–88). Low levels of literacy, the cost of books and the lack of opportunity and inclination to read them all conspired to make access to books merely a further dimension of social privilege, and it must have become clear that there was a contradiction

in using this privilege as the basis of a common culture of the *Volk*.
Bürger's doubts about his original literary-political project are further
shown by his plans towards the end of his life for an exclusive
*Prachtausgabe* of his poems, and also by his return to the term *Mensch*, a
typically Enlightenment category which he had formerly rejected in
favour of *Volk*.[27]

Bürger was clearly able to empathize with the social and economic
predicaments of particular underprivileged sections of society which he
knew well, and – for example, in *Der Bauer* – to give a voice to the
exploited peasant, but his references to the *Volk* were throughout his life
generalized and abstract in nature. In 1783, the year of his most radical
indictment of the dependence of what people call 'taste' on wealth and
education in *Über deutsche Sprache*, he decided to give up his post as
magistrate, and from the following year until his death lectured at
Göttingen university, and this change of experience may have played a
part in shifting his attitude towards society. Bürger's notion of
*Volkspoesie* was based on the idea of a culturally homogeneous *Volk*
which, as he came to realize, did not exist in eighteenth-century
Germany; nor could *Volkspoesie* produce that *Volk*. Later, the notion of
a *Volk* would be used in Germany to legitimate racial supremicism, but
in the eighteenth century its prime role lay in the regeneration of a
middle-class sensibility. This should not be underestimated: Bürger's
ideals of 'Anschaulichkeit und Leben' (*SW*, 14) are the same ideals which
allowed Goethe, Lenz, Bürger – and Schiller too – to write a poetry which
reproduced the directness of individual experience.[28]

## Notes

1. See Roy Pascal, *The German Sturm und Drang* (Manchester, 1953), pp. 80–4.
2. Gottfried August Bürger, *Sämtliche Werke*, ed. Günter and Hiltrud Häntzschel
   (Munich, 1987), p. 14. References to this edition henceforth *SW* plus page
   number.
3. 'Über Bürgers Gedichte' in *Schillers Werke. Nationalausgabe*, vol. 22, ed.
   Herbert Meyer (Weimar, 1958), pp. 245–64, here p. 247. References to this
   edition henceforth *NA* plus page number.
4. Johann Christoph Adelung, *Versuch eines vollständigen grammatisch-kritischen
   Wörterbuches Der Hochdeutschen Mundart*, vol. IV (Leipzig, 1780), cols
   1612–14, from which the following quotations are taken. See also his
   *Grammatisch-kritisches Wörterbuch der Hochdeutschen Mundart*, vol. IV (Leipzig,
   1798 and Vienna, 1811).
5. At this point there occurs the only substantial amendment in the second
   edition, which adds the phrase 'welche sich von der Handarbeit nähren'
   (col. 1225).

6. Johann Carl Wezel, *Kritische Schriften*, ed. Albert R. Schmitt, 3 vols (Stuttgart, 1971–75), I, pp. 127–37, here p. 130. This review covers the whole of the first number of the *Deutsches Museum* of 1776, which had also included an essay by Bürger introducing samples of his translation of the *Iliad*. The fact that Wezel makes no connection between the two shows that he did not know the identity of the author of *Aus Daniel Wunderlichs Buch*.

7. Wezel, *op. cit.*, I, p. 133.

8. *Eyn feyner kleyner Almanach vol schönerr echterr liblicherr Volckslieder, lustigerr Reyen unndt kleglicherr Mordgeschichte, gesungen von Gabriel Wunderlich weyl. Benkelsengernn zu Dessaw, herausgegeben von Daniel Seuberlich, Schusternn zu Ritzmück ann der Elbe* (1777; reprinted in Friedrich Nicolai, *Gesammelte Werke*, ed. Bernhard Fabian and Marie-Luise Spieckermann (Hildesheim, 1985), vol. IV). Nicolai mockingly suggests that the intellectuals of the *Sturm und Drang* should renounce their social privileges if they want to write folk-poetry: 'Eß muß traun gantz getan seyn, oder muß gar bleyben. Wolan, ir Genyes, wollt ir teutscher alter Volckspoeterei aufhelfen, laßt alle Cultur, Uppigkeit unndt gelartes Wesen, werdet erliche Handwerckslewtt, Schuster, Weber, Schreyner, Gerber, Schmide, arbeitet vile Wochenlang mit Macht, biß eyn Tag kommt, ds ir den Drang fulet, Volckslider z' dichten' (IV, pp. 18f.).

9. We do, however, know that his friend Boie recommended it to him (Boie to Bürger, 19 November 1778, in Adolf Strodtmann (ed.), *Briefe von und an Gottfried August Bürger. Ein Beitrag zur Literaturgeschichte seiner Zeit*, 4 vols (Berlin, 1874), II, p. 321).

10. Thus Boie in a letter to Nicolai of 9 December 1776: 'Nach einigen Jahren wollen wir sehen, was er gelernt hat aus den Volksliedern. Er hat sie studiert, wie vielleicht wenige Deutsche, und hat *gelebt* mit dem, was wir Volk nennen.' See Lore Kaim-Kloock, *Gottfried August Bürger. Zum Problem der Volkstümlichkeit in der Lyrik* (Berlin, 1963), p. 98.

11. For example: 'Teutschheit, gedrungene, markige, nervenstraffe Teutschheit, find' ich auf dem Weg, den ich wandle, und sonst auf keinem andern. Sie allein vermags, den Geist Homers mächtig zu packen, und ihn, wie Sturmwind, aus Ionien nach Teutschland zu reißen' (*SW*, 658).

12. See his letter to Boie of 18 June 1773: 'O Boie, Boie, welche Wonne! als ich fand, daß ein Mann wie Herder, eben das von der Lyrik des Volks und mithin der Natur deutlicher und bestimmter lehrte, was ich dunkel davon schon längst gedacht und empfunden hatte' (Strodtmann, *op. cit.*, ed. cit., I, p. 122). For an incisive discussion of Herder's various uses of the term see Wulf Koepke, 'Das Wort "Volk" im Sprachgebrauch Johann Gottfried Herders', *Lessing Yearbook*, 19 (1987), pp. 209–21.

13. Johann Gottfried Herder, *Sämmtliche Werke*, ed. Bernhard Suphan, 33 vols (Berlin, 1877–1913), I, p. 18.

14. Ibid., XVIII, p. 308.

15. Adelung, *Grammatisch-kritisches Wörterbuch*, IV, col. 1225.

16. Koepke, *op. cit.*, p. 217.

17. Herder, *op. cit.*, V, p. 181.

18. 'Zum Volke gehört, wer, ohne sich über das *Mittelmäßige* zu erheben, schreibt, oder öffentlich lehrt, oder die Wissenschaften in gemeinem Leben anwendet; ferner gehören diejenigen dazu, welche so wenig von dem wissen, was würdig ist, gewußt zu werden, (es kommt hier auch mit in Betracht, wenn sie sich auf

zu viel Unwissenswürdiges eingelassen haben) daß sie nicht zünftig sind. Außer diesen wird die Zahl des Volkes auch noch durch die schwankenden Kenner, und diejenigen Jünglinge vermehrt, welche von sich hoffen lassen, daß man sie bald in eine Zunft werde aufnehmen können' (Friedrich Gottlieb Klopstock, *Ausgewählte Werke*, ed. Karl August Schleiden (Munich, 1962), pp. 875f.).

19. 'Ein Mitglied des Pöbels verdirbt die wenigen Naturgaben, die es etwa noch haben mag durch das Studieren' (Klopstock, *op. cit.*, p. 877).
20. *Ibid.*, p. 875.
21. Koepke, *op. cit.*, p. 215. But in the introduction to his second collection of folk-songs of 1779 he is much more negative: 'Zum Volkssänger gehört nicht, daß er aus dem Pöbel seyn muß, oder für den Pöbel singt. ... Volk heißt nicht, der Pöbel auf den Gassen, der singt und dichtet niemals, sondern schreyt und verstümmelt' (Herder, *op. cit.*, XXV, p. 323).
22. Jakob Michael Reinhold Lenz, *Werke und Briefe*, ed. Sigrid Damm (Leipzig, 1987), III, p. 326.
23. A similar generalizing, inclusive formulation is to be found in Bürger's report of the instructions he had given to Chodowiecki for the title vignette: 'Ich hatte Chodow. einen *simpel aber modern gekleideten Sänger oder Spieler*, der eines andächtigen Zuhörerschaft aus *allen Ständen* auf einer Harfe oder sonstigen popularen Instrum[ente] was vorspielte, vorgeschrieben' (letter to Boie of 30 April 1778, Strodtmann, *op. cit.*, II, p. 278). The picture Chodowiecki produced (*SW*, 165) received Bürger's approval, apart from the portrait of a rather academic, bewigged harpist, and shows aristocratic males on one side of the harpist, while on the other there are men, women and children of lower social standing but no examples of hardship.
24. Adelung, *Versuch eines vollständigen grammatisch-kritischen Wörterbuches Der Hochdeutschen Mundart*, col. 1107. Bürger had himself used the word 'pöbelhaft' with negative connotations alongside 'komisch', 'niedrig' and 'schmutzig' in his early *Etwas über eine deutsche Übersetzung des Homers* (*SW*, 598).
25. This essay cannot be dated with any certainty. It is based on material intended for the 1778 edition of his poems but was first published posthumously and may well contain later additions. Similarities of formulation with the preface to the 1789 edition of poems suggest that the following quotation is one such addition.
26. Herder, *op. cit.*, VIII, p. 424.
27. Poetry, whose value is measured by its *Popularität*, he now calls 'diese so allgemein menschliche Kunst' (*SW*, 14), and he quotes the *Spectator* to the effect that 'Human Nature is the same in all reasonable creatures', saying 'Dies ist ungefähr meine Meinung von Volkspoesie' (*SW*, 15). Contrast Lessing's Nathan, who presents *Mensch* as a higher category than *Volk* (admittedly in the narrower sense of a religious community): 'Was heißt denn Volk? / Sind Christ und Jude eher Christ und Jude, / Als Mensch?' (Gotthold Ephraim Lessing, *Werke*, ed. Herbert G. Göpfert *et al.* (Munich, 1970–79), II, p. 253).
28. This does not mean that they ignored traditional poetic devices but that they integrated them more completely. See for example Anna Carrdus, *Classical Rhetoric and the German Poet 1620 to the Present. A Study of Opitz, Bürger and Eichendorff* (Oxford, 1996).

# 4
# Moments of Emancipation: The Nineteenth-Century Heroine in German Literature

*Ruth Whittle*

The complex relationship between Fanny Lewald (1811–1889), Ida Hahn-Hahn (1805–1880) and Johanna Kinkel (1810–1858) invites a comparison.[1] Lewald was acquainted both with Hahn-Hahn and Kinkel. Whereas the former publicly satirized what she perceived as Hahn-Hahn's aristocratic and therefore limited view of society – for example, in her satirical novel *Diogena*[2] – she was a friend of Kinkel's. All three women were able to widen their horizons through extensive travelling and wrote about their observations and adventures. These accounts alone established them as serious writers. Whereas Hahn-Hahn presented her letters to friends in *Orientalische Reisebriefe* (1844),[3] Lewald published her observations on her first journey to Italy in *Italienisches Bilderbuch* (1847).[4] This account is prepared as if it were a work of fiction and it includes independent novella-like chapters where the author is only the narrator and not one of the actors. Kinkel's *Hans Ibeles in London* (1860) is the semi-autobiographical account of the author's own emigration to London and her first years there.[5] Beyond the expression of her own experience the novel is a carefully worked piece of fiction including a number of didactic passages. Both Kinkel and Lewald were very accomplished and independent women before they married, Kinkel being a composer and pianist in her own right and Lewald having a career as a journalist and writer. All three knew considerable personal hardship, dissenting from the social norms imposed on them by their families.[6] The added twist here is that Hahn-Hahn and Lewald were in love with the same man, Heinrich Simon. Though Simon did not love Lewald he gave up Hahn-Hahn, partially in order to not hurt Lewald. It is thus with some reason that the works of these three writers should be examined together for their potential models of emancipated women and for ways of dealing satisfactorily in art with the challenge they had set themselves. A brief discussion of the socio-historical background between 1800 and 1850 will help to appreciate the task they undertook.

In 1789, the year of the French Revolution, the philanthropist and Rousseauist Joachim Heinrich Campe, a prolific and widely read author of educational books, wrote down his fatherly advice for his daughter. He reminded her of the fact that as a woman she was condemned to a sedentary lifestyle. Whilst it was indeed men who designed the restrictive clothing which prohibited girls and women from running or moving around swiftly and naturally, they, by comparison, had designed their environment so that they could play and go about their business with ease. He concludes:

> Es ist also der übereinstimmende Wille der Natur und der menschlichen Gesellschaft, daß der Mann des Weibes Beschützer und Oberhaupt, das Weib hingegen die sich ihm anschmiegende, sich an ihm haltende und stützende treue, dankbare und folgsame Gefährtin und Gehilfin seines Lebens sein solle.[7]

Campe does not deny that the woman's position in marriage, despite some attractions on the surface, can cause feelings of oppression and despondency (p. 28), and this is noteworthy. On the other hand, he relieves the man from any direct responsibility for her situation because man is an 'in einigem Grade stolzes, gebieterisches, herrschsüchtiges, oft auch aufbrausendes und in der Hitze der Leidenschaft bis zur Ungerechtigkeit hartes und fühlloses Geschöpf' (p. 29). His behaviour is dictated by nature, not by his mind, and Rousseau would have subscribed to this notion.

Other enlightened educational writers confirm such views about the nature and destiny of women, including Betty Gleim who, having herself been educated in the spirit of the *Reformpädagoge* Pestalozzi, founded one of the first and at the time only public schools for girls (*höhere Mädchenschule*) in Bremen in 1806.[8] Gleim set up a modern curriculum including German grammar, religious education, history, geography, physics, drawing, singing, reading the classical writers, arithmetic, handwriting and needlework, the latter taking up eight and a half hours per week. Pupils were expected to converse in French during their needlework lessons. Gleim's aim was to develop her students for the sake of their own individual lives.[9] Their original and natural destination, however, was still considered to be marriage and children, and only where this route was not possible was the carrying out of other caring tasks envisaged. Education was to make women more attractive by neither boring others in conversation nor being bored by knowing nothing. The nature of the woman as a carer and the one who has feeling and sentiment was not in question. At least in Germany, arguing against the natural gifts of women would, during the first decades of the nineteenth century at least, have meant being far too radical, and a person arguing against such female gifts would not have succeeded in gaining any position of influence such as that of a headmistress.

However, since the 1830s the perception of women and their self-worth had changed. Women came to realize that there was a contradiction between the reality of their own position, characterized as it was by male dominance, and the demands made by the Enlightenment and early Socialism for freedom and equality.[10] The fields in which change was seen to be essential were education, marriage and political rights. This is not to say, however, that all articulate women demanded the same things or were of the same opinion in all these fields. Emancipation as preached and practised by Louise Aston, for example, meant leaving one's family duties in order to fight for one's own rights. Such a stance was not condoned by other women, who found this either too dangerous or morally unacceptable.[11] When attempting to realize emancipatory ambitions in life proved difficult and a matter of controversy even among friends, it follows that achieving such ambitions within writing must have been all the more challenging.[12] It is also clear that all three women wrote in full awareness of the ongoing discussions among educationalists and writers and of their own critics.

The experience of travelling must therefore be analysed against this background. Leaving one's own shores was clearly an emancipatory moment for the travellers and, in the case of Hahn-Hahn and Lewald, problematic for those who gave them permission to go. Travelling provided one important alternative to education of the conventional kind. The latter stopped for girls with their fourteenth year, thus stifling the development of any independent thinking from the outset.[13] It is significant that both Lewald and Hahn-Hahn (among so many others) experienced their travels as liberating and as an opening of new horizons for their lives. This was even more the case as they both travelled South, into spheres which had hitherto only been alive in their dreams.[14] In her *Italienisches Bilderbuch*, for example, Lewald explains:

Der Wagen fuhr mir, obgleich es bergab und schnell genug ging, viel, viel zu langsam. Jetzt, da der Vorhang aufgezogen war, sollten sich mir auch gleich alle Schönheiten enthüllen, die ich geahnt hatte und die ich erwarten durfte ... Und wie ein Kind hätte ich immerfort rufen mögen: Mehr! mehr! (p. 10)

She sways between childlike expectations of a fairy-tale unfolding and fears of the brutality and surprise of the new world she is about to enter (p. 6). Hahn-Hahn's impressions, on the other hand, were dominated by a passionately adventurous spirit and thirst for knowledge; as expressed, for example, in a letter to her mother from Vienna just prior to her departure into the unknown:

und was ich noch nicht kenne – gerade das möchte ich kennenlernen; denn kennen ist wissen, und Wissen ist eine noch schönere Sache als die Freude über den St Stephan, über die bacchantischen Jubelwalzer von Strauß ... Allein ich kann nun einmal nicht anders als streben und immer streben, und daher geht mir der Drang zur Erkenntnis über das, was ich bereits erkannt habe.[15]

In this context she refers to the phoenix. Imitating its fabulous resurrection from the ashes, she is intent on practising her strengths again and again by feeding the fire in which she must burn to be reborn with ever more knowledge.

The difference between the two women is significant for two very different approaches to discovering the as yet unknown. Whereas Lewald feels the abundant curiosity of a child characterized by a mix of fear and pleasure, Hahn-Hahn's strife has an all-consuming quality, as the phoenix imagery suggests. It is this passionate, completely untamed side which Lewald takes up in her critique of Hahn-Hahn, particularly in *Diogena*, where the eponymous protagonist has only regard for the exalting, erotic, Dionysian side of life and love. The narrator last meets Diogena in an asylum for the mentally deranged and she lets a young male doctor analyse Diogena's incurable condition:

Unkluge Nachbeter der geistreichen George Sand haben in glänzendem Mißverstehen dessen, was diese große Frau meinte und bezweckte, eine Theorie der weiblichen Selbstsucht geschaffen, deren Höhepunkte in der deutschen Frauenliteratur jetzt erreicht ist. (p. 144)

The impatient search for 'den Rechten' in every corner of the world in *Diogena* will, according to Lewald, in the end not lead to more insight but be a sign of egotism, arrogance and lack of insight into one's own condition, thus leading to derangement. This attempt at emancipation from Apollonian values is clearly rejected. The narrator not only puts Diogena and her like into their places, but also aims her criticism at this approach to women's writing as a whole.

Johanna Kinkel and her narrator are not likely to fall into the category on which Lewald pours her scorn, but neither are they capable of Lewald's childlike enjoyment of nature as it unfolds itself around her from the (fairly common) vantage point of her carriage. In contrast to Johanna's real-life experience,[16] Dorothea, the female protagonist in *Hans Ibeles in London*, represents the ideal of a housewife, and her usual environment is her home – albeit in England. Dorothea had always been skilful in making a good home for her sensitive artist husband, family and visiting friends, but she had not learnt anything with which one could earn a living and thus she had to leave this task entirely to her husband Hans. The experience of running a household in financially strained circumstances in a foreign environment actually forces her to develop in a way which is fertile for both herself and her family.

After the initial hard years, when the family was a little better off because Hans had found more students than he really cared to teach, Dorothea realized to her disappointment that he had directed his leisure interests entirely away from the family towards more fashionable circles such as the salon of the Duchess of Blafoska, a passionate political manipulator with little patience either for her children or any real political action. There he was also lured by another manipulator, Livia. This woman was on the lookout for a man who would be naive enough to want to protect her and thus secure her disguise as a lady in distress whereas she had really become an outcast of society through having been suspected of murdering her husband. It was the unselfish Dorothea who reunited the family, not by yet another manipulative ploy, but by cultivating her family and herself and making the home environment attractive for her husband again despite hesitations as to whether she would be able enough to do so (p. 246). In the decisive argument with her husband she is thus described as a strong woman:

Ihr Ehrgefühl war ganz so stark wie das, welches der Mann ihr gegenüber geltend machte; auch sie wollte um des persönlichen Glücks willen weder das Unwürdige tun noch dulden. Es war ihr ein viel tieferes Seelenbedürfnis, den Mann, den sie liebte, zu achten, als ihn zu besitzen. (p. 376)

Once the couple have realized each other's worth through a deep crisis where they nearly lost each other, both partners communicate again, and the father picks up the children's musical education where the mother had left it: 'So manchen Keim des Talentes in den jungen Seelen der Kinder, den die Mutter mit banger Hand gehütet und gepflegt, entfaltete ein Strahl aus dem liebenden Vaterauge zu reicher schwellender Blüte' (p. 381). Even though it may be unsatisfactory for the contemporary reader that it is the 'Vaterauge' that helps the children's skills to develop their full potential, it must be noted that he took it upon himself to teach his two older *daughters* whom he had not really deemed worthy of his attention before and had therefore neglected (p. 242). One of Hans's biggest disappointments during the first years in England had been the fact that both his boys, whom he had firmly expected to follow him in his career as a composer and musician, refused to go on taking lessons from him and demanded a more practical career (p. 239f.). This is in stark contrast to the fate the German governess Meta described in her diary to which one chapter of *Hans Ibeles* is dedicated: her father preferred to spend his money on her brothers for them to become 'dumme Professoren' rather than 'gescheite Handwerker' (p. 141). This meant that nothing was left for Meta and she was thus barely equipped to fend for herself.

The concluding scene of the book depicts Hans's two girls playing one of his own compositions and shows how he is forced to realize, 'daß er fortlebe in zwei dem besten Mann ebenbürtigen Künstlernaturen' (p. 382). He knows that this is a result of his wife's care and attention during the time when he had his head in the clouds. Without criticizing the boys for following their own desires, he allows his ambitions to be transferred to the girls whilst at the same time recognizing and acknowledging the part his wife played in developing his daughters' talents. The book concludes with a predominantly bright outlook both in terms of this family's future and with respect to the daughters' professional possibilities.[17]

Whilst Dorothea the protagonist is professionally not as emancipated as her 'creator', she has very little of the meek and subservient housewife. It is true that she is in a serving role, much along the lines of Campe's 'folgsame Gefährtin und Gehilfin' in so far as she wants to help her husband to find his feet in London without putting pressure on him to earn money at the expense of his artistic soul. At the same time, the narrator repeatedly explains their relationship during the couple's good days together.

> Dorothea war die vertraute Freundin ihres Mannes, nicht bloß weil sie die Mutter seiner Kinder war, sondern das heimatliche Band hatte sich in der Fremde fest und fester um ihre Gemüter geschlungen ... kein Verhältnis hätte Ibeles Spaß gemacht, wenn er nicht mit seiner Frau davon hätte reden können. (p. 182, see also pp. 181, 377)

Thus they communicate on equal terms with each other. The crisis shows that where this type of communication is lacking, unhappiness and suffering result, but blame is not directly allotted. The narrator is telling her tale from a position of inner strength and mature insight. It is rather a few remarks about men scattered around the book and meant for the 'Leserinnen' (p. 234) which throw a critical light on men. Real criticism is poured over the likes of Duchess Blafoska, and in the context of the argument of the time this must also extend to Hahn-Hahn, Aston and others:

> Wenn berühmte Künstler die Zeit, die sie weihrauchstreuenden Verehrerinnen widmen, darauf wendeten, ihre Angehörigen zu sich emporzuziehen, so würden ihre Frauen nicht so oft in niedriger Beschäftigung geistig verkommen und ihre Kinder nicht verdummen oder mißraten. Darum offener Krieg gegen jede Emanzipierte, die einen andern Pflichtenkreis als ihren eigenen aufsucht ... Die Emanzipierten mögen sich an ihrer Freiheit genügen, aber ihren Schwestern, die sich demütig und gehorsam dem Joch der Ehe gefügt haben, die Liebe und das *ganze* Herz ihres Mannes lassen. (p. 184)

Although men are here being called upon to help raise their family's culture to their own level, the neglect of this duty may possibly be forgiven, if only because of men's nature, as Campe had taught; fellow women, on the other hand, are openly attacked, and for much the same reason as in Lewald's *Diogena*. Kinkel does not simply approve or disapprove of the women's situation; she demands loyalty among women and recognition for those who keep the family unit together regardless of the constraints imposed on them. Marriage for her is not so much an institution as a task for which wives give their energy and forgo pleasures. In return they should also receive their husband's full confidence and love. Women with other than housewifely ambitions should not compete with devoted spouses. Kinkel's stance on marriage is thus a practical and a moral one and less of a political one. In a bizarre twist of fate, Johanna Kinkel died under mysterious circumstances (suicide, murder or accidental death?) around the point in her own life where her heroine Dorothea is depicted as regaining her man and the family's happiness is restored. Whilst her husband had been unfaithful to her in a similar way as Hans to Dorothea, she herself could not experience in reality the same kind of dramatic climax followed by a 'blauer Himmel des Glücks' (p. 383) she portrayed in fiction, but died soon after completing the novel. Did Kinkel allow her heroine to gain such power of insight and inner strength as a substitute for a solution to her own seemingly intractable situation? This could then be interpreted as a success at emancipation through writing where such success is elusive in real life.

The travel situation in any case creates the need for deeper exploration of oneself and others. Hahn-Hahn, Lewald and Kinkel take the opportunity of travel to write about central truths of their existence. Above all, they compare their situation at home. A few examples will suffice to illustrate the point.

In Kinkel's novel, Dorothea Ibeles is confronted once more with her past just when she has settled in moderate comfort in London. Born a baroness, she had to adapt rapidly to the ways of a bourgeois wife when she married Hans Ibeles (p. 245). As the family's financial circumstances improve, she recognizes that it is now no longer suitable for her to do all the housework alongside her one servant. She puts it to her husband that 'Frauen auf derjenigen Stufe der Gesellschaft, die unserem gebildeten Mittelstand ungefähr entspricht, degradieren nicht bloß sich selbst, sondern auch ihren Mann, wenn sie materielle Arbeit tun' (p. 244). She recognizes the need, for her husband's sake just as much as for her own, to avoid any rumour that Hans had married his cook rather than a lady (p. 247), and therefore wants to employ another maid. At the point in time where Dorothea discusses this plan with her husband he is already much estranged from the goings-on in his own house; he is oblivious of social dictates in so far as they pertain to his wife's standing, and thus has no sympathy at all for her. The narrator's argument about the lack of satisfaction offered by housework as, in a woman's eyes, it is never ending, whilst men only recognize those tasks which have not been done (p. 249), has a modern ring which appeals to the contemporary reader. The description of how one ought to hire a new girl is both amusing as well as a good example of how Dorothea studied the local mores and became efficient in the English way of life.[18] She developed into a real lady; not because of her wealth, little though it was, or the number of servants in her employ, but because of her ability to adapt whilst always remaining true to her own self. Emancipation in this sense appears to be advocated as an inner sense of liberation, often achieved through adjustment, not through rebellion. In *Orientalische Briefe*, Hahn-Hahn's attitude towards conformity is quite different. Imbued with passion, she is rather impatient in her observations. Whilst objects of architecture are enjoyed and well described, she sizes up people very quickly and with the same yardstick as at home. A particularly interesting area for the study of her time and how she shares its prejudices is her preoccupation with the conventional notion of beauty. She visits the slave market in Constantinople where she finds that the female slaves are ugly when measured against her Pre-Raphaelite ideal of beauty.[19] Devoid of such beauty, a woman cannot possibly have any ability to feel. Hahn-Hahn mentions 'das nichtssagende Auge', the 'Mund mit der affrösen tierischen Bildung der vorspringenden Kinnladen, und mit den klaffenden *schwarzen* Lippen' and is repelled particularly by 'das unerhört Tierische der ganzen Erscheinung, Form und Ausdruck inbegriffen ... Ich muß ehrlich gestehen, daß mich bei der ganzen Prozedur nichts so anwiderte als ihre Häßlichkeit' (p. 50; original emphasis). Needless to say, these creatures can therefore not be endowed with any intelligence either and are not just likened to but classed as animals. Oriental men on average fare a little better. In Constantinople she complains that she cannot see enough young male Turks in the streets for her analysis, but:

Alle Türken sehen alt aus. Einen weißen Bart zu haben gilt bei ihnen als schön: so brauchen sie denn ebenso eifrig Mittel um ihn weiß zu machen, als man in Europa braucht um ihn schwarz zu färben ... Haar haben sie nicht, es wird abgeschoren; den Fez drücken sie auf die Augenbrauen, das rote fleischige Gesicht umgibt der graue Bart, die Gestalt ist breit und schwer – nirgends eine Spur von jugendlicher kräftiger Schönheit! Im höheren Alter sehen sie besser aus. Merkwürdiger ist es wohl, alt und schön zu sein; doch hübscher ist es jung und schön! (p. 56)

In contrast she puts forward her Greco-Italian ideal of male beauty. Some Turks can be handsome, but they are of the wrong age in her opinion. She thus misses a very important opportunity to gain a deeper insight into herself and how her male and female protagonists are stereotyped all too often as the unhappy victims of their inextricably linked beauty and intelligence. In *Hans Ibeles in London* Kinkel criticizes exactly this resort to stereotype. Dorothea is portrayed as not being particularly pretty but she has a good measure of *Bildung* together with sympathy for and knowledge of the political ideas of the democratic avant-garde. It is because of this that she can become mistress of her own destiny rather than being subjected to a mix of bad luck and male calculation. Another example is Meta. According to her own description she is 'weder hübsch noch vermögend' (p. 144). She does not have *Bildung* but the account of her life shows her independent critical eye together with a high degree of self-esteem.[20] The latter is severely impaired when she finds that her love for the intellectual Stern is recognized but not requited as he has fallen for the pretty and much tamer Hulda. In the end Meta emigrates to Australia where, Dorothea believes, 'eine Persönlichkeit wie die Ihre in einer frisch sich bildenden Gemeinschaft an ihrem Platz sein werde' (p. 338) rather than either looking for a career in England, where she is not regarded as being talented and refined enough, or for a husband for whom she is not sufficiently pliable with her high degree of 'scharfer Verstand' (p. 336). Thus with her more subtle appreciation of human personality, Kinkel is able to convey a sense of resignation that social parameters are not yet right in England or Germany for a complex and unstereotypical woman like Meta to have a fulfilled life. It is interesting that Kinkel had recourse to a diary within a semi-autobiography. If Dorothea had not been such an assiduous reader, Kinkel's reader might never have heard of Meta's background. Kinkel thus re-emphasizes that writing is a productive means of expression about one's condition, although it is made clear that Meta's diary does not see publication and so it is in more than one sense that Meta remains unfree.

Both Hahn-Hahn's and Lewald's travel writings were meant to be published after their return, partly in order to provide funds for further travelling and partly because such literature was very popular. In *Orientalische Briefe*, Hahn-Hahn's reader is made aware of the fact that her letters are not simply to her friends and relatives but are for the reading public, as she intersperses short didactic deliberations on certain values she particularly cherishes; for example, on marriage and divorce (p. 325). Similarly, Lewald's *Italienisches Bilderbuch* contains brief interpretations of this kind; encounters with Jews (that is, her own, Jewish, past) being a frequent topic.[21] Furthermore, she weaves independent novellas into the diary format. The longest such story is at first glance merely a description of the Roman Carnival.[22] However, it is really a love story of two couples, Horazio and Maria, and Hermann and Giuditta, who find a way of marrying each other against the odds because of the particular circumstances offered to them through the carnival.[23] This annual week-long feast with its masked balls and crowded carnival processions allows lovers to meet without being noticed by their guardians. If all goes well, it is also possible to ask for the permission of these guardians to allow otherwise unlikely matches by taking advantage of the playful and relaxed atmosphere of the festivities. Giuditta had been promised to Horazio in order to fulfil their common uncle's wish and as a prerequisite to inheriting his wealth. However, both love other people and can in the end marry for love rather than convenience and with their (guardian) aunts' blessings.

Lewald puts on a kind of narrational mask and mixes in the crowds in order to detect all the ways in which human instinct and ingenuity find personal happiness and fulfilment. Significantly, the Roman Carnival chapter was written after a long break from writing: Lewald had herself met and fallen in love with the then married Stahr.[24] It was only after they had admitted their love to each other that she felt able to write again. On the one hand, she achieves in writing what she had finally achieved in real life: a passion which was requited. On the other hand, she lays herself open to criticism by society in a new way. For in an illicit affair she lives her womanhood to the full for the first time, at what was considered a fairly advanced age. In her Carnival chapter, however, she manages to disguise herself and her sex completely. She thus puts herself beyond the reach of the reader at the very point where she had made herself vulnerable in real life.

In so far as the doctrines on education and marriage of the emerging nineteenth century can be used as a yardstick for describing the emancipatory positions of Hahn-Hahn, Kinkel and Lewald, interesting parallels and distinctions emerge. Whilst Kinkel and her hero Dorothea were brought up in the spirit of Campe, they developed further – Kinkel herself went further than her heroine Dorothea and thus Gleim, though the protagonist was made to find more recognition and happiness in her life than her creator ever did.

The educated teenager Fanny Lewald realized that whilst she had been encouraged to learn in her early years, she was of the wrong sex to be allowed to go on studying and become independent of the family. By striving for independence, she had to go beyond Gleim, not least because no suitable lover appeared at the 'right' time and she had refused arranged matches. To call her writings fresh because of a lack of formal literary education would be to attempt to make a virtue out of a desperate situation.[25] Partly because of her upbringing and partly because of her previous unrequited love affairs, Lewald had no experience of relying successfully on her feelings until she met Stahr and they confessed their love to each other. The Carnival story reveals an interest in the novella form, a genre which had just been revived at the beginning of the nineteenth century by Goethe and others, whom Lewald would have read. Furthermore, *Italienisches Bilderbuch* presents a breakthrough where Lewald reveals herself as a writer and an intellectual who is looking for ways of allowing her protagonists personal freedom and happiness.

Hahn-Hahn is in many respects the opposite to Lewald. Not only does she work with clichés in thought and imagery, but she could also be called more exclusive – in the sense that she limits the social range of her characters by choosing aristocrats, who, because of their social standing, can usually afford unconventional views, emphatic judgements and fiery passions without being exposed to recrimination.

The kind of close reading attempted here should ultimately lead to a more sensitive appreciation of the individuality of each woman author and the question of emancipation with which they struggled. Many more readings of a similar nature will be required in order to allow a fuller and more integrated view of women's writing in the nineteenth century, and this may in turn shed a brighter light on our own intellectual situation today.

*The author gratefully acknowledges the financial support of the British Academy which enabled her to gather archival material for this chapter through a Small Research Grant.*

## Notes

1. Of the three, Kinkel is the least discussed writer in secondary literature and this situation is unlikely to change dramatically as she was not included in the state-of-the-art sourcebook by E.P. Frederiksen and E.G. Ametsbichler (eds), *Women writers in German-speaking countries: a bio-biographical critical sourcebook* (Westport, CT, 1998). Hahn-Hahn and Lewald have been discussed as antipodes on numerous occasions; for example, by Bernd Goldmann in 'Ida Hahn-Hahn und andere schreibende Frauen des beginnenden 19. Jahrhunderts' in *Frauen sehen ihre Zeit, Katalog zur Literaturausstellung des Landesfrauenbeirates Rheinland-Pfalz* (Mainz, 1984), pp. 13–25.
2. Fanny Lewald, alias Iduna Gräfin H.H., *Diogena* (1847), edition quoted here: Königstein, 1996. This work satirizes a number of novels in one fell swoop, particularly *Gräfin Faustine* (1840), *Gräfin Sibylle, eine Selbstbiographie* (1846),

*Sigismund Forster* (1843) and *Zwei Frauen* (1845): see Ulrike Helmer's postscript in *Diogena*, pp. 152ff.

3. Edition quoted here: Wien, 1991.
4. Edition quoted here: Frankfurt am Main, 1992.
5. Edition quoted here: Frankfurt am Main, 1991. Kinkel's novel was only finished in 1858 and published by her husband in 1860, around ten years after the political events of the *Vormärz*. However, these events are its starting point and are discussed throughout the novel. The Restoration affected an émigré family of intellectuals in a different way from the way in which it affected a family in the German states or Austria.
6. For details, compare the respective entries in Gisela Brinker-Gabler *et al.*, *Lexikon deutschsprachiger Schriftstellerinnen 1800–1945* (Munich, 1986).
7. J.H. Campe, 'Väterlicher Rat für meine Tochter ...' (1789), in S. Lange (ed.), *Ob die Weiber Menschen sind* (Leipzig, 1992), pp. 24–37, here p. 27.
8. Betty Gleim, for example, in 'Über die Bildung der Frauen und die Behauptung der Würde in den wichtigsten Verhältnissen des Lebens' (1814), in *Ob die Weiber Menschen sind*, pp. 86–111. The most important situation in life for a woman is marriage.
9. See Becker-Contarino, *Der lange Weg zur Mündigkeit* (Stuttgart, 1987), pp. 194–6.
10. See Germaine Goetzinger, 'Demokratismus vs Restauration, Autorinnen zwischen Politik, Frauenfrage und Macht', in Gisela Brinker-Gabler (ed.), *Deutsche Literatur von Frauen*, vol. 2 (Munich, 1988), pp. 86–104, here p. 88.
11. For example, Louise Otto and others in the *Frauen-Zeitung* (1849), as quoted in Goetzinger (*op. cit.*, p. 90f.), clashed further concerning the degree of education, and with respect to the degree of radicalism when demanding political rights. Bourgeois women were to varying degrees aware of and concerned with the very different needs of proletarian women. In the context of this essay these fields are of minor importance and are therefore neglected.
12. Goetzinger characterizes the situation with the term 'double bind' (*op. cit.*, p. 104).
13. *Ibid.*, p. 92ff.
14. Lewald speaks of Italy as 'jenes Fabelland' (*Italienisches Bilderbuch*, p. 5).
15. *Orientalische Briefe*, p. 17.
16. Johanna herself was an accomplished pianist and composer by the time she married Gottfried Kinkel. She helped him in his democratic *Vormärz* ambitions and had to bear the brunt of the consequences when he was caught and incarcerated. She lost her piano pupils and had to fend for her four children, her husband and herself. Once they had been able to emigrate to England, both of them tried to eke out a living: Johanna by teaching the piano; Gottfried by lecturing in art history and the history of literature.
17. Characteristically, the narrator does not paint the girls' future in entirely bright colours. Enough was said on the difficult life of artists in the book to appreciate that it cannot be a dream (see particularly Chapter 7: 'Die vornehmen Proletarier').
18. See *Hans Ibeles in London*, Chapter 18: 'Der Sklavenmarkt und die freien Töchter Albinos' (*sic*), pp. 252–62.
19. See, in *Gräfin Faustine* (1840) (Bonn, 1986), for example, the image of the virgin statue in a temple (p. 10f.) in an all-black silk dress with immaculate

light skin (p. 93), Faustine as she was transfixed (her gaze is compared to a Girandola) (p. 141), and similarly in other pre-1850 novels.

20. *Hans Ibeles in London*, Chapter 11, pp. 143–59, 'Die deutsche Governeß (Manuskript)'.

21. Of special importance is the description of the beginning of the Roman Carnival, marked by a ceremony in which the Jews of the Roman Ghetto bring a token tribute to the Roman Senate and Citizens in order to have their right of residence extended by another year (p. 162) and the description and discussion of the Baptism of Jews before Easter (p. 205).

22. See 'Aus dem Karneval', pp. 162–92.

23. See Horazio's comment on this chance opportunity (*Italienische Reisebilder*, p. 177).

24. See Ulrike Helmer's postscript to *Italienische Reisebilder*, p. 339. Stahr does not figure at all in this volume. Lewald dedicated a private diary of their time in Italy to him later.

25. See Brinker-Gabler *et al*. (*op. cit.*, p. 198f.).

# 5
# 'Apollo aber schließlich die Sprache des Dionysus': Harmony or Hegemony in *Die Geburt der Tragödie*?

*Ronald Speirs*

It is commonly held that Nietzsche conceived the relationship between the Dionysiac and the Apolline to be one of balance or even synthesis.[1] In what follows I shall argue that such a view conflicts with crucial parts of Nietzsche's argument, and attempt to explain why.

It is certainly not difficult to find passages which appear to support a synthesizing interpretation of *Die Geburt der Tragödie* [The Birth of Tragedy]. Indeed, the very first paragraph of the book asserts that the distinct artistic drives of the Apolline and the Dionysiac became paired thanks to a metaphysical miracle of the Hellenic 'Will', and that they 'in dieser Paarung zuletzt das ebenso dionysische als apollinische Kunstwerk der attischen Tragödie erzeugen' (22).[2] The creator of this supreme form of tragedy is characterized by Nietzsche as 'zugleich Rausch- und Traumkünstler' (26), while the creation itself is described as 'das gemeinsame Ziel beider Triebe, deren geheimnisvolles Ehebündnis, nach langem vorhergehenden Kampfe, sich in einem solchen Kinde – das zugleich Antigone und Kassandra ist – verherrlicht hat' (38). Correspondingly, Nietzsche's declared aim is to grasp the 'dionysisch-apollinischen Genius' or at least to attain to 'das ahnungsvolle Verständnis jenes Einheitsmysteriums' (38).

51

The final sentence of Section 21 of *Die Geburt der Tragödie* in particular is sometimes cited[3] as evidence of Nietzsche's belief that the supreme aim of tragedy was only to be achieved through a balance or 'fraternal bond' between the Apolline and the Dionysiac:

> So wäre wirklich das schwierige Verhältnis des Apollinischen und des Dionysischen in der Tragödie durch einen Bruderbund beider Gottheiten zu symbolisieren: Dionysus redet die Sprache des Apollo, Apollo aber schließlich die Sprache des Dionysus: womit das höchste Ziel der Tragödie und der Kunst überhaupt erreicht ist. (136)

It is my contention, however, that Nietzsche's use of the word 'schließlich' here, far from being a rhetorical flourish, indicates that he understands the experience of musical tragedy (whereby the music is of the essence, not some dispensable decoration) to be a dynamic process which ends in the dominance of the Dionysiac over the Apolline drive at that culminating moment when 'Apollo finally speaks the language of Dionysus'. To demonstrate this it is necessary simply to follow the argument of Section 21 step by step.

As Nietzsche defines it in this section, the role of the Apolline in musical tragedy is to create a screen of images that will shield the spectator-listener, for the duration of the action, from the exorbitant power of the music that threatens to suck the individual into the annihilating maelstrom of the primal, universal Being, of which Dionysiac music is the symbol. So effectively does this veil of imagery function that it can produce the illusory impression in the mind of the audience that the music is merely a means of presenting and enlivening the action:

> Die Tragödie stellt zwischen die universale Geltung ihrer Musik und den dionysisch-empfänglichen Zuhörer ein erhabenes Gleichnis, den Mythos, und erweckt bei jenem den Schein, als ob die Musik nur ein höchstes Darstellungsmittel zur Belebung der plastischen Welt des Mythus sei. (130)

In truth, Nietzsche maintains, the reverse is the case: the mythical drama actually subserves the aim of the music, in that it permits music to attain to a degree of expressiveness far more intense than the listener could bear if his (or her) attention were not partly distracted by the veil of action:

Dieser edlen Täuschung vertrauend darf sie [die Musik] jetzt ihre Glieder zum rhythmischen Tanze bewegen und sich unbedenklich einem orgiastischen Gefühl der Freiheit hingeben, in welchem sie als Musik an sich, ohne jene Täuschung, nicht zu schwelgen wagen dürfte. (130)

In return for such expressive freedom, the music imparts to the dramatic figures an otherwise unattainable suggestiveness, enabling them to become *almost* transparent for the universal metaphysical reality to whose creative and destructive energies the mythical action points:

Dafür verleiht die Musik, als Gegengeschenk, dem tragischen Mythus eine so eindringliche und überzeugende metaphysische Bedeutsamkeit, wie sie Wort und Bild, ohne jene einzige Hilfe, nie zu erreichen vermögen. (130)

During the course of the dramatic action the Apolline illusion manages, just, to contain the boundless emotions stirred by the music by focusing them on the sufferings of the 'individual' figures on stage:

So gewaltig auch das Mitleiden in uns hineingreift, in einem gewissen Sinne rettet uns doch das Mitleiden vor dem Urleiden der Welt, wie das Gleichnisbild des Mythus uns vor dem unmittelbaren Anschauen der höchsten Weltidee, wie der Gedanke und das Wort uns vor dem ungedämmten Ergusse des unbewußten Willens rettet. Durch jene herrliche apollinische Täuschung dünkt es uns, als ob uns selbst das Tonreich wie eine plastische Welt gegenüber träte. (132–3)

The key word here, however, is 'Täuschung': delusion. If in tragedy music *appears* merely to illustrate the action, it is because Apollo's ambition in converting Dionysiac music into dramatic action was to gain control over the alien invader Dionysus[4] and because Apollo's magic is powerful indeed. But that power has its limits. The action is merely a weak reflection of the higher reality symbolized by music: 'die Musik ist die eigentliche Idee der Welt, das Drama nur ein Abglanz dieser Idee, ein vereinzeltes Schattenbild derselben' (134). There remains an uncrossable gulf separating the world of appearances, represented by the dramatic action, and the noumenal being whose energies are adumbrated by the rhythms, melodies and harmonies of music:

Sie [die Gestalt] bleibt immer nur die Erscheinung, von der es keine Brücke gibt, die in die wahre Realität, ins Herz der Welt führte. Aus diesem Herzen heraus aber redet die Musik. (134)[5]

Seen against the background of this argument, the proper sense of the conclusion of Section 21 of *Die Geburt der Tragödie* emerges clearly. The unbridgeable chasm separating the transcendent world of which music speaks from the phenomenal world of the action is crucial to Nietzsche's understanding of the final effect of musical tragedy, an effect which shatters the beguiling spell of the Apolline images. To make sure that no one could mistake his meaning, Nietzsche stressed the key point typographically:

in dem allerwesentlichsten Punkte ist jene apollinische Täuschung durchbrochen und vernichtet. Das Drama, das in so innerlich erleuchteter Deutlichkeit aller Bewegungen und Gestalten, mit Hilfe der Musik, sich vor uns ausbreitet, als ob wir das Gewebe am Webstuhl im Auf- und Niederzucken entstehen sehen – erreicht als Ganzes eine Wirkung, die *jenseits aller apollinischen Kunstwirkungen* liegt. In der Gesammtwirkung der Tragödie erlangt das Dionysische wieder das Uebergewicht; sie schließt mit einem Klange, der niemals von dem Reiche der apollinischen Kunst her tönen könnte. (135)

At its climax, tragedy tears apart the protective veil of the illusory world that has entranced the listener/spectator in order the more powerfully to induce surrender to the invisible world underlying the music and its illustrative images:

Und damit erweist sich die apollinische Täuschung als das, was sie ist, als die während der Dauer der Tragödie anhaltende Verschleierung der eigentlichen dionysischen Wirkung: die doch so mächtig ist, am Schluß das apollinische Drama selbst in eine Sphäre zu drängen, wo es mit dionysischer Weisheit zu reden beginnt und wo es sich selbst und seine apollinische Sichtbarkeit verneint. (135)

When the force of the Dionysiac is released in tragedy (not its full force, admittedly, since this would be utterly unbearable for even the strongest of human beings), the captivating-protective Apolline illusion ('Schein'), which has permitted the action to unfold to its terrible climax, is revealed to be mere delusion ('Täuschung'). Hence the 'schließlich' – which, despite all Nietzsche's emphases, is so often passed over in silence by commentators – in the concluding sentence of this section. Dionysus is given the last word not simply because he gestures towards the realm of truth and away from delusion, but also because the Dionysiac experience provided by musical tragedy is the most intense expression tolerable to human beings of their relation to that otherwise unknowable realm.[6] Though the Dionysiac may have adopted the mantle and spoken the language of the Apolline for a while, finally Apollo speaks the sublime, awe-inspiring language of Dionysus. Ultimately, the drama (the symbolic equivalent of the world conjured up by Schopenhauer's *principium individuationis*) is compelled by the more powerful magic of the Dionysiac to deny or annul its Apolline visibility. Nietzsche compressed this complex of ideas into an aphorism which he combined with a gnomic Latin apophthegm in one of his jottings from the period: 'Der Genius ist die sich selbst vernichtende Erscheinung. Serpens nisi serpentem comederit non fit draco.'[7]

Nietzsche's aim in constructing this argument was to answer a perennial problem of aesthetics, namely: why do, why can men take pleasure in tragic subjects? His answer has both a negative and a positive aspect. Put negatively, pleasure in tragedy is not of the same kind as pleasure in the visual arts, such as sculpture or epic poetry, both of which transfigure, celebrate, 'justify', and thus bind men to the world of appearances. Although tragedy too employs the arts of Apollo, it does so in order to induce an effect quite at variance with what Nietzsche's contemporaries sought to subsume under the aesthetic of the beautiful. The spectator of tragedy knows that his experience does not aim at 'die in jenem Anschauen erreichte Rechtfertigung der Welt der individuatio, als welche die Spitze und der Inbegriff der apollinischen Kunst ist' (136). On the contrary, despite its beauty and nobility, the tragic spectator negates the very world the stage presents to his gaze: 'Er schaut die verklärte Welt der Bühne und verneint sie doch.' In Nietzsche's view the purpose for which the tragic hero is created is, precisely, to be defeated and destroyed;[8] indeed, therein lies both his paradoxical 'victory' and the kernel of the spectator's pleasure as he 'sieht den tragischen Helden vor sich in epischer Deutlichkeit und Schönheit und erfreut sich doch an seiner Vernichtung' (136). Delight in tragedy springs from that point in human beings at which their view of the phenomenal world is in sympathy with that of the awesome, hidden, Saturn-like creator and destroyer of the world which plays with substanceless, finite symbols of its own infinite being. Through the experience of tragedy humans are at least partly released from the vanity of this world and all its sufferings by the knowledge of its delusory, insubstantial nature. This is the human counterpart to the release ('Erlösung') given, in a rather different way, to the infinite creative energies of the Primal Unity by the fact that the entire temporal world exists and is justified ('gerechtfertigt') only as part of an infinitely repeated process of destruction and renewal through procreative discharge ('Erguß'):

> wie dann aber sein ungeheurer dionysischer Trieb diese ganze Welt der Erscheinungen verschlingt, um hinter ihr und durch ihre Vernichtung eine höchste künstlerische Urfreude im Schoosse des Ur-Einen ahnen zu lassen. (137)

Human beings may have an intimation ('ahnen') of that joy, but as creatures of the phenomenal world they can never truly share it. The most they can attain to is to learn to live with an unfulfillable longing ('Sehnsucht') to become one with the truth of being from which they are forever separated by an infinite chasm. Humans' knowledge, unique amongst the creatures of this world, that their being is no more substantial than that of painted figures on a veil, is what makes the human condition tragic. It is what prompts them to seek to assuage their pain in the beautiful illusions of the Apolline. But it is also what gives rise to the higher, sublime art of Dionysiac tragedy, and humanity's strange pride and pleasure in it; something which Nietzsche likens to the pleasure-in-pain of unresolved musical dissonance:

> Verstehen wir doch jetzt, was es heißen will, in der Tragödie zugleich schauen zu wollen und sich über das Schauen hinaus zu sehnen: welchen Zustand wir in betreff der künstlerisch verwendeten Dissonanz ebenso zu charakterisieren hätten, daß wir hören wollen und über das Hören hinaus uns zugleich hinaussehnen. Jenes Streben ins Unendliche, der Flügelschlag der Sehnsucht, bei der höchsten Lust an der percipierten Wirklichkeit, erinnern daran, daß wir in beiden Zuständen ein dionysisches Phänomen zu erkennen haben. (149)

Whether one approves of it or, like Walter Benjamin, deeply disapproves of such aesthetic nihilism,[9] this is the artistic experience the young Nietzsche considered most appropriate to human beings or, as he once defined them, to the 'Menschwerdung der Dissonanz' (151). Dionysus-Zagreus, the god who can be reborn – restored to unity – after being torn limb from limb by his worshippers, is Nietzsche's metaphor for such unresolvable pleasure-in-pain as a metaphysical principle, a principle to which even the mighty Apollo yields when, in tragedy, he 'schließlich' speaks the language of Dionysus.

## Notes

1. The widely used annotated translations by Walter Kaufmann are perhaps the main source of this perception, at least in the English-speaking world. His introduction to the Vintage edition of *The Birth of Tragedy*, for example, asserts that: 'Apollo and Dionysus reached a synthesis in tragedy.' *The Birth of Tragedy and The Case of Wagner*, translated, with commentary, by Walter Kaufmann (New York, 1967), p. 12. More than thirty years on, and despite a cavil at Kaufmann's alleged preference for the Apolline, the same view has been restated by Nicholas Martin: 'The tragedies of Aeschylus and Sophocles (and, by implication, Wagner) are the supreme form of art in Nietzsche's view because they achieve a perfect blend of Apollinian and Dionysian impulses.' *Nietzsche and Schiller: Untimely Aesthetics* (Oxford, 1996), p. 186. The contrary view, namely that Nietzsche at this stage favoured a Dionysian-pessimistic interpretation of tragedy, has been put most forcibly by Julian Young, in *Nietzsche's Philosophy of Art* (Cambridge, 1992); my purpose here is to support Young's reading by highlighting a particular section of the argument. (The early Nietzsche, incidentally, was the subject on which Wilfried van der Will chose to write for the *Festschrift* in honour of his colleague, Richard Hinton Thomas; hence my own choice of topic on this occasion.)
2. References in this form are to Colli and Montinari's critical edition of *Die Geburt der Tragödie* in *Werke* III/1 (Berlin, De Gruyter, 1967–77).
3. By Nicholas Martin, for example, *op. cit.*, p. 162.
4. 'Der alte Dithyramb rein dionysisch: wirklich verwandelt in Musik. Jetzt tritt die apollinische Kunst hinzu: sie erfindet den Schauspieler und den Choreuten, sie ahmt den Rausch nach, sie fügt Skene dazu, mit ihrem gesammten Kunstapparat sucht sie zur Herrschaft zu kommen: vor allem mit dem Wort, der Dialektik. Sie verwandelt die Musik in die Dienerin.' *Werke*, III/3, pp. 67–8.
5. The point is rightly stressed by Robert Rethy: 'Despite the ontological primacy of the primordial one, there is no path from its dark unity to the "shining show" of the world. Refusing to affirm Kant's apothegm that "appearance must be the apearance of something" in the case of semblance, Nietzsche asserts the underivability and independence of *Schein* from *Sein*.' Robert Rethy, '*Schein* in Nietzsche's philosophy', in Keith Ansell-Pearson (ed.), *Nietzsche and Modern German Thought* (London, 1991), p. 65.
6. As Henry Staten argues, the Dionysian or whatever other inadequate circumscription is applied to the hidden ground of the world demands to be expressed through negation of all that is circumscribed: 'This *limit of individuation*, which is the only irreducible kernel of Nietzsche's allegory in *The Birth of Tragedy*, is not itself capable of being represented, yet there is, phenomenologically or aesthesiologically, something that corresponds to it as its effect or affect: it is the passage to the limit of sensation, its extreme, ultimate intensification along both dimensions to the point that pleasure and displeasure cease to be distinguishable and a rupture of the scale occurs. This is the *excess* of nature (*BT*

IV;46), the Dionysian *Rausch* the expression of which is said to be music.'
Henry Staten, *Nietzsche's Voice* (Ithaca/London, 1990), p. 208.

7. *Werke* III/3, Nachgelassene Fragmente, Herbst 1869 – Herbst 1872, p. 209.

8. 'Die allgemeinste Form des *tragischen* Schicksals ist das siegreiche Unterliegen oder das im Unterliegen zum Siege Gelangen. Jedesmal unterliegt das Individuum: und trotzdem empfinden wir seine Vernichtung als einen Sieg. Für den tragischen Helden ist es notwendig, an dem zu Grunde zu gehen, womit er siegen soll. In dieser bedenklichen Gegenüberstellung ahnen wir etwas von der schon einmal angedeuteten höchsten Wertschätzung der Individuation: welche das Ureine braucht, um sein letztes Lustziel zu erreichen: sodaß das Vergehen ebenso würdig und verehrenswerth erscheint als das Entstehen und das Entstandene im Vergehen die ihm als Individuum vorgesetzte Aufgabe zu lösen hat.' *Werke* III/3, p. 200.

9. 'Denn was verschlägt es, ob der Wille zum Leben oder zu seiner Vernichtung vorgeblich jedes Kunstwerk inspiriere, da es als Ausgeburt des absoluten Willens mit der Welt sich selbst entwertet. Der in den Tiefen der bayreuther Kunstphilosphie behauste Nihilismus vereitelte – es war nicht anders möglich – den Begriff der harten, der geschichtlichen Gegebenheit der griechischen Tragödie.' Walter Benjamin, *Ursprung des deutschen Trauerspiels* (Frankfurt am Main, 1963), pp. 104–5.

# 6

# Ernst Stadler in Oxford: Addenda, Corrigenda and Two Unpublished Letters[1]

*Richard Sheppard*

When Francis Wylie (1865–1952), the Oxford Secretary and future Warden of Rhodes House, wrote to all the relevant Oxford colleges in January 1931 asking them whether they had included or intended to include the names of German Old Members who had fallen in the Great War on their college war memorials, Magdalen College, where the Expressionist poet Ernst Stadler studied as a Rhodes Scholar from 1906 to 1908 and again in 1910, conspicuously failed to reply. Stadler had simply been forgotten. But on the eightieth anniversary of his death, Magdalen finally put up a memorial plaque and asked me to write a monograph on him.[2] The archival work which I did then and a subsequent series of coincidences led me to additional material on German Rhodes Scholars in general[3] and Stadler in particular that was unknown or unavailable to Engelmann and the editors of Stadler's writings.[4] This postscript aims to make this new material public.

First, when Stadler went to Munich in 1904 to work on his doctorate, his 'Meldekarte' in the Stadtarchiv there indicates that he lived near the University and the Bayrische Staatsbibliothek at Arcisstraße 43/2 from 27 (not 26) April to 25 July 1904 (cf. *DSB*, p. 811). Oddly enough, however, although the same 'Meldekarte' describes the purpose of his stay in Munich as 'Studium', the University Archives contain no record of his presence at the University either as an 'ordentlich immatrikulierter Student' or as a 'Gasthörer'.[5]

Second, when Stadler arrived at Magdalen, he was unwittingly treading on ground that was even more unprepared than I had surmised in my monograph. There had been one German Rhodes Scholar at Magdalen before Stadler: Hélie, Le Marquis de Talleyrand-Périgord (1882–1968), a personal nominee of the Kaiser (see below). One of the very first intake of Rhodes Scholars in 1903, he had arrived more than a fortnight after the beginning of term, without proper testimonials or examination certificates, provoking Magdalen's formidable President Thomas Herbert Warren (1853–1930) to write a stiffly worded letter of protest to the German authorities on 10 November 1903.[6] Talleyrand seems to have been a very personable young man and began his studies well, scoring an alpha in the Terminal (college) Examinations at the end of his first term. But he then seems to have got in with the fast set, specifically the notorious Bullingdon Club, and encouraged it, one summer evening 'by way of a spirited finish' to a 'successful dinner', 'to raid the Magdalen Deer Park, secure a deer and brighten up the High [Street]', thereby incurring the wrath of Warren even though the raid was unsuccessful.[7] On 23 June 1905, just before he left Oxford, he was summoned to the Chancellor's Court to pay a tailor's bill of £28 9d – a not inconsiderable sum when you remember that an Oxford carter's yearly income at the time was just under £71 a year.[8] And on 12 June 1906, he failed his B.Litt. on Roman Law so badly that the Law Faculty resolved to dispense with a viva on the grounds that nothing could be done to redeem the dissertation. Stadler fell foul of Magdalen's authorities for very different reasons but Warren nevertheless tarred him with the Talleyrand brush. In April 1911, responding to a circular letter from Wylie on the progress of German Rhodes Scholars to date, Warren described Talleyrand as 'attractive' but 'idle' and complained about Stadler's 'shilly shallying with his work' (RH File 1682). Similarly, when a third German Rhodes Scholar applied to come to Magdalen in 1911, Warren wrote to Wylie on 10 June 1911 that they would accept him only if they received guarantees that 'he is kept at work which we had not in the case of either Stadler or Talleyrand-Périgord' (RH File H.F.T. Ries). As I suggested in my monograph, the Magdalen authorities simply failed to grasp that Stadler had better things to do with his time than produce tutorial essays during his first period in Oxford or to appreciate the difficulties that beset him while he was writing his B.Litt. thesis during his second period at the University (*ES*, pp. 10–16).

Third, documents in the Berlin-Brandenburgische Akademie der Wissenschaften in Berlin indicate that the Königlich-Preußische Akademie der Wissenschaften agreed on 12 March 1908 to commission Stadler to edit 'Abteilung 2 Band 1 bis 4 (Shakespeare)' of the *Historisch-kritische Gesamtausgabe* of Wieland's works.[9] A formal contract, mentioning an unspecified fee (which Stadler would have found useful at Oxford in general, where even careful German Rhodes Scholars found it hard to manage on the Rhodes Scholarship of £250 per annum and Magdalen in particular, which was one of the most expensive colleges) was signed by Stadler and the Secretary of the Akademie on 23 March 1908. The fourth volume was to have contained an introduction and a textual apparatus, but in the end, Stadler included his eight-page 'Nachwort' and forty-four pages of detailed 'Lesarten' and 'Erläuterungen' in the third volume. But despite the publication dates that appear in the three volumes themselves, the records of the Akademie show that they first appeared in print in November 1908, the second in December 1909, and the third in April 1911[10] – suggesting a further reason why Stadler took so long to complete his Oxford B.Litt. and annoy Magdalen's governing body in the process. Although the *Gesamtausgabe* had first been proposed in 1903 by Professor Erich Schmidt (1853–1913), a former Director of the Goethe-Archive in Weimar and Professor of German at the University of Berlin since 1887, a contract for publication (with the Weidmannsche Buchhandlung) was not signed until 16 November 1907.[11] This means that within three months of getting an important scholarly project off the ground, one of the most prestigious academic bodies in the German-speaking world would formally commission a young unknown who had published nothing hitherto on Shakespeare in Germany to edit a major part of that project. This happened a whole year earlier than had been assumed until the publication of *ESF* (cf. *DSB*, p. 811; *ES*, p. 9): that is, *during* (not after) Stadler's first period in Oxford and about four months *before* he handed in his *Habilitationsschrift*, *Wielands Shakespeare* (which would not be published until 1910). Stadler wrote the 'Vorwort' for that published version around Christmas 1909, and in it he said:

Die nachfolgende Untersuchung über Wielands Shakespeare-Übersetzung, die sich an den vom Verfasser besorgten Neudruck der Übersetzung in der von der Kgl. Preußischen Akademie der Wissenschaften veranstalteten Gesamtausgabe von Wielands Schriften anschließt, dankt ihre Entstehung der gütigen Anregung Erich Schmidts.

This acknowledgement means that Schmidt knew of Stadler from a fairly early date (1905–6) via Stadler's *Doktorvater* Professor Ernst Martin (1841–1910), to whom the *Habilitation* is dedicated, with whom Schmidt had studied under Wilhelm Scherer, and who, with Schmidt and Alois Brandl, edited the scholarly series *Quellen und Forschungen zur Sprach- und Culturgeschichte der Germanischen Völker* (in which Stadler's *Habilitation* appeared as *Heft* 107). Given the pre-history of the Wieland edition described above, the same acknowledgement probably also means that Schmidt encouraged Stadler to write his *Habilitation* and begin preparatory work for what would be his 'Abteilungen' of that edition in tandem, in the first half of 1906 – that is, after he had completed his first doctorate and before the formal contract with the publishers was secured. But even more interestingly, it also suggests that it may have been Schmidt who encouraged Stadler to apply for a Rhodes Scholarship so that he could study Shakespeare on his home ground.

Fourth, before the Great War, one Dr Friedrich Schmidt (1860–1956), a senior (and rising) official in the Prussian Ministry of Education,[12] was personally responsible for selecting potential German Rhodes Scholars, drawing up a shortlist of about seven candidates, and assessing them more or less warmly in an annual report on the German Rhodes Scholarship scheme. This then went to the Kaiser via the Prussian Foreign Ministry (whose head was also the *Reichskanzler*) and the Privy Council. The Kaiser then selected five candidates personally (as he was entitled to do under the codicil to Cecil Rhodes's seventh will), normally following most of Schmidt's recommendations (some, but by no means all of which derived from nominations that had originated with the Kaiser). But to get on Schmidt's list, a candidate had to have powerful backing – academic, personal, political, or imperial – and to come from reasonably well-off families because of the cost of studying at Oxford. As Stadler's name went forward in a document dated 2 June 1906,[13] it seems very likely, given the academic scenario described above, that Schmidt was Stadler's backer and recommended him strongly. But Stadler's application may have had even more powerful backing than Schmidt's. Stadler's father Adolf worked as an official in the Strasbourg Ministry of Justice from 1886 to 1906; worked as the deputy *Kurator* – a state-appointed administrator whose duties combined those of a modern English Registrar and Vice-Chancellor – of the recently founded (Prussian) University of Strasbourg from 1906 to 1909 and was its *Kurator* from 1909 until his death in November 1910. One of the major duties of *Kuratoren* of Prussian universities was to liaise with the Prussian Ministry of Education, and ten official (ms.) letters during 1903–7 from

Adolf Stadler to Friedrich Althoff (1839–1908), then the Prussian Minister of Education, are still extant in Althoff's *Nachlaß* in the GSPK.[14] Althoff had himself been an administrator at the University of Strasbourg from the time of its foundation in 1871 to 1880 – when he became a Professor in its Law Faculty for two years before moving to the Prussian Ministry of Education in Berlin in 1882 as a *Geheimer Regierungsrat und Vortragender Rat* with special responsibility for universities. He had also been an honorary member of the Königlich-Preußische Akademie der Wissenschaften since 21 December 1899 (of which, of course, Schmidt was also a member).[15] Given that the Prussian *Beamtentum* formed a compact elite group and that several of Schmidt's nominees came from that echelon, Althoff, too, may have heard about Ernst Stadler from Schmidt and, knowing his father, have put in a good word for him with Schmidt (who had taken over from Althoff as *Abteilungsdirigent für Kunst und allgemeine wissenschaftliche Anglegenheiten* in 1903 and worked directly under him until Althoff's retirement on grounds of ill-health in 1907). Whoever Stadler's backers were, their judgement was certainly vindicated since Schmidt's annual report-cum-shortlist dated 29 April 1907 specifically states that Oxford wants 'ältere Studierende und eigentliche Students (Gelehrte) ..., die auf die englische Jugend vorbildlichen Einfluß zu üben geeignet sind. Daß sich derartige Studierende, wie Dr Erbe, Dr Drechsler und Dr Stadler in Oxford besonderer Würdigung erfreut haben, ist nicht zu verkennen.'[16]

Fifth, it transpires from a letter of 12 July 1906 from the Prussian Ministry of Education to the Prussian Foreign Office[17] that Stadler had originally applied not for Magdalen but for Corpus Christi – probably because Corpus had a high academic profile in German academic circles[18] – and that a Prussian aristocrat, Baron Gunther von Diergardt (1884–1965), whose mother was the sister of the Kaiser's *Ober-Hofmeisterin* and whose father was a *Königlicher Kammerherr*, had applied to Magdalen. But von Diergardt had studied one semester of Law at the University of Munich and on 26 June 1906 Wylie wrote to Schmidt advising him that Magdalen's President – probably with Talleyrand's recent B.Litt. débâcle very much in mind – did not want a law student as a German Rhodes Scholar that year and would prefer a student of science or philology. Consequently, he, Wylie, had decided to send Stadler to Magdalen and would try to get the well-connected von Diergardt a place at Christ Church – in those days the aristocratic college *par excellence* – as Corpus had no more vacancies. Although Wylie's decision was not particularly fortunate from Stadler's point of view, it certainly meant that Magdalen got the better deal since in June 1908 von Diergardt failed the Diploma in Economics (a two-year course which had been instituted in June 1903 and which was particularly suited to the needs of German Rhodes Scholars), having taken the first paper and then withdrawn from the examination.[19] As a result, he was sent down a week early and it transpires from Wylie's carefully understated letters to Schmidt of 11 February and 6 August 1908[20] that this failure was due to the fact that von Diergardt's interests ran more along social than academic lines.

Sixth, as I showed in my monograph, Stadler was temperamentally not 'a good college man' and incapable, unlike most of the other pre-war German Rhodes Scholars,[21] of becoming one. Moreover, because he had originally registered as a student of English literature who intended to take his BA in two years, Magdalen treated him like any normal undergraduate during his first period of study – he had to deliver regular tutorial essays and take termly collegiate examinations – and consistently refused to recognize either of his doctorates during his two stays in Oxford. Magdalen was probably not unique in this respect since Oxford's Regulations gave Germans Junior Standing (which allowed them to take a BA in two years) if they had any kind of doctorate and Senior Standing (which allowed them to take a postgraduate degree) only if they had a doctorate *magna* or *summa cum laude* – which implied in effect that a good German doctorate was reckoned the equivalent of a good BA! Nevertheless, Merton gave Dr Theodor Erbe (1880–c.1915) the privilege of wearing a scholar's gown 'in recognition of the distinction he has in the PhD of Göttingen',[22] and Wylie, after an initial reluctance, always referred to German Rhodes Scholars with doctorates by their academic titles. Indeed, Wylie had a special respect for German Rhodes Scholars whose interests were primarily academic. Schmidt's report to the Kaiser in April 1907[23] was undoubtedly based on material sent to him by Wylie for in his letter of 6 August 1908,[24] Wylie yet again singled out 'Dr Stadler' and 'Dr [Robert] Drechsler' (1880–1961) (the one pre-1914 German Rhodes Scholar from the working class) as the kind of 'professed *students*' of whom he would like to see more. Probably because he felt so out of place in Magdalen, Stadler, in the summer term of 1907, took the very unusual step of asking to spend the academic year 1907–8 in lodgings.[25] Magdalen was not happy with this request, being of the opinion that a college was a community in which everyone should play an active and many-sided part, and it is in this context that Stadler wrote from Strasbourg the following (unpublished) letter to Wylie (RH File 1431), dated 29 July 1907:

Dear Mr Wylie,

I thank you very much for your kind letter and for the permission of going to lodgings next year. I have communicated the decision of the Rhodes-Trustees to the Dean of Magd. College who however thinks it very unsuitable for me to go out of College. As you yourself seem not to agree to my intention I have decided to renounce and to keep my rooms in College. The more as I am constrained by some reasons to contrive an other [*sic*] scheme in regard of my degree and my stay at Oxford.

As you know I intended to become a university-lecturer in Strassburg after my second Oxford-year. For that purpose I have above all to write a rather big thesis. I had the intention to do that in Summer 1908 after having come back from England. But now I understand that the professor for whom I have to write the thesis will retire from his post in July 1908 and so I have to go in for my german [*sic*] university-examination before the end of July 1908. As I am must [*sic*] occupy myself now during the vacation and afterwards with the preparations for this examination, I shall of course not be able to take my degree at Oxford next summer. So I have decided (if it is possible) to stay a third year at Oxford and to take my degree in Summer *1909*.

In winter 1909 after having taken up my residence as university-lecturer I should have to deliver a course of lectures at the university of Strassburg and therefore not be able to come to Oxford during Michaelmas Term 1909. But for summer 1909 I should easily get leave from the university of Strassburg and consequently arrive at Oxford immediately after our German 'winter-semester' (which would be about the middle of February) and stay continuously till the end of summer term (end of June) so that in fact I could quite well keep the time which is required for residence at Oxford. I should be exceedingly grateful to you, if you would lay this scheme and my valid reasons for it before the Trustees and inform me if you think that they will allow to give me the Scholarship in these circumstances for a third year.

Herr Geheimrat Schmidt in Berlin to whom I communicated my intentions consents entirely to my plan except if the Rhodes Trustees and the College Authorities objected [to] it. But as there is no other possibility left for taking *my* english [*sic*] degree as well as going in for my german [*sic*] examen [*sic*] at the only time I can do it, I hope, they will [give] their permission. I am very sorry to trouble you again and I thank you in advance for your pains.

> Believe me,
> yours very sincerely,
> Ernst Stadler

On 2 September 1907 Wylie wrote to the Secretary of the Trustees backing this request on the grounds that 'Stadler is a good man', and the Secretary approved it in a letter to Wylie of 12 September 1907 (RH File 1431). In his report to the Kaiser of 25 April 1908, Schmidt passed on Stadler's request to spend the spring and summer terms of a third academic year in Oxford,[26] and this duly received the imperial blessing. Seventh, most Rhodes Scholars spent three years at Oxford, but because of the difficulty of reconciling the informal structure of the Oxford course with the more formally organized conditions of study in Germany, most German Rhodes Scholars stayed for two years only (which is why so many of them took the Diploma in Economics). But if, as the above exchange of letters implies, a German Rhodes Scholar wanted to stay on for a third year, then the Rhodes Trustees were only too glad to fund that year on the grounds that it corresponded better with Rhodes's original intentions. And if, like Erbe and Drechsler, you wanted to use that third year to read for a higher degree, then the German authorities were equally happy since they felt that the acquisition of a B.Litt. enhanced the 'Ansehen' of the German scholars in Oxford in general and the eyes of the Rhodes Trustees in particular.[27] So when, in late 1908, while he was spending his term in Strasbourg as envisaged in the above letter, Stadler decided to use his third year to read for a B.Litt. rather than a BA, he must have assumed that his change of status would be approved fairly automatically. Thus, it must have come as a considerable surprise when both Magdalen and the Board of English Studies made difficulties (*ES*, p. 10). As I have shown, his change of status was not approved until 30 October 1909 (*ES*, p. 11), and it was immediately after obtaining this approval that he wrote the following (unpublished) letter to Schmidt, dated 14 November 1909:

Sehr verehrter Herr Geheimrat,

Nach einer mir aus Oxford zugegangenen Mitteilung hat der Board of Modern Languages mein Gesuch um Zulassung als B.Litt Candidat nun genehmigt, und ich werde mich also im nächsten Sommer mit einer Thesis über 'History of German Shakespeare Criticism' um den Grad bewerben. Um mich der Arbeit an dieser Thesis ungestört hingeben zu können, habe ich mich entschlossen, für nächstes Semester um Beurlaubung von meiner hiesigen [in Strasbourg (RWS)] Dozententätigkeit nachzusuchen, und beabsichtige dann, unmittelbar nach Schluss des Winter-Semesters nach Oxford zu fahren, um zugleich meine englischen Sprach-Kenntnisse aufzufrischen und zu

erweitern. Ich darf wohl hoffen, dass die mir für 1908/09 gütigst erwirkte Verleihung des Cecil Rhodes Stipendiums auf ein drittes Jahr nun auch für 1909/10 in Kraft bleiben wird. Herr Wylie hatte mir entsprechend der Anzahl der in Oxford zugebrachten Terms 1/3 resp. 2/3 des Stipendiums in Aussicht gestellt. Indem ich mich mit Unterbrechung meiner hiesigen Studien dem englischen Examen unterziehe, dessen Ablegung im letzten Jahre durch dringende Gründe vereitelt wurde, hoffe ich zugleich im Sinne von Ew. Hochwohl-geboren zu handeln.
In ausgezeichneter Hochachtung bin ich Ihr sehr ergebener
Dr Ernst Stadler
Privatdozent a.d. Universität Strassburg[28]

Eighth, on 15 May 1912, Graf Albrecht von Bernstorff (1890–1945), a German Rhodes Scholar at Trinity who would be executed for anti-Nazi activities in April 1945,[29] gave a paper to the Oxford Anglo-German Society (founded 1909) which then grew into an anonymous, privately printed booklet entitled *Des Teutschen Scholaren Glossarium in Oxford* for discreet circulation among new German undergraduates at Oxford. Although the booklet concentrates on the problems of being a German student at Oxford, it devotes considerable space to the work of the Oxford and Cambridge settlements in the slums of the East End of London (notably Cambridge's Toynbee Hall, founded in Whitechapel in 1884, and the High Church Oxford House, founded in the Parish of St Andrew's, Bethnal Green, in the same year). Von Bernstorff wrote:

Ich erwähnte vorhin den Umstand, daß von hier viele große Bewegungen ausgegangen sind. Besonders hervorzuheben ist die humanitäre Bewegung, die in den achtziger Jahren einsetzte. Da fingen einzelne Colleges an, in den Armenvierteln von London sogenannte Settlements einzurichten, das sind Niederlassungen von Studenten. Der Zweck ist der, erstens mit den dortigen Zuständen bekannt zu werden ... und zweitens das moralische und soziale Niveau durch persönlichen Einfluß zu heben dadurch, daß man etwas von dem, was man hier gelernt, dort verbreitet ... Viele Studenten, darunter selbst die vornehmsten, gehen dort für einige Tage während der Ferien hin, um in den niederen Volksschichten unterzutauchen und dieses unbeschreibliche Elend möglichst zu mildern (pp. 11–12; see also pp. 29–33).

Another German Rhodes Scholar who was at Trinity College from 1905 to 1908, Conrad Frederick Roediger (1887–1973), also felt that this aspect of Oxford life was sufficiently unusual to merit extensive comment in an (unpublished) autobiographical essay written some time after 1966:

> Durch die starke Betonung kirchlicher Fragen unterschieden sich die englischen Universitäten damals nicht unerheblich von den deutschen. Durch die Teilnahme an den Sitzungen der Church-Society konnte ich manchen interessanten Einblick in das englische Denken gewinnen. Bemerkenswert war, daß im Gegensatz zu Deutschland die studierenden Engländer sich sehr für die Fragen der Inneren Mission interessierten, auch solche Studenten, die nicht die kirchliche Laufbahn einzuschlagen gedachten. Trinity College hatte in den Elendvierteln von London eine eigene Missions-Station mit Clubs usw. für die arbeitende Bevölkerung. Es war selbstverständlich, daß jeder Studierende diese Mission nicht nur finanziell unterstützte, sondern auch häufiger zu kurzen Aufenthalten besuchte, um die dortigen Verhältnisse aus eigener Anschauung kennenzulernen und dabei mitzuarbeiten.[30]

Magdalen, like other Oxbridge colleges, had its own mission in the East End,[31] and according to A.H. Halsey, President Warren was one of the 'Oxford notables' who 'followed the lead of T.H. Green and Arnold Toynbee to promote an active citizenship among the privileged and gifted Oxonians seeking national integration in a divided society' by encouraging undergraduates to participate in such missions.[32] Roediger knew Stadler and actually says in his memoir that 'Ein Gespräch mit dem geistsprühenden Ernst *Stadler* war für alle, insbesondere für seine Freunde, stets ein besonderer Genuß'.[33] Given which, it is highly likely that German Rhodes Scholars discussed the above unfamiliar institutions, and by no means improbable that Stadler acquired the minimal experience of urban, working-class poverty which enabled him to write his poems 'Judenviertel in London' and 'Kinder vor einer Londoner Armenspeisehaus' through the agency of one of these settlements. Certainly, the kind of Fabianism and Christian Socialism from which such settlements drew much of their inspiration was very close in spirit to the kind of humanitarian/religious politics which attracted Stadler to the work of Péguy and to which he would, almost certainly, have moved closer had he survived the War (*ES*, pp. 21–2).

Ninth, although Stadler and Brinkmann felt especially uncomfortable in the collegiate atmosphere of pre-1914 Oxford, their discomfiture was actually a more extreme form of three problems with which all German students at Oxford had to contend. To begin with all German students who studied at or just visited Oxford were appalled by the restrictions which the collegiate system imposed on their personal freedom. At the end of his one and only year at Oxford, Hans von Lindeiner-Wildau (1883–1947), one of the very first German Rhodes Scholars and a future *Reichstagsabgeordneter* of the ultra-right-wing DNVP from 1924 to 1928, said that 'student life in England reminds one more of life in our great public schools than in our universities', and concluded that 'English undergraduates during their time at college, remain to some considerable extent in ignorance of real life and its dangers. Afterwards, as soon as they really enter life and stand on their own feet, they are confronted by temptations unknown and unaccustomed.'[34] The author of a letter to the Berlin newspaper *Die Tägliche Rundschau* who had studied at Oxford described the requirement that every undergraduate be in his college by midnight as 'abschreckend'.[35] Bertram Graubner, the leader of a party of eighty-six German students who visited England from 10 August to 24 September 1910 and who were in Oxford from 23 to 30 August, said in an interview:

> As you press me, however, I may tell you that we were surprised to find that at your University the young men are treated as though they were schoolboys. No undergraduate is allowed out except in his distinctive cap and gown, and all have to be in by twelve o'clock in the evening. In Germany students are treated as men. They go where they like and return home when they like, and they have no uniform of any description ... The German student nowadays, as you will see, is absolutely free. It is better, in my opinion, that this should be so. Freedom begets a sense of responsibility and habits of self-reliance.[36]

And the Expressionist dramatist Walter Hasenclever, who spent about six months in Oxford learning English in spring–summer 1908 (until his father decided that he was enjoying himself too much and recalled him),[37] wrote in 1914:

> [Der Oxforder Student] zieht sich dreimal am Tage um, und möglichst jeden Tag anders. Er hat seinen Schneider, seinen Friseur, seine Bäder, seinen Lawn-Tennis-Platz, sein Reitpferd, sein Segelboot – aber weder Bier noch Frauen. Letzteres ist ihm aufs strengste untersagt, sowie alle abendlichen Zusammenkünfte in Cafés oder Kneipen und Weinhäusern. Wenn er sich betrinken will, dann darf er das nur zu Hause

in seinem College, d h. unter Kontrolle. Und zwar nach dem Abendessen, zwischen 9 und 12, denn um 12 Uhr ist Schluß.[38]

This state of affairs caused Hasenclever to echo von Lindeiner's remark that the life of an Oxford student was more akin to that of a schoolboy. Then again, many German students at Oxford were clearly dismayed, not to say alienated, by the anti-intellectualism of so many of their British counterparts. Von Bernstorff, who was passionately pro-British and whose avowed aim in his *Glossarium* was to emphasize the good sides of Oxford (p. 2), nevertheless admitted:

Überhaupt hat der Engländer in der Art, das Leben anzupacken, viel mehr Individualität als wir, schon ganz allein deshalb, weil er sich um das Urteil der Außenwelt gar nicht kümmert. Auf geistigem Gebiet mag die Sache anders liegen. Das hängt hauptsächlich damit zusammen, daß der Engländer möglichst wenig denkt – er ist ein Mann der Tat, nicht des Überlegens – und er sich deshalb in geistigen Fragen auf das stützt, was er zu Hause oder in der Schule gehört hat, um sich dann nicht weiter viel darum zu kümmern. (pp. 6–7)

And:

Wir Deutschen sind geneigt, auf die geistige Arbeit des Engländers herabzusehen. Ganz fraglos ist, daß der Engländer, wenn er von der Schule kommt, ein viel geringeres Wissen besitzt wie unsere Oberprimaner ... Sind Sie also ein intellektueller Snob, so empfehle ich Ihnen, weniger mit dem brauchbaren Durchschnittstypus, als mit dem gelehrten Scholar zu verkehren. Der Durchschnittsengländer in Oxford begnügt sich mit merkwürdig wenig Intellektualität unter seinen Freunden. Wenn er mit ihnen zusammensitzt, begnügt er sich mit einer Konversation, die aufrechterhalten wird durch banale Bemerkungen, die der eine oder der andere von Zeit zu Zeit aus unbewegten Lippen reßt. Im allgemeinen dreht sich seine Konversation um den Sport, den er am Tage getrieben hat, wobei er sich mit erschreckender Sicherheit jedes einzelnen Schlages beim Golf erinnert, oder sich stundenlang über eine komische Episode beim Spiel amüsieren kann. (pp. 7–8)

Even Hasenclever, by no means a great intellectual himself, noted:

Oxford und Cambridge ist die Blüte der englische Erziehung. Äußerlich-innerlich weiß ein Obersekundaner bei uns mehr ... [Das Leben des englischen Studenten] ist der Sport. Theater kennt er kaum. Zu den wissenschaftlichen Übungen und Vorlesungen kommt er gezwungen, aber sie stören ihn nicht. Er muß ja schließlich da sein, und so ist er da. Fehlen gibt es nicht und wird streng bestraft. Er sitzt mit den anderen da in den breitgetafelten alten Räumen an nackten Holztischen, schreibt auf, was ihm diktiert wird, fühlt den Sommer draußen, das Blühen der Bäume und die alten Kathedralen, während seltsame Köpfe in Spitzenkragen und Bilder aus vergangenen Jahrhunderten lächelnd und ernst auf ihn niedersehen.[39]

This is something of a caricature of course, and Roediger, who was in Oxford for much longer than Hasenclever and acquired both a Diploma in Economics with Distinction and a B.Litt., saw that although sport was paramount, 'das Geistige' had its place – especially in the debates in the Union (which he correctly perceived to be a 'Klub der Ausbildung des politisch interessierten Engländers, insbesondere der Vorbildung für das Parlament').[40] Nevertheless, these latter considerations explain very clearly why the one real friend whom Stadler made at Magdalen, Alan Grant Ogilvie (1887–1954), was middle-class, Scottish and, like Stadler, a future academic.[41]

In his *Glossarium*, the perceptive von Bernstorff divided Oxford undergraduates into four categories:

Erstens in die 'Scholars', das sind die stillen Arbeiter, die zukünftigen Gelehrten und Beamten, Männer in der englischen Heim- und Kolonialverwaltung; zweitens diejenigen, die sich gern in der Öffentlichkeit zeigen und die organisatorisches Talent besitzen, wie zum Beispiel die Redner in der Union. Das gibt die zukünftigen Politiker, Staatsanwälte und Großkaufleute; dann die große Mittelklasse von Leuten, die sich mit einem gewöhnlichen 'Degree' begnügen, um später als niedere Beamten, Geistliche oder Kaufleute das Rückgrat Englands zu bilden. Schließlich 'the ornamental loafer', der sich schön anzieht und unproduktiv bleibt. (p. 3)

Clearly, Stadler would have instinctively gravitated to the first group and away from the other three (which were, as far as I can tell, well represented in Warren's Magdalen). He was from the *Bildungbürgertum* and had done his military service. Despite his youthful looks,[42] he was the third oldest German Rhodes Scholar during the period 1903–10 (at matriculation, two were aged seventeen, eight were eighteen, eleven were nineteen, eight were twenty, four were twenty-one, four were twenty-two, one (Stadler) was twenty-three and two were twenty-four). He was one of four German Rhodes Scholars between 1903 and 1910 to arrive at Oxford with a German doctorate or to gain one while they were there. His command of English was sophisticated when he matriculated and steadily improved during his stay. He was exceptionally hard-working and studied an untypical subject to a higher degree than was usual (only four other German Rhodes Scholars obtained a B.Litt. during the years 1903–10) and that while finishing his *Habilitation* and preparing a three-volume edition and one other, smaller, edition.

Finally, it is also probable that Stadler, partly because he was short-sighted and partly because he was something of a loner, would have been more than usually alienated from the prevailing ethos of pre-war Oxford because of the crucial importance of team sport. Although German universities by no means lacked sporting facilities, all the pre-war German commentators were very forcibly struck by the excessive importance of sport in Oxford. Hasenclever wrote:

> Der Oxforder Student ist zugleich Schuljunge, Aristokrat und Sportsmann. Sehr viel mehr als Tennis, Cricket, Hockey und Rudern interessiert ihn nicht ... In der Nacht wird geschlafen und nicht Tennis gespielt. Das ist der Unterschied zwischen Tag und Nacht.[43]

Roediger said: 'Wesentlich war, daß die deutschen Studenten sich in Oxford an dem regen sportlichen Leben beteiligten, denn hier ergab sich die beste Gelegenheit einer engeren Fühlungnahme mit Engländern',[44] and then devoted two pages to sport at Oxford before addressing 'das Geistige' in one paragraph.[45] And although in his *Glossarium* von Bernstorff understood the importance of sport in the creation of an imperial elite (p. 56) and spent a whole section of his lecture discussing it (pp. 24–7), he described sport at Oxford as 'übertrieben' (p. 4) and saw that this situation was likely to pose problems for a young German, especially one with intellectual pretensions or aspirations. Given which it was doubly unfortunate that Wylie had elected to send Stadler to Magdalen since, in an appendix to von Bernstorff's *Glossarium* which provided thumbnail sketches of the various colleges, we read:

> Zur Zeit Oskar Wildes, der dort wohnte [1874–1878], war Magdalen der Mittelpunkt der ästhetischen Richtung, bis nach dessen Sturz [1895] dem College absichtlich ein anderer Charakterzug verliehen

wurde dadurch, daß der Präsident [that is, Warren] sich Eton rowing-men erbat; seitdem ist Magdalen im Rudern stets an der Spitze gewesen. Das College zeichnet sich durch großen Reichtum aus und durch ein starkes Zusammenhalten seiner Studenten, die auf die übrigen Colleges herabzusehen geneigt sind. (p. 44)

Stadler was not a pretentious man, but he was first and foremost a serious-minded intellectual and his early poetry had been heavily marked by *fin de siècle* aestheticism. So when he discovered not only that he was a member of Oscar Wilde's old college but also that the cult of aestheticism had been displaced to a significant extent by one of muscular anti-intellectualism, he must have experienced the difficulties described by von Bernstorff even more acutely than most of his German peers. When Stadler left Oxford in June 1910, he gave a dedicated copy of his first doctoral thesis to H. Krebs, the Librarian of Oxford's Taylor Institute, which is still preserved there, and in February 1912 he sent what seems to have been a copy of his *Habilitation* to the Rhodes Trustees for their newly established collection of Rhodes Scholars' Publications (now dispersed) which an unidentified respondent acknowledged in a letter of 4 March 1912 (RH File, E.M.R. Stadler). But he never sent any of the publications which derived from his time in Oxford either to Magdalen's library or to his tutor P.V.M. Benecke (cf. *ES*, p. 8), which possibly ties in with the fact that in the second group photograph[46] the maturer and markedly more self-confident Dr Stadler is standing in a Wildean pose, with a faint look of Wildean hauteur on his face and his more than averagely floppy hair parted down the middle (instead of down the side like most of the shorter-haired athletes surrounding him). This may be fanciful, but I cannot help wondering whether this was not a subdued but pointed reminder of that 'aesthetischen Radikalismus' which Stadler would approvingly impute to Wilde in an essay that he wrote about his friend René Schickele c. 1912 (see *DSB*, pp. 288 and 690) and which he had signally failed to find in Magdalen. After the crude nationalism generated by the 1998 World Cup, I, at least, would like to think so.

## Notes

1. The information contained in this essay comes from many sources and I would like to express my particular thanks to Mr Simon Bailey (Oxford University Archives); Dr Robin Darwall-Smith and Dr Janie Cottis (Magdalen College Archives); Professor W.E.W. Roediger, the nephew of Conrad

Roediger; Ms Caroline Brown (Rhodes House Archives) and Ms Jill Hughes (The Taylor Institution Library, Oxford) for their help and patience. Stadler's first letter is reproduced by kind permission of the Warden and Trustees of Rhodes House (RH); his second letter by kind permission of the Geheimes Staatsarchiv Preussischer Kulturbesitz (Berlin) (GSPK); and both are reproduced through the good offices of Frau Nina Schneider (Hamburg) to whom I am also indebted for her very helpful advice and perceptive criticisms. Thanks are also due to the Bundesarchiv (Berlin) (BAB), the Berlin-Brandenburgische Akademie der Wissenschaften (Berlin) (BBAW) and the Archiv des Auswärtigen Amtes (Bonn) for their hospitality in summer 1998. A final debt of gratitude is owed to the DAAD whose generosity enabled me to do much of the research involved in this essay.

2. Richard Sheppard, *Ernst Stadler (1883–1914): A German Expressionist Poet at Oxford*, Magdalen Occasional Paper No. 2 (Oxford, 1994). Subsequent references in the text as *ES* plus page number.

3. See in particular Werner Engelmann, *Die Cecil-Rhodes-Stipendiaten. Ihre Vorgeschichte und ihre Bedeutung für die deutschen Stipendiaten* (Heidelberg, 1965).

4. See Ernst Stadler, *Dichtungen, Schriften, Briefe*, ed. Klaus Hurlebusch and Karl Ludwig Schneider (Munich, 1983). Subsequent references in the text as *DSB* plus page number.

5. Letter to me from the Universitätsarchiv, Munich, 25 October 1996.

6. See the letter from Warren to Professor Franz Kielhorn, 10 November 1903; Rep. 92 Schmidt-Ott, B XXXXII (Cecil-RhodesStiftung), Bd. 1 (GSPK). Kielhorn (1840–1903) was Professor of 'Indische Philologie' and the *Kurator* of the Georg-Augustus University, Göttingen. He spoke perfect English (having taught in India for many years) and knew Oxford well (having studied there under Max Müller and been awarded an honorary D.Litt. on 24 June 1902). For these reasons, he was deputed to visit Oxford with Friedrich Schmidt-Ott (see below) in November 1902 to take preliminary soundings about the German Rhodes Scholarships and he liaised with Oxford's colleges in spring 1903 over the terms and conditions on which they would be prepared to accept German Rhodes Scholars from October 1903.

7. Sir Francis Wylie, 'First Arrivals', in *The First Fifty Years of the Rhodes Trust and the Rhodes Scholarship*, ed. Lord Elton (Oxford, 1955), pp. 80–1.

8. C. Violet Butler, *Social Conditions in Oxford* (London, 1912), pp. 126–41.

9. See Akten II-V-84, pp. 18–19 and II-VIII-17, pp. 115–16 (BBAW); also Nina Schneider (ed.), *Ernst Stadler und seine Freundeskreise* (Hamburg, 1993), p. 92. Subsequent references in the text as *ESF* plus page number.

10. See Akten II-VIII-17 and II-VIII-18; also II-V-87, p. 25 (dated 27 April 1911) where the delivery of the third and final volume is noted in the Academy's minutes (BBAW).

11. See Akten II-VIII-16 and II-VIII-17 (BBAW).

12. See Friedrich Schmidt-Ott, *Erlebtes und Erstrebtes 1860–1950* (Wiesbaden, 1952). As is evident from Stadler's first letter, Friedrich Schmidt-Ott was originally just Friedrich Schmidt. He added the 'Ott', his wife's maiden name, in 1920.

13. R 901 (Auswärtiges Amt) (Cecil-Rhodes-Stiftung), Bd. 5 (Nr. 38951) (BAB).

14. Rep. 92 Althoff, Abt. B, Nr.179 (GSPK).

15. See Akten II-V-75, p. 98 and II-III-130, p. 66 (BBAW).
16. R 901 (Auswärtiges Amt) (Cecil-Rhodes-Stiftung), Bd. 6 (Nr. 38952) (BAB).
17. *Ibid.*, Bd. 5.
18. See the letter from Kielhorn to Geheimrat Eilsberger, c. April 1905; Rep. 92 Schmidt-Ott, B XXXXII (Cecil-Rhodes-Stiftung), Bd. 1 (GSPK). In von Bernstorff's *Glossarium* (see below), it is said of Corpus: 'Während der ganzen Dauer seiner Existenz hat sich C.C.C. ausgezeichnet als eine Hüterin der Wissenschaft' (p. 50).
19. See the letter from Francis Wylie to Schmidt of 13 June 1908; Rep. 92 Schmidt-Ott, B XXXXII (Cecil-Rhodes-Stiftung), Bd. 2 (GSPK).
20. *Ibid.*
21. See Wylie's correspondence with Oxford colleges on their experience of German Rhodes Scholars of April 1911 (RH File 1682).
22. Report from Schmidt to the Kaiser of 15 January 1904 (which includes the transcript of a letter from Wylie to Schmidt of 20 November 1903); R 901 (Auswärtiges Amt) (Cecil-Rhodes-Stiftung), Bd. 2 (Nr. 38948) (BAB).
23. See note 16 above.
24. See note 19 above.
25. The only other pre-1914 German Rhodes Scholar who asked (successfully) to move out of College was also a budding academic, Carl Brinkmann (1885–1954), who became a Professor of History at the Universities of Berlin, Heidelberg and Tübingen and who, like Stadler, stayed for three years at Oxford to read for a B.Litt. The note by Wylie of 28 February 1911 following a conversation with the Senior Tutor of Queen's College (RH File 1682) records that Queen's were willing to grant Brinkmann's request because it was evident that he 'will probably be a distinguished Professor in the future'. But then, significantly, Wylie added that 'from the Rhodes point of view, he was too much of a recluse'.
26. R 901 (Auswärtiges Amt) (Cecil-Rhodes-Stiftung), Bd. 7 (Nr. 38953) (BAB).
27. Report from Schmidt to the Kaiser of 3 June 1905, *ibid.*, Bd. 4 (Nr. 38950) (BAB).
28. Rep. 92 Schmidt B XXXXII (Cecil-Rhodes-Stiftung), Bd. 2 (GSPK). On the top of the letter, someone, probably Schmidt, has noted: 'Dr Stadler möchte ein 3. Jahr in Oxford zubringen.' Cf. Stadler's letter to Wylie, 21 November 1909 (*DSB*, pp. 474–5).
29. See Knut Hansen, *Albrecht Graf Bernstorff: Diplomat und Bankier zwischen Kaiserreich und Nationalsozialismus* (Frankfurt am Main/Berlin/Berne/New York/Paris/Vienna, 1996).
30. Conrad Frederick Roediger, 'Jahrelange Beziehungen eines Deutschen zu England', unpublished typescript of 28 pp.
31. See Janie Cottis, 'The Magdalen Mission, 1884–1940', *Magdalen College Record* (1994), pp. 68–75. Here, we learn that Magdalen's Mission had four successive bases: in Stepney from 1884 to 1886, in Shoreditch from 1886 to 1896, at Portsea (Portsmouth) from 1896 to 1908 and finally in Somers Town, Euston, from 1908 until it was closed down in 1940. So if Stadler got to know the East End via Magdalen's Mission, it was during his second Oxford period. Otherwise he would have gone there under the aegis of Oxford House or a Mission run by another college.

32. A.H. Halsey, 'A Job in the City', *Oxford Today*, 4.1 (Michaelmas Term 1991), p. 58. See also David Peake, 'Oxford House Today', *ibid.*, p. 59. For the essay which set the trend in motion, see Samuel A. Barnett, 'The Universities and the Poor', *The Nineteenth Century*, 15.84 (February 1884), pp. 255–61.
33. See note 30 above.
34. Anon., 'A German At Oxford', *The Daily Mail* (27 December 1904).
35. H[arald] A.F. Loeffler, 'Die Rhodes-Studenten: Eine Ergänzung', *Die Tägliche Rundschau* (16 December 1910). Loeffler had matriculated as a non-collegiate student at Oxford in 1908.
36. Anon., 'German Students in England: University Life Compared', *Morning Post* (London) (26 September 1910).
37. See Bert Kasties, *Walter Hasenclever: Eine Biografie der deutschen Moderne* (Tübingen, 1994), pp. 45–55.
38. Walter Hasenclever, 'Oxford: Erinnerungen eines deutschen Studenten', *St Petersburger Zeitung* (14 June 1914). A shorter version had been published in the *Breslauer General-Anzeiger* on 5 June 1914.
39. *Ibid.*
40. Roediger, *op. cit.*, pp. 10–11.
41. Stadler clearly failed to keep in contact with nearly all the other German Rhodes Scholars after he left Oxford. For when Wylie wrote round to the survivors in 1922 trying to establish who had been killed in the war, only one respondent mentioned Stadler's death.
42. Two hitherto unpublished pictures of Stadler have recently come to light in Magdalen's Archives as part of group photographs taken in 1907 and 1910. Looking at the earlier picture, it is hard to believe that we are seeing a twenty-three-year-old with military service behind him.
43. Hasenclever, *op. cit.*
44. Roediger, *op. cit.*, p. 8.
45. *Ibid.*, p. 11.
46. See note 42 above.

# 7
# Historicity and All That: Reflections on Bertolt Brecht's *Die Maßnahme*

*Martin Swales*

History can play strange tricks.

In 1930 Bertolt Brecht, together with the composer Hanns Eisler, worked on *Die Maßnahme*, which was premiered in December 1930. The impact was considerable; partly in response to various criticisms Brecht reworked the text, and the result was the version of 1931 – on which this essay is based.[1] The play concerns a group of Communist agitators from Moscow who return from an expedition, the aim of which was to spread Communist propaganda ('das Abc des Kommunismus' (76), as it is described in the text) in a Chinese province.[2] One of their number found himself unable to adhere to the discipline of the Party – not only psychologically (the rebellious spirit, *der junge Genosse*, was simply too unguarded in his behaviour) but also intellectually (he acknowledged the promptings of immediate response, of compassion, and in consequence failed to perceive that only the long-term agenda, that is, the goals and methods of the Party, count for anything). Because he had put their mission in danger, the agitators killed the Young Comrade – with the permission of their victim. On their return, they explain their actions to a (quasi-judicial) Kontrollchor – who agree that there was nothing else to be done. The necessary measures simply had to be taken.

In the years after 1945 Brecht had misgivings about public performances of the work.[3] On one occasion he explained (with that casuistry that so often characterizes his linguistic – and other – moves) that it would not be appropriate to perform it because it had been conceived merely as a kind of practice piece for actors (an unlikely story, given the musical forces involved). In any event, in the 1950s Brecht strenuously resisted any notion of public performance. The interdiction was respected by the heirs – with the result that *Die Maßnahme* disappeared from public view until September 1997 when it was revived by the Berliner Ensemble. I happened to be in Berlin in July 1998 and saw a performance, which was, on the particular evening in question, followed by an open discussion with the audience. I found the whole occasion quite extraordinary. I had, after a fashion, known Brecht's text, which always struck me as largely unexciting – a piece of (given the time of its creation) understandably vigorous propaganda in a not unworthy cause, a statement that sought to explain why Communists, although fired by a humanist message, could not be humane people on the ground. The problem is, of course, that Brecht's words have been overwhelmed by history – by endless show trials in Moscow, by Stalin's Gulag, by the collapse of Communism in the 1980s. In *Die Maßnahme* Brecht is concerned neither to debate the ideas nor to celebrate the ideals of Communism; rather, he validates the Party as an all-or-nothing institution. And there, precisely, is the rub – the all has become nothing. *Die Maßnahme* has been completely overtaken, both aesthetically and politically.

I am aware that this judgement may seem unacceptably harsh, so let us reconsider Brecht's text for a moment. Of course there are impressive and pained passages in it which sustainedly express the bad conscience about the hard line being adopted. On several occasions, instances of human physicality and immediacy are invoked – and with them a world not regimented by Party discipline. A key injunction to the Young Comrade is 'Verfalle aber nicht dem Mitleid' (106). Later, as the agitators debate the only judgement which they can reach, they ruefully invoke the lure of inadmissable human responses:

Wie das Tier dem Tiere hilft
Wünschten auch wir uns, ihm zu helfen, der
Mit uns gekämpft für unsere Sache. (123)

Here, then, they acknowledge the force of the Young Comrade's 'Der Mensch muß dem Menschen helfen' (101). (The motif of immediate need is one I shall return to later.) Even in the moment of final decision there is an intimation of fellow feeling:

Furchtbar ist es, zu töten.
Aber nicht andere nur, auch uns töten wir, wenn es nottut (124)

which expresses itself in the injunction:

Lehne deinen Kopf an unsern Arm
Schließ die Augen. (125)

In such moments, registers of compassion and beauty are heard. But ultimately they are not allowed to prevail. It is, of all people, the Young Comrade who, early in the play, has warned us against yielding to beauty without first checking the political context. When he hears the 'Gesang der Reiskahnschlepper', he responds by saying: 'Häßlich zu hören ist die Schönheit, mit der diese Männer zudecken die Qual ihrer Arbeit' (107). All such promptings are submerged by the rhetoric of necessary struggle, by the sense of

wieviel
nötig ist, die Welt zu verändern. (125)

The note of regret may be impressive – and nowhere more so than when the Young Comrade tears off his mask and exposes the helpless flesh which has then to be disavowed. But in the last analysis the note of regret is not just muffled but choked by the hard-line conclusion.[4] Sensuousness has to be denied, then. It is important that the agitators have come not to bring immediate material help – neither vehicles nor tools, nor food; instead, they bring leaflets; they bring the teachings of Communism, and nothing else. Both thematically and stylistically *Die Maßnahme* is austere – even, in the final instance (and it is a play in which only final instances count) arid.

Yet it was not arid in the Berliner Ensemble's production which I saw in July 1998 – nor in the anxious, troubled discussion between cast and audience that followed the performance. I had, of course, expected that a measure of life could and would be breathed into the work by a production that would enshrine our present unease with it. And that was certainly the case. No attempt was made to understate the fiercely forensic character of he play. For the most part the four agitators stood behind music stands which held the text of their reports and self-defence. Only when it was unavoidable did they move away from the self-justificatory pose in order to provide palpable enactment of the events reported. Yet all this bodily and gestural fixity was constantly belied by other energies and intimations. The four young actors who played the agitators did so with evident discomfort at the linguistic and physical ruthlessness that had to define their performances. Occasionally the strain showed as the tensedly immobile body trembled. Vocally, too, the disquiet manifested itself – the actor who most memorably impersonated the Young Comrade often took his voice back to the level of near-whispering; moreover, at key moments he stuttered painfully. And a powerful strand of intertextuality was in evidence because many of the solo numbers were entrusted to a kind of Master of Ceremonies figure – somewhat in the Joel Grey mode from the film *Cabaret*. He wore evening dress; the face was luridly made up. And he had an acerbic tenor voice that unforgettably captured the fierceness of the 'Song von der Ware', sung by the successful tradesman who knows the identity of nothing but the price of everything. There was, then, much to admire in the production. I intend no belittling of the corporate intelligence of the Berliner Ensemble when I say that I had anticipated from them – as I would from any other company of note – some such evidence of textual critique of *Die Maßnahme*. By definition, a perfomance in the late 1990s of a play from the early 1930s must take issue with the historical gap which separates the work as of then from the performance as of now. Precisely that interplay was forcefully expressed in a moment late in the play when the four agitators admit that they only had five minutes to weigh up the necessity of passing sentence on the Young Comrade:

Bei der Kürze der Zeit fanden wir keinen Ausweg.
Wie das Tier dem Tiere hilft
Wünschten auch wir uns, ihm zu helfen, der
Mit uns gekämpft für unsere Sache.
Fünf Minuten im Angesicht der Verfolger
Dachten wir nach über eine
Bessere Möglichkeit.
Auch ihr jetzt denkt nach über eine
Bessere Möglichkeit.
*Pause* (123–4)

The 'Pause' in question was the longest I have ever experienced in the theatre. It felt like an eternity; and it became, in the last resort, an eternity of unease and embarrassment because the house lights were brought up, and we, in the late 1990s, in Brecht's own theatre, found ourselves looking at (and being looked at by) an uneasy contemporary performance of a work from the 1930s which radiates a kind of conviction that was no longer available to any of us, on either side of the footlights. As the pause continued, the motionlessness of the actors contrasted ever more powerfully with the audience's anguished shifting in its seats. The odd nervous laugh was heard; an occasional half-suppressed giggle. The feeling of relief when the house lights went down and the play continued was palpable. And yet that relief was both confirmed and challenged by the first words to be spoken after the agonizing pause:

Also beschlossen wir: jetzt
Abzuschneiden den eigenen Fuß vom Körper. (124)

At one level, it was good to know that a decision had been made, that the chasm of silence and waiting had been finally crossed. Yet at a price. Somehow, in that moment, the complex and pained historicity of Brecht's play, of its present-day performance, and of our present-day attendance at that performance was fully articulated. The air was thick with good, bad and mixed consciences – and consciousnesses.

For this – or something like it – I was prepared. But something alse was in evidence that evening for whose impact I was not prepared – and that was Hanns Eisler's music. Because of the lack of performances during the past forty years or so I had known only half the text – Brecht's words, but not Eisler's music. It was a revelation; and part of that revelation had to do with the fact that the music was superbly performed in the Berliner Ensemble production; the chorus consisted of 'Mitglieder des Konzertchors der Deutschen Staatsoper Berlin' (no less); the band was the 'Kammerensemble Neue Musik Berlin', a small ensemble consisting of three trumpets, two trombones, two horns and four percussionists. They were, as far as I can judge, of virtuosic calibre. Eisler's score is magnificent in its expressive range: on the one hand, highly rhythmic, often jazzy, with syncopated figures and rasping wah-wah sounds from the trumpets and trombones particularly; on the other, weighty, sonorous, full of echoes of the great tradition of German sacred music – particularly of Bach's chorales. It was essentially these sounds, essentially these colours and textures and phrasings that were deployed in validation of the Party, of the 'ABC of Communism'. One's initial response (in my case, at any rate) was one of disbelief and dissent. How *could* that kind of music be aligned in the service of *that* kind of creed? Yet my disbelief and dissent did a double-take – because Eisler's music seemed to speak not just of one collective, of the narrow Communist Party line, but rather of the collective, choric dimension as such, of church, university, club, society, of any institution sustained by a common belief and purpose. In an unforgettable moment the agitators put to the Young Comrade the case for solidarity, above all the case for the institution as provider of ontological shelter; they answer the question 'Wer aber ist die Partei?' in the following terms:

Wir sind sie.
Du und ich und ihr – wir alle.
In deinem Anzug steckt sie, Genosse, und denkt in deinem Kopf.
Wo ich wohne, ist ihr Haus und wo du angegriffen wirst, da kämpft sie. (119)

It is, of course, a hugely powerful appeal. And Eisler's music gives it immense emotional authority. Yet at the same time we recall that it is an authority that accepts the claims all institutions make – to know better, to know of some greater good that has to take precedence over the individual's immediate sense of humane value. The Young Comrade seeks to countermand the choric appeal of the music by invoking the evidence of his own eyes – 'mit meinen zwei Augen sehe ich, daß das Elend nicht warten kann' (120). He resists the Kontrollchor's 'Lob der Partei' by asserting his own selfhood, by claiming 'ich ... tue das allein Menschliche' (120). We know what he means, of course; but he has no chance against that choric dimension which, by virtue of Eisler's music, speaks not just in tones of a cerebral 'knowing (the ABC of Communism) better', but also with the emotional pull of pre-individuated, and by that token, corporate expression – rhythm, cadence, sonority. As Eisler knew full well, music generalizes emotion like no other form of artistic expression.

Precisely that musical dimension sets up urgent intertexts. One is, as I have already indicated, the Bach chorale. But there are others. One, most painfully, is Beethoven's *Fidelio*. At the beginning of the play, the Young Comrade says: 'Der Mensch muß dem Menschen helfen' (101); and one hears powerfully an echo of

Es sucht der Bruder seine Brüder,
und kann er helfen, hilft er gern

from the finale of *Fidelio*. By contrast, at the very end of Brecht's play, one of the agitators says: 'Auch wenn er nicht einverstanden ist, muß er verschwinden, und zwar ganz' (124). The last little word says it all – 'ganz'. Brecht's play is about the total extinction of the human subject for the sake of long-term goals. Beethoven's *Fidelio* is about that liberation from inhumanity that resides both in the removing of chains, and in the loving acknowledgement of the wholeness of individual selfhood. It is Leonore who truly makes Florestan whole:

> Euch, edle Frau, allein,
> euch ziemt es ganz ihn zu befrein.

On the word 'ganz' the orchestra ascends passionately, expansively, wondrously. In Brecht's play, by contrast, 'ganz' intimates brutality and not transfiguration. But then, in Beethoven's opera humanity is achieved as a moment of liberation from the imprisoning institution. Whereas in Brecht's play humanity is ineffectual unless entrusted to an institution. And that, too, has to do with historicity ...

It is interesting to note that Brecht expressed considerable unease about the power of music – particularly when it became an assertive presence in the oratorio-like 'Lehrstücke' (*Der Ozeanflug, Das Badener Lehrstück vom Einverständnis, Die Maßnahme*). He criticized the 'konzertante Aufführung' that used a full professional cast, because (he said) the listener 'wurde zur Empfindung angeregt und im Ganzen handelte es sich um eine künstlerische Suggestion, die auf den Hörer ausgeübt werden sollte, um in ihm Illusionen zu erzeugen'.[5] This may or may not speak well of Brecht's aesthetic judgement. In any event, in the 1990s one may have to insist that so many of those stern ideological and political commitments which Brecht could, with a measure of historical tenability, espouse in the late 1920s have now become untenable. In consequence, *Die Maßnahme* becomes an historical text only performable with the irony and manifest unease that comes from hindsight. But Eisler's music, with its eloquent validation of the choric collective, makes the irony more complex and uncomfortable. The Party becomes any and every institution that persuades itself and its followers, in the language of Blairite England, that there are always hard choices that have to be made – choices which override the sensuous authority of the evidence of one's own eyes – about human suffering in the here and now.

Many of the issues of Brecht's *Die Maßnahme* re-emerge, in more radicalized form, in Heiner Müller's *Mauser* (1970). Once again, the choric voice of the Party demands allegiance from its individual members; natural responses and promptings are deferred in the name of a revolutionary solution which alone can address those needs in the long run:

Denn das Natürliche ist nicht natürlich
Sondern das Gras müssen wir ausreißen
Und das Brot müssen wir ausspeien
Bis die Revolution gesiegt hat endgültig
In der Stadt Witebsk wie in andern Städten
Damit das Gras grün bleibt und aufhört der Hunger.[6]

In the midst of these litanesquely asserted passages there is a drama of
human transgression. The (just about) individuated voices of A and B
express horror at having to kill peasants who are 'Feinde der Revolution
aus Unwissenheit' (58). Somewhere in this drama there is, presumably,
a human subject; but it is difficult to register its presence because
humankind is largely being replaced by trained killing machines:

A:      Ich bin ein Mensch. Der Mensch ist keine Maschine.
        Töten und töten, der gleiche nach jedem Tod
        Konnte ich nicht. Gebt mir den Schlaf der Maschine.
Chor:   Nicht eh die Revolution gesiegt hat endgültig
        In der Stadt Witbesk wie in andern Städten
        Werden wie wissen, was das ist, ein Mensch. (66)

At the end, the Chor is the triumphant agent. Humanity, sensuous
indwelling in present material reality has to be deferred until revolutionary goals have been achieved. The price, as Brecht and Müller knew,
was enormous. As A puts it (and we remember the Young Comrade's
invocation of the evidence of his own eyes):

Und am Abend sah ich mein Gesicht
Das mich ansah mit nicht meinen Augen
Aus dem Wandspiegel. (61)

The life lived, then, has to offer an exemplary abstention from
sensuousness. And what of the plays that chronicle those lives? Both
Brecht and Müller knew of the call of sensuousness (one thinks of Baal,
of the Fondrak figure in Müller's *Die Bauern*). As Brecht unforgettably
put it in a great poem:

In mir streiten sich
Die Begeisterung über den blühenden Apfelbaum
Und das Entsetzen über die Reden des Anstreichers.
Aber nur das zweite
Drängt mich zum Schreibtisch.[7]

Yet perhaps Brecht manages to sustain as paradox the interplay (both experientially and aesthetically) of sensuousness and its negation. Certainly this is the case, as I have tried to suggest, in the worded and musical text of *Die Maßnahme* – and in the finest of his poetry and drama. Whereas Heiner Müller seems to me to be destroyed by an internecine warfare between contradictory impulses, as bodiliness is now affirmed, now disparaged. The upshot, in such later texts as *Todesanzeige* and *Hamletmaschine* is a near-obsession with the brutalized (female) body.[8] In any event, such issues have profoundly to do with the hazardous enterprise of writing drama that seeks to subordinate the evidence of eyes, ears, and bodies to long-term political goals. And the difference in literary quality that separates Brecht and Müller has, I venture to suggest, to do (once again) with historicity.

## Notes

1. For a discussion of the various versions see Bertolt Brecht, *Stücke 3* (Große kommentierte Berliner und Frankfurter Ausgabe, edited by Werner Hecht *et al.*) (Berlin/Weimar/Frankfurt am Main, 1988), pp. 433–9.
2. All page references are to the Berlin and Frankfurt edition, cited in note 1 above.
3. *Stücke 3*, p. 444. It is interesting to conjecture about the political misgivings that may have been at work. Clearly the play can be seen either as a doctrinaire defence of Party discipline or as a denunciation of the ruthlessness of the Party; for example, its predilection for show trials.
4. For contrasting views on the doctrinaire – and other – intimations of *Die Maßnahme* specifically and of the 'Lehrstücke' generally, see Reiner Steinweg, *Das Lehrstück Brechts: Theorie einer politisch-ästhetischen Erziehung* (Stuttgart, 1972), and Rainer Nägele, 'Brechts Theater der Grausamkeit: Lernstücke und Stückwerke', in Walter Hinderer (ed.) *Brechts Dramen: neue Interpretationen* (Stuttgart, 1984), pp. 300–20.
5. Quoted in Bertolt Brecht, *Fünf Lehrstücke*, edited by Keith Dickson (London, 1969), p. xxxiii.
6. Heiner Müller, *Mauser* (Berlin, 1994), p. 59. All page references are to this text.
7. Brecht, 'Schlechte Zeit für Lyrik' (Berlin/Frankfurt am Main), vol. 14, p. 432.
8. For a very different view of Müller's theatre see Elizabeth Wright, *Postmodern Brecht* (London/New York, 1989), pp. 125–36.

# 8
# 'Zwischen den Zeilen?': The Development of Dolf Sternberger's Political 'Sprachkritik' from the 'Wörterbuch der Regierung von Papen' (1932) to 'Ein guter Ausdruck' (1937)

*Bill Dodd*

The journalistic 'Sprachkritik' published during the Third Reich is a somewhat neglected area in German Studies, perhaps because it stands in the shadow of a Weimar 'Golden Age' of political 'Sprachkritik' and such masters of the genre as Brecht, Kraus and Tucholsky, whose work was typically produced before or outside the Third Reich. But one would be wrong to assume that with the advent of the Nazis this form of political critique was destroyed within the borders of the Reich. In fact, it lived on, though for understandable reasons it was increasingly obliged to develop and refine the possibilities of a 'verdeckte Schreibweise', to use Dolf Sternberger's phrase.[1] Sternberger himself occupies an important position within this tradition. The two essays at the centre of this paper were published just five years apart, but they belong to very different eras. My aim is to explore the continuities between them, continuities all the more remarkable given the dangerous times in which the second of these essays appeared, on the front page of the *Frankfurter*

*Zeitung.* Uncovering these continuities, however, is a delicate and difficult task. Even in 1949, Fred Hepp stressed the problems in reconstructing communicative acts performed during the Third Reich: 'weil das Sensorium des heutigen Betrachters vielfach nicht so geschärft ist, um die zwischen den Zeilen zu lesenden Aktionen und Reaktionen der Schreibenden ganz würdigen zu können'. Nevertheless, Hepp continued, it is necessary to attempt such an evaluation, 'denn schließlich haben wir es hier mit einem Faktum zu tun, dem in der Geschichte des deutschen Journalismus damit der gebührende Rang zugeordnet werden soll'.[2] Whilst fully acknowledging Erwin Rotermund's arguments[3] for a systematic hermeneutics and poetics of the 'verdeckte Schreibweise', and hoping that the present study will contribute in some small part to that debate, I would suggest that even for today's reader much of Sternberger's oppositional discourse is often barely concealed, as likely to be found 'in' as it is 'between' the lines.

It was perhaps inevitable that those who continued to publish in the Third Reich would be charged with moral compromise or, worse, complicity. However, Thomas Mann's remark (which he later withdrew) that everything published in the Reich was suspect met with a strong rebuttal from Wilhelm Hausenstein, editor of the *Frankfurter Zeitung*'s 'Literaturblatt' and 'Frauenbeilage' during these years, who pointed to a long list of authors whose published work refuted Mann's point.[4] It is not surprising that Sternberger's name appears in this roll of honour. As his tribute to Herbert Küsel, his fellow editor on the *Frankfurter Zeitung*, makes clear, Sternberger saw himself as one of a select group whose task it was to be 'hellhöriger' than others, 'empfindlich für die leisesten Anklänge an den fatalen Wortschatz, den die herrschende Partei ausschüttete', to remain vigilant against the slightest acquiescence in the ruling discourse, and to subvert it wherever possible, while appearing to observe, or at least not to mount a 'frontal' challenge to, the 'Sprachregelungen' of the authorities.[5] These were the conditions in which 'Ein guter Ausdruck' was produced. Before coming to this essay, however, it is instructive to read the essay which the twenty-four-year-old Sternberger published in 1932, before the advent of the Nazi state.

## 'Wörterbuch der Regierung von Papen im Auszug' (1932)

This essay appeared in the journal *Deutsche Republik* on 30 July 1932, with the full title '"Fressendes Gift" bis "Wiedergeburt": Wörterbuch der Regierung von Papen im Auszug' (cf. *Schriften* XI, pp. 25–32).[6] Reading it is instructive because one gains a vivid impression of Sternberger's unfettered style in a time when 'frontal' assault was still possible and tactical considerations of a 'verdeckte Schreibweise' were considered unnecessary. In short, pointed commentaries, he seeks to expose the real, pragmatic and ideological value of selected 'ungewohnte Vokabeln' which he identifies as vital elements in the public pronouncements of the von Papen government. This counterfactual lexicon deconstructs a series of key expressions in the public discourse of the government: 'fressendes Gift', 'gottgewollt', 'Kräfte', 'Lebenswille', 'Liebe', 'Mark', 'organisch', 'sittliche Grundlagen', 'Schicksal', 'Sohn', 'Staat', 'Stände', 'Wiedergeburt'. To take just one example, Sternberger picks up the phrase 'fressendes Gift' and enquires why this term is preferred to, for example, 'bedrohliche Tendenzen', since it is clear to everyone what is meant. His answer to this question is both penetrating and prophetic:

> Mit einem Gift *kann man und braucht man sich nicht auseinanderzusetzen*, ein Gift hat keine Gründe, keine Argumente, überhaupt keine vernünftigen Ursachen, Gift ist eine Naturerscheinung, von Anfang an böse und gefährlich, böse eben von Natur. Das schmuckende Beiwort 'Fressend' erhöht die Suggestion des physiologischen Vorgangs, gemahnt an Schlangenbisse und ähnlich von Urzeiten her finstere, dämonische Ereignisse, ja vielleicht auch noch an Baldurs oder Herakles' Tod durch Gift. – Hat man bestimmte menschliche, und also begründete Ansichten und Bedürfnisse (z.B. Hunger) wenn auch nur gleichnisweise – in Gift verwandelt, so erübrigt sich alle weitere Beschäftigung mit ihnen, ausgenommen die *Ausrottung* solcher giftproduzierenden Unwesen mit Feuer und Schwert. (p. 26f.)

These lines reveal a fierce critical acumen and, even in 1932, a degree of civil courage which were to be the hallmarks of Sternberger's language-critical work even in the radically different circumstances of the Third Reich. The prophetic quality of this particular remark needs to be seen, of course, pragmatically, in Sternberger's reading of the political tendencies of the time, rather than in purely hermeneutic terms. Having said this, it is also characteristic that he sees a direct social and political logic proceeding from the semantics of the phrase, which is not chosen arbitrarily, he insists: it has its own logic, and the task of the critical commentator is to expose these hidden consequences, and with them the concealed political programme. Important positions are already being taken by Sternberger here which would inform his subsequent linguistic criticism: the need for vigilance against the insidious power of an unchallenged dominant discourse, and the conviction that despite attempts at concealment, the public language of the elite always betrays their real intentions. Thus, the metaphor of 'Gift' is taken literally and what is said 'nur gleichnisweise' is resituated in a discourse of 'Ausrottung', whose real political consequences are spelt out. It is worth noting that Sternberger's method here is essentially one of 'Stilkritik' (or 'Sprachverkehrskritik'), in that it is focused on the usage of a particular individual or class of individuals.[7] The language of political leaders, he insists in the opening sentences of this essay, needs to be weighed with particular care, because of its deceptively 'ordinary' quality:

> Regierende sprechen anders als Nichtregierende. Vielmehr sie sprechen nicht anders – sie haben sogar meist eine ungewöhnlich gewöhnliche oder normale Sprache -, sondern diese ihre Sprache hat als solche eine andere Bedeutung, ein anderes Verhältnis zur Wirklichkeit ... Die Worte in staatsmännischen Reden gleichen vielfach Kapseln, die *außen farblos* sind, deren *Inhalt aber geheim* bleibt, und die ebendeswegen unzähliger Kommentare bedürfen. (p. 25)

One wonders whether this essay would be more widely known today if it had, for example, Brecht's name over it – which, as far as content and method are concerned, it conceivably could.[8] But whereas the 'canonical' masters of the genre, confronted with Nazi dictatorship, either fell silent, at least in public (Kraus), or continued their criticism of the regime from abroad (Brecht), or fled the Reich only to fall victim to despair (Benjamin, Tucholsky), Sternberger and others chose a path which was at least as difficult – to contribute to an oppositional public discourse within the Reich itself by whatever means and for as long as circumstances allowed. Of course, 'frontal' assaults on the new political masters were fraught with danger, necessitating a move towards more oblique modes of expression, but not necessarily, in Sternberger's case, to an emasculated criticism.

## The *Frankurter Zeitung* as redoubt

Sternberger joined the editorial staff of the *Frankurter Zeitung* in 1934, remaining until the paper was finally closed down on 1 August 1943, on the personal instruction of Hitler.[9] A detailed account of the *FZ* during these years, and of Sternberger as one of its most daring journalists, 'listig und erfindungsreich', can be found in Günther Gillessen's book *Auf verlorenem Posten*, for which Hepp's study is an important source.[10] One can hardly overstate the importance of the 'Redaktionskonferenz' of the increasingly beleaguered *FZ* as the nerve centre of a 'geistiger Widerstand' which increasingly turned to cultural topics as a vehicle for insinuated dissent and which saw the particular value of language, and language criticism, as camouflaged sites of this dissenting discourse. The cultivation of an untainted style was pursued with vigour, in order to distance the paper stylistically from the 'Jargon der Zeit', in Wilhelm Hausenstein's phrase:

Auch einem literarisch strengen Mitarbeiter konnte es einmal passieren, dass er, im Eifer des Entwurfs, sich die Bequemlichkeit eines Ausdrucks gestattete, in die Nachlässigkeit eines Ausdrucks abglitt, der eher aus der Jargon der Zeit als aus ursprünglicher Unverdorbenheit der Sprache herrührte. Ich habe beispielsweise nie den schauderhaften adverbialen Gebrauch des Participiums 'weitgehend' akzeptiert (das doch den Bezug auf ein auftretendes Subjekt voraussetzt); das preziöse, überdies missbräuchliche 'benötigen' habe ich stets durch 'nötig haben' oder durch das schlicht-massive 'brauchen' ersetzt; das flaue 'wissen um ...' konnte nicht bleiben: für gestanzte Modewörter wie 'einmalig', 'unerhört', 'erlesen', die unerträglich geworden waren, habe ich regelmäßig Synonyma gesucht und auch gefunden. (quoted from Gillessen, p. 364)

Max von Brück's recollections of the editorial conference also confirm this extraordinary sensitivity to language issues. He recalls the *FZ* as a 'Bastion', an 'Oase' in a 'Sprachwüste' and cites, for example, the insistence on spelling the words 'Telegraph' and 'Telephon' with 'ph' rather than 'f', the proscribing of the word 'bekanntlich', and the avoidance of 'zumal' as a conjunction ('zumal da' was the house style). To a later age, such examples of the *FZ* 'Hauscodex' may seem petty, even futile gestures, based purely on personal whim. But Hausenstein's distinction between the 'Jargon der Zeit' and an underlying, pre-existing 'Unverdorbenheit der Sprache', with its Romantic overtones, reveals the ideological and political basis of these judgements, as emblematic of a moral and political stance against the insidious power of the ruling discourse. 'Sauber' und 'redlich' are words which Max von Brück uses in describing the language of the *FZ*, which retained its integrity 'wo sie Distanz spüren ließ, und zwar, sofern ein Widerspruch gegen den Inhalt nicht mehr möglich war, jedenfalls und immer Distanz durch Stil, Syntax, Wort, Sprachklima'.[11] Hepp (p. 183) comments:

Die Sprache hat in diesem Kampf eine wichtigere als nur äußerlich-ästhetische Bedeutung. Aus der bewahrenden Grundhaltung heraus unterscheidet sie sich essentiell von der Sprache des Totalitarismus. Sie ist Wesensaussage, das Signum des Geistes gegenüber dem Ungeist.

Alongside this emblematic 'Sprachpflege' the *FZ* also engaged in a sustained programme of 'Sprachkritik' which provided a rather more prominent site for oppositional discourse. Sternberger was arguably the most important author in this regard, though certainly not the only one.[12] In 1936 he initiated an occasional series of language glosses, 'Vademecum für den Gebrauch von Sprichwörtern' (cf. *Schriften* IX, pp. 35–55),[13] offering commentaries on popular idioms such as 'Wer A sagt, muß auch B sagen', and 'Ende gut, alles gut.' Even today, one hardly needs to read 'between the lines' to appreciate these thinly veiled attacks on the regime. In his commentary on 'Eine Krähe hackt der andern kein Auge aus', for example, the equation of the crows with the Nazis, though nowhere explicit, is plain enough: 'Aber warum sollten Krähen gerade auf dem Gipfel ihrer Macht und Sicherheit zu Tauben werden?' (p. 41). Essentially the same technique underlies his later essay 'Figuren der Fabel' (*FZ*, 25 December 1941; cf. *Schriften* IX, pp. 13–26), which nearly cost him and his Jewish wife Ilse their lives. Sternberger's commentary on the fable of the wolf and the lamb in this piece – an obvious metaphor for the Nazis' treatment of the Jews – finally prompted the Propaganda Ministry to open a file on him. The remarkable story of how the Berlin office of the *FZ* interceded on his behalf, and how the Press Department official Hans Fritzsche tore up the file, is recounted in Gillessen (pp. 350–4).

Sternberger's attacks in these years on expressions characteristic of bureaucratic registers[14] – and, by implication, of the ruling discourse – also frequently function (as in 'Figuren der Fabel') as oblique commentaries on atrocities. For example, his critique of the terms 'behandeln', 'Krankengut', and 'Krankenmaterial' in the provocatively entitled 'Menschen als Material' (*FZ*, 21 April 1940; *Schriften* XI, pp. 316–7) alludes to the 'removal' of 'lebensunwertes Leben' from German society (and this is also the underlying topic of 'Der Wert des Menschen', *FZ*, 26 January 1941). A close study of these materials reveals a line of more or less direct descent from the 'aesthetics of resistance' practised by the *Frankfurter Zeitung* to much of the political 'Sprachkritik' of the early post-war era, including, of course, 'Aus dem Wörterbuch des Unmenschen'.[15] The thesis of an 'inhuman accusative', for example, clearly has its roots in this tradition, which could aptly be characterized using Peter von Polenz's phrase 'Faschismuskritik in Form von Sprachkritik.'[16]

## 'Ein guter Ausdruck' (1937)

In turning now to 'Ein guter Ausdruck' we need of course to attempt to reconstruct the conventions of a 'verdeckte Schreibweise'. My reading suggests that whilst Sternberger certainly employs strategies for writing 'between the lines' – notably, transferred meaning – these strategies are far from abstruse and the encoded messages, if I read correctly, have changed little from the 'frontal' assault typical of the von Papen essay. 'Ein guter Ausdruck' is relatively unknown, undeservedly so.[17] Compared with more obviously subversive titles such as those of the 'Vademecum' glosses or 'Menschen als Material', 'Ein guter Ausdruck' seems rather unpromising. Against that, one needs to consider that it appeared on the front page of the *FZ* on 22 August 1937, prominently placed across two columns just beneath the title banner, with a continuation on page 2. This prominent position is itself remarkable – though perhaps slightly less so in the idiosyncratic *FZ* with its reputation for giving prominence to cultural issues. This very idiosyncracy, however, might itself be an elaborate camouflage.

The essay, just over two thousand words in length, has five substantial paragraphs of several hundred words each and a short final paragraph of sixty-two words. It is prefaced by a quotation from Lichtenberg: 'Ein guter Ausdruck ist so viel wert wie ein guter Gedanke, weil es fast unmöglich ist, sich gut auszudrücken ohne das Ausgedrückte von einer guten Seite zu zeigen.' The ostensible point of departure is a 'Jahresbericht' for 1934/5 which laments the poor state of 'Deutschunterricht' and language awareness in the schools of Hessen-Nassau. At times the article reads like a book review, quoting with approval a recent style guide, Fritz Rahn's *Schule des Schreibens*. But these matters emerge only halfway into the article, and the first two paragraphs, expanding on Lichtenberg's aphorism, make several pointed statements which amount to an appeal to see language as a political institution which is everyone's business. Since there is no thought without language, Sternberger argues, in terms reminiscent of Karl Kraus,[18] language is 'niemals bloße Formsache'. 'Gerade uns Deutschen', he pointedly remarks, 'liegt es nahe, die Sprache als bloße Form in die zweite Reihe zu schieben'. The nation stands in need of a stringent induction to grammar and style, not for aesthetic reasons but for the urgent practical benefits this would bring. This malaise, though not new, is now increasingly a cause for concern: 'Es steht nicht erst seit gestern schlecht um den Gebrauch der deutschen Sprache. Aber seit gestern oder sogar erst seit heute ist die Einsicht im Wachsen, daß es schlecht steht.' The issue is no longer 'der Kampf gegen die Fremdwörter' (a cause which Sternberger had disparaged only months before in an attack on the 'Deutscher Sprachverein'[19]). A general call to arms is issued: 'Heute beginnt der Kampf um die deutsche Sprache selber, der ein Kampf *für* die Sprache ist, für die Genauigkeit und Gelenkigkeit des Ausdrucks, eine öffentliche Angelegenheit zu werden. Er *ist* eine öffentliche Angelegenheit, und eine vom höchsten Rang.' Language is not the specialism of particular groups (Sternberger disingenuously cites first of all 'die Dichter und Schriftsteller'), and moreover – a statement which invites re-reading: 'es gibt niemand, der sich der Forderung der Sprache ungestraft entziehen könnte. Die Sprache aber fordert nichts anderes, als daß der Mensch sich ihrer bediene.' But if one could make an inventory of the occasions on which one makes use of one's language and those on which 'er ... von der Sprache sich gebrauchen läßt – das Ergebnis würde schaudern machen'. In a programmatic statement, Sternberger continues:

> Wer einen schlechten Ausdruck, ein schiefes Bild, eine falsche Satzform anwendet oder ungeprüft stehen läßt, der zeigt nicht bloß, was entschuldbar wäre, Mangel an Schönheitssinn oder 'Stilgefühl', sondern zum wenigsten Mangel an Genauigkeit, Redlichkeit, Zuverlässigkeit, Selbständigkeit, Männlichkeit, also auch Mangel an Charakter. Er spricht die Sprache nicht selber, sondern er ist der Knecht dessen, was einmal irgendwann gesprochen wurde. Er ist fast so gut wie stumm – nein, schlimmer als stumm, denn er brauchte es nicht zu sein.

Ethical responsibilities follow from being a member of a language community, it is implied, and since this is a given in human society, Sternberger is in effect arguing for Germans ('gerade uns Deutschen liegt es nahe') to remain on their guard against the seductive notion that the dominant discourse is 'only' words. Hepp, citing excerpts from the above passage, rightly calls it a 'freimütige Feststellung', and comments: 'Hier hat Sternberger den Kern des Sprachverfalls unter dem National-sozialismus getroffen: er ist ein Symptom für den Verfall des Charakters' (p. 145). Setting on one side the merits of the contentious dual premise of a linguistic decay attributable to National Socialism, it is clearly the case that Sternberger here exploits this dual premise. By placing the (alleged) 'recent' decline in national standards in 'Deutschunterricht' at the ostensible centre of the article, he is able to use (the German) language as a metaphor, or more accurately, in an age of increasing 'Gleichschaltung', a metonym, for the (German) polity, making possible an implied criticism of the (recent) decline of (national) character. Fully reconstituted, this argument looks like a thinly disguised attack on the state of Germany under the Nazis. A political critique is presented in the guise of a treatise on the democratic institution of language. The claim, for example, that there are signs of an increasing awareness that the struggle for the language is the struggle for each speaker 'was seiner würdig ist – sie souverän zu gebrauchen', has a clear political analogue. The subtext is essentially the same message Sternberger had delivered 'frontally' in 1932: take control of your language or be controlled by it, the words of your political masters are often 'Kapseln, die *außen farblos sind, deren Inhalt aber geheim* bleibt'. But at times this 'subtext' seems very insistent and 'close to the surface'.

The latter half of the essay focuses more directly on the 'Jahresbericht' and on *Schule des Schreibens*, quoting examples of bad style which may have a strong association with the usage of the political elite, such as the following: 'Gleich nach erfolgter Ankunft in Weimar unterzogen wir das Goethehaus einer eingehenden Besichtigung.' The language is a medium of exchange ('Verständigung'), Sternberger observes, but a prerequisite is 'der sprachliche Verstand'. 'Wie kann man sich verständigen auf Kosten des Verstandes?', he asks, and replies:

> Der sprachliche Verstand knetet die Wortmassen, gliedert und bildet die Sätze, spricht und spricht an. Wo aber solche unförmige Ballen hingelegt werden – die sich freilich mit einem gewissen Brustton füllen lassen und dem Sprecher Bedeutung zu verleihen scheinen –, da verständigt man sich nicht mehr mit dem Angeredeten, sondern man unterwirft sich allenfalls gemeinsam mit ihm einem Fetisch von starrem Ausdruck.

The brief final paragraph audaciously goes through the motions of approvingly citing Hitler by way of endorsement. This is of course a cynical pragmatic device, apparently rendering the obligatory tribute willingly and sincerely, and endorsing the Führer (who is, however, referred to as 'Adolf Hitler') as the arch stylist and thinker. One can understand the reasons for such a defence mechanism against a suspicious censorship:

Die von Adolf Hitler gebrauchte Definition 'Deutsch sein heißt klar sein' verpflichtet auch im Bereich der Sprache und gerade dort. Denn ein guter, das ist ein genauer, bewegter, tüchtiger, bildlich treffender und also wahrhaft 'gebildeter' Ausdruck ist so viel wert als ein guter Gedanke. Indem man sprechen lernt, lernt man sogleich auch denken. Und was wäre nützlicher, was auch angenehmer als dies?

The purpose of this conclusion is presumably to fool the less intelligent censor and make it difficult for more perceptive readers within the regime to make a case against the author. The really intriguing question for later commentators is whether this concluding paragraph actually takes the assault on Nazism to new, and daring, heights. It is difficult to know whether one's instincts here are appropriate, but on a 'resistant' reading, fostered by the tenor of the essay as a whole, this final paragraph seems actually to set up the Führer himself as the ultimate object for scrutiny. Hitler's words, the readers are told, impose obligations on them 'auch im Bereich der Sprache und gerade dort'. The sentence venerably quoted is, on closer inspection, elliptical and vague, a wonderfully chosen example of self-contradiction. It fulfils none of the criteria of a 'good expression' listed immediately afterwards. Whatever its rhetorical appeal, it scores poorly on clarity. 'Clear', Sternberger seems to be inviting us to ask, 'about what?'. As Sternberger might have said in 1932, the expression is empty, or at least 'outwardly colourless', deceptively ordinary. Perhaps one can imagine the competent readers of 1937 – on both sides of the political divide – tracing the parabolic logic of the piece through to this unutterable conclusion. Today's readers, however, must be wary not only of missing what is 'between the lines' in a text such as this, but also of inserting it there ourselves, equipped as we are with our inadequate 'Sensorium'. Having said this, the sentence from Hitler looks, on a 'resistant' reading, as though it belongs rather to the class of 'unförmige Ballen ... die sich freilich mit einem gewissen Brustton füllen lassen und dem Sprecher Bedeutung zu verleihen scheinen'. This would admittedly be a daring, even reckless gambit on Sternberger's behalf; but, on the other hand, it would not be entirely out of character. The more dangerous the subtext, of course, the more cunningly it needs to be concealed. The brevity of that final paragraph, its awkward connection to the rest of the text, functioning apparently merely as a pragmatic cliché, could actually be subtle pointers to its hidden significance. Writing under the nose of the tyrant, the writer must conceal and reveal his true meaning at the same time, to different audiences. His true meaning is constructed using the devices of a 'verdeckte Schreibweise', parabolic and, most importantly, deniable: 'deutlich zu erkennen, aber nur selten eindeutig nachzuweisen', as Gillessen (p. 250) says.[20] 'Ein guter Ausdruck' is far from being a harmless, parochial piece of pedantry on the state of language teaching, or a glorified book review. Here, as elsewhere in the *Frankfurter Zeitung*, Sternberger uses language criticism as a camouflaged site of resistance. Read in these terms, the essay has a consistently political import. Even on a superficial reading it is difficult not to be struck by passages such as the ones quoted above in which the meaning 'behind' or 'beneath' the surface is in plain view for those with eyes to see it. For understandable reasons, the 'frontal' assault on the political elite in the 'Wörterbuch der Regierung von Papen' has given way to the coded, parabolic techniques of a 'verdeckte Schreibweise'. But, I would suggest, the 'code' is readily accessible, and the import and much of the impetus from the 1932 essay have survived the intervening five years, remarkably so if my reading of the final paragraph is correct. Even in such an unpromising article, one finds evidence to support Gillessen's assessment: 'Sternbergers Beiträge enthielten keine Konzessionen. Sie waren mit Spitzen gestickt und raffiniert geschliffen' (p. 423).

## Notes

1. See Sternberger's 'Nachbemerkung' to the first book edition of *Figuren der Fabel*, reproduced in subsequent editions (Berlin/Frankfurt am Main, 1990), p. 179.
2. Fred Hepp, *Der geistige Widerstand im Kulturteil der 'Frankfurter Zeitung' gegen die Diktatur des totalen Staates 1933–1943*. Inaugural-Dissertation zur Erlangung der Doktorwürde der Philosophischen Fakultät der Ludwigs-Maximilians-Universität zu München (1949), p. 5f.
3. Erwin Rotermund, 'Herbert Küsels 'Dietrich-Eckart'-Artikel vom 23. März 1943. Ein Beitrag zur Hermeneutik und Poetik der "verdeckten Schreibweise" im "Dritten Reich"', in D. Borchmeyer (ed.), *Poetik und Geschichte* (Tübingen, 1989), pp. 150–62.
4. Cf. Günther Gillessen, *Auf verlorenem Posten. Die 'Frankfurter Zeitung' im Dritten Reich* (Berlin, 1986), p. 532.
5. Dolf Sternberger, 'Einleitung', in Sternberger (ed.), *Herbert Küsel. Zeitungs-Artikel* (Heidelberg, 1973), p. 15. For a discussion of the nature, extent and significance of the 'Sprachregelungen' see Michael Townson, *Mother-tongue and Fatherland. Language and Politics in German* (Manchester, 1992), pp. 140–6.
6. References in the body of the text are to Dolf Sternberger, *Schriften* (Frankfurt am Main = Vol. IX, *Gut und Böse*, 1988), and (Frankfurt am Main/Leipzig = Vol. XI, *Sprache und Politik*, Peter Haungs et al. (eds), 1991).

7. This is of interest because Sternberger's post-1945 work was criticized by Saussurean linguists for being merely 'Sprachsystemkritik'. Karl Kraus's language criticism, on the other hand, is characterized by Hans Jürgen Heringer as 'Stilkritik' ('Karl Kraus als Sprachkritiker', in *Muttersprache*, 9 (1967), pp. 256–62). For an analysis of the issues involved see Peter von Polenz, 'Sprachkritik und Sprachnormenkritik', in Heringer (ed.), *Holzfeuer im hölzernen Ofen* (Tübingen, 1982), pp. 70–93. Von Polenz's terms 'Sprachverkehrskritik' and 'Sprachbrauchkritik' are also relevant to the present discussion.

8. Compare for example Brecht's 1934 deconstruction of the use of 'Volk', 'Boden', 'Disziplin', and 'Ehre' in 'Die List, die Wahrheit unter vielen zu verbreiten' (in 'Fünf Schwierigkeiten beim Schreiben der Wahrheit', in *Bertolt Brecht. Werke. Berliner und Frankfurter Ausgabe*, I. Gellert *et al.* (eds), Bd. 22, Berlin/Weimar/Frankfurt am Main, 1993, pp. 81f.).

9. The co-authors of the 'Wörterbuch des Unmenschen' also had close links with the paper. Süskind joined the paper's editorial staff in 1934, working mainly on the 'Kulturbeilage', and Storz, although not on the staff of the *FZ*, contributed language-critical articles on a regular basis during this period.

10. Gillessen, *op. cit.* (quotation from p. 354).

11. Max von Brück, 'Die Bastion der Sprache', in *Die Gegenwart. Sonderheft 'Frankfurter Zeitung'*, Jg. 11 (1956), pp. 26–8 (quotation from p. 28).

12. The work of Fritz Kraus, Walter Dirks, Nicholas Benckiser, and Sternberger's later collaborators in the 'Wörterbuch des Unmenschen', Storz and Süskind, also deserves mention here.

13. However, only the first eight glosses have been reprinted (cf. also *Figuren der Fabel*, pp. 38–59). A ninth, entitled 'Frucht und Wespe', appeared in the *Frankfurter Zeitung* on 30 June 1936.

14. Cf. his critique of bureaucratic nominalization in general ('Das Universalverbum' *FZ*, 28 January 1940; *Schriften* XI, pp. 314–15), and the verbs 'durchführen' ('Verschriebene Schreiber', *FZ*, 6 June 1937; *Schriften* XI, pp. 311–13) and 'erfolgen' (also in 'Das Universalverbum').

15. Cf. the entries on 'wissen um', 'Betreuung', 'charakterlich' and 'menschlich', for example, which have direct antecedents in the *Frankfurter Zeitung* ('Die Darumwisser', *FZ*, 5 July 1942; *Schriften* XI, pp. 321–3; 'Menschlich', *FZ*, 22 June 1941; *Schriften* XI, pp. 318–20).

16. Hans Jürgen Heringer, 'Der Streit um die Sprachkritik: Dialog mit Peter von Polenz', in *Holzfeuer im hölzernen Ofen*, pp. 161–75 (esp. p. 163). Von Polenz actually uses the term to characterize 'Aus dem Wörterbuch des Unmenschen' and other language critical works of the immediate post-war period. The thesis of the 'inhuman accusative', rejected by Saussurean linguists in the 1960s, makes more sense as an oblique political critique of National Socialist ideology and practice, a way of talking about atrocities by focusing on characteristic, officially promoted euphemistic usage (for example, of 'betreuen'). The most important language-critical essay on this theme to appear in the *FZ* was by Walter Dirks, just days before the paper was closed down ('Bekochen und beschirmen', *FZ*, 25 August 1943). Werner Betz makes the point that euphemisms such as 'behandeln' were perfectly understood by Germans at the time, and that it is individual speakers who are culpable, not the language system ('Nicht der Sprecher, die Sprache lügt?',

in F. Handt (ed.), *Deutsch – gefrorene Sprache in einem gefrorenen Land?*, Berlin,
1964, pp. 38–41). These valid criticisms, in addition to explaining the
inadequacies of Sternberger's post-war 'Sprachkritik', may also help to explain
the value of these linguistic targets to a 'Sprachkritik' which between 1933
and 1945 was in effect an underground 'Systemkritik'.

17. Gillessen (*op. cit.*, p. 367) was unable to locate the article, mistakenly dating
it 1939. His account is therefore based on Hepp (*op. cit.*, p. 145). Rotermund
(*op. cit.*, p. 153) quotes from Gillessen.

18. There are strong echoes of Kraus's 1932 essay 'Die Sprache' (Karl Kraus, *Die
Sprache*, ed. Heinrich Fischer, Munich, 1954, pp. 436–8), which Sternberger
must have known.

19. 'Man nehme', *FZ*, 11 February 1936; cf. *Schriften* XI, pp. 243–4.

20. Cf. Rotermund on the difficult balancing act required of the 'verdeckte
Schreibweise': 'kritischen Lesern entsprechende Aussagen zu übermitteln und
zugleich systemkonforme Rezipienten über die eigentliche Bedeutung
ebendieser Aussagen zu täuschen' (p. 150).

# 9
# The Paradox of Simultaneity: 'Vergangenheitsbewältigung' in Paul Schallück's *Engelbert Reineke*

*John Klapper*

In the 1950s the dashing of many writers' hopes for a completely new, united, socialist Germany, allied to suspicions of *Restauration*, led to a substantial divide between the world of letters and the political establishment. Evidence of this estrangement, a re-enactment of the old *Geist* and *Macht* dichotomy, is found in Koeppen's *Das Treibhaus* (1953) and Weisenborn's *Auf Sand gebaut* (1956). It is also to be seen in writers' opposition to a number of political developments: the 1952 censorship legislation, the deepening division of Germany, anti-Communism, rearmament, NATO membership and, most strikingly, proposals to equip the Bundeswehr with nuclear weapons. In wide-ranging speeches, articles and manifestos authors as diverse as Ilse Aichinger, Alfred Andersch, Stefan Andres, Hans Henny Jahnn, Peter Rühmkorf and Reinhold Schneider contributed to a literary protest movement bitterly opposed to the policies of the Adenauer government.

Underlying many of these issues was concern at Germany's relationship with its Nazi past. Whereas historians had begun soon after the war to explore the origins of National Socialism and the nature of its power structure, considerably less attention was paid to social aspects of the Nazi terror and to the everyday life of ordinary individuals between 1933 and 1945. Such historical awareness was considered superfluous in a society intent on consolidating its material and military security. Indeed, even in otherwise critical fictional biographies from the 1950s such as Hartung's *Wir Wunderkinder* (1957) and Nossack's *Der jüngere Bruder* (1958), National Socialism is a notable lacuna. By contrast, keen to make up for the lost opportunities and frustrated aspirations of the late 1940s, writers such as Böll in *Haus ohne Hüter* (1954), Koeppen in *Der Tod in Rom* (1954) and Schnurre in his short stories explored the continuing relevance of the Nazi past against the background of a society in which nascent economic prosperity and Cold War manoeuvrings were blinding people to moral imperatives and making it difficult to submit to self-examination and to accept personal guilt or responsibility. This literary 'Vergangenheitsbewältigung' began to reach its height at the end of the decade, with the work of, in particular, Böll, Grass and Walser acting as catalysts for a more general reappraisal of the past and prompting the remembrance and mourning most people had hitherto avoided. The process of working through the past, rejecting the temptation mentally to draw a line under it,[1] was given added momentum by the Auschwitz trials (1963–5) and the subsequent questioning of the past by the generation of 1968, and was eventually to prove the first real challenge to the stability of the post-war republic.

One of the less well known figures in this process was Paul Schallück whose literary,[2] publicistic and editorial work over a period of twenty-five years combined to establish his reputation as a sharp and critical observer of post-war society. Born 1922 in Warendorf, Westphalia, he was seriously wounded in the war, abandoned his subsequent studies and took up writing full-time in 1952. An early member of the Gruppe 47, he was one of the representatives of the post-war *junge Generation* who endeavoured to re-establish contact with a humanistic and democratic tradition which had been trampled under foot during the Nazi years. He was particularly active in opposing rearmament and in promoting German–Jewish understanding,[3] belonged to the SPD-sponsored *Kampf dem Atomtod* and the *Grünwalder Kreis*, Hans Werner Richter's short-lived political counterpart to the Gruppe 47. He was a close ally and neighbour of Böll and the two shared both literary concerns and public platforms, most notably alongside Grass during the 1969 election campaign on behalf of the SPD. Disappointed by the critical failure of his over-ambitious final novel *Don Quichotte in Köln* (1967), Schallück devoted himself increasingly to publicistic work, in particular the journal *Dokumente* which he edited with distinction from 1971 until his death from lung cancer in 1976.

The novel *Engelbert Reineke* (1959) was to remain Schallück's one major literary achievement and, had it not appeared in a cheap paperback edition in the same year as *Die Blechtrommel, Billard um halbzehn* (with which it shares a number of narratorial similarities) and *Mutmaßungen über Jakob*, it might well have enjoyed greater success.[4] Its principal themes are prefigured in four essays on contemporary Germany where Schallück identifies complacency with regard to the past, political indifference and self-centred resignation as the inevitable corollaries of the furious economic activity and burgeoning consumerism of the 'Wirtschaftswunder' society.[5] In 'Von deutscher Tüchtigkeit' (1954), with its moral dissection of the 'Volk in Hemdsärmeln', he points to a people with no inclination to reflect on the recent past, to a society of 'Streber' with no time to listen to the insistent call of conscience or to address personal and communal shortcomings. Similarly, in 'Von deutscher Vergeßlichkeit' (1956) contemporary West German society is accused of limiting the exercise of memory to official acts of remembrance with no longer-lasting consequences. Life goes on as though the ruins and mass graves were the result of some inexplicable sudden natural catastrophe, rather than of specific human crimes, and most Germans consequently appear rootless, living in a present without a past. The fervent post-war hopes for a new beginning have been exchanged for material comforts; though an understandable reaction to physical deprivation and suffering, this is seen to have led to widespread spiritual impoverishment. Coming close to the Mitscherlichs' later diagnosis of a society unable to mourn, psychologically incapable of facing up to the past,[6] he sees pathological signs in the average German's submersion of conscience in the furious activity and competitiveness of the *Leistungsgesellschaft* with its dubious nationalist pretensions: 'die Vergangenheit und die Toten lassen sich wohl kaum auf die Dauer durch neue Fabriken und gehobenen Lebensindex, durch blühenden Export, wiedererlangte Souveränität und materielles Wohlbefinden verdrängen'.[7] Elsewhere deceit in dealing with the past is linked to political resignation: in the 'Scheindemokratie' of the FRG the state is allowed to dictate the intellectual agenda, people relinquish political opinions and fall victim to the old 'Autoritätskomplex',[8] that fateful obeisance before the authority of the anonymous state and the 'strong man' which had been at the root of so many German ills in the past.

Schallück lends expression to these ideas in his story of a young teacher and his father. After the war Engelbert Reineke returns to Niederhagen to teach at the same grammar school his father, Dr Leopold Reineke, nicknamed Beileibenicht, had taught German and History. Throughout the Nazi years Reineke senior had refused to compromise with the regime, using his position to offer subtle resistance and to promote an enlightened humanistic education, the very antithesis of the barbarism enveloping both town and school. Helpless to stop the rising tide of intimidation and nationalist cant, he was eventually denounced and taken to Buchenwald where he was tortured and later died. Many of Beileibenicht's former colleagues, whose weakness and cowardice had made them partly responsible for his fate, are still working at the school. Representatives of a generation whose past failings are compounded by a lack of remorse, they are depicted as average citizens of small-town Germany past and present. They see Engelbert's mere presence as an uncomfortable reminder of the past, a silent reproach to them, and therefore try to blacken his reputation and make life difficult for him. Yet Engelbert has done nothing to fan the flames of their resentment; initially, he is not in the least concerned with seeking revenge for his father's death and indeed would like nothing better than to ignore the call of conscience and forget the past. In the face of the hostility of his older colleagues his inclination is to give in, leave Niederhagen and take a job in industry.

The novel covers approximately ten hours of one day, beginning with the morning post which brings the job offer, through to the evening and his final decision to stay and fight. In the intervening period, as he wanders through the town, people, places and events from the past come flooding back, with one incident sparking off another, and mere sights, sounds and gestures triggering long forgotten or suppressed memories. Try as he might, he cannot shut out the past and is forced to explore and face up to his recollections of pre-war days, of life as a pupil in Beileibenicht's class during the war and of his return to the school as a teacher.

Important figures from the past include Hildegard, the daughter of the staunchly nationalistic headteacher; she had become Engelbert's fiancée during the war at a party during which Beileibenicht had been arrested. Her father, Wolfgang Sondermann, now relieved of his headship, seeks to put a gloss on his past moral failings and to depict himself as an innocent victim of the de-nazification process. Siegfried Sondermann, his son, was the Hitlerjugend leader in Engelbert's class who betrayed Reineke senior to the Gestapo and was subsequently killed during the war. Yet ultimately it is Paul Sondermann, Wolfgang's cynical brother, an unscrupulous and amoral industrialist, whom Engelbert holds responsible for his father's fate. Finally, Arthur Lehmköster, the former art teacher and close friend of Beileibenicht, whose Jewish wife was gassed by the Nazis, plays a key role in Engelbert's inner struggle. An eccentric recluse long since forgotten by the town, living alone surrounded by the writings and symbols of Judaism to which he has converted, Lehmköster's demand for repentance and his devotion to the memory of Beileibenicht represent a challenge to Engelbert and prevent him taking the easy option of flight from the past. Engelbert's decision to stay is confirmed in a meeting with Bludau, one of his young, activist colleagues, who has learnt about past events at the school and wishes to work with Engelbert to bring about change.

The novel presents a damning verdict on the failure of a town, its school and industry to come to terms with the past. Niederhagen embodies petit-bourgeois small-mindedness and hypocritically turns a blind eye to moral wrong-doing while continuing to live 'den Traum von der bieder-ständigen Redlichkeit des Bürgers ... von der Ordnung im Schatten des Kirchturms' (53).[9] Obsessed with superficial order and cleanliness, it reveals virtually no trace of its culpable past. The one exception is the synagogue where the 'Schönheitschirurgen' (84) have renovated just the front: round the back, out of sight, the charred remains of the original building can still be found, a symbol of post-war society and attitudes to the past. The new beginning – 'hygienische Reinlichkeit als unbekümmerten Neubeginn' (84) – is a deceitful façade, lacking depth, substance or meaning.

The town's *Gymnasium* has not changed fundamentally either. Used as a military hospital during the war, the ease with which all traces of the past have been removed from the school buildings reflects the all-too-simple 'washing away' of moral responsibility practised by many of its teachers and the town as a whole. The school's easy bridging of recent German history and its religious insincerity are linked to German reluctance to acknowledge acquiescence in the rise of National Socialism: 'Bis die schwarzen Tafeln mit steil geschriebenem "Friedrich Wilhelm der Große Kurfürst", oder "Das fünfte Gebot Gottes lautet: Du sollst nicht töten", ... zurückgeholt werden konnten in ihre Bestimmung' (54). Like the synagogue, the school's democratic veneer lacks substance. The opportunistic PE teacher Steltenkamp, who during the Nazi years had removed 'Gott' from his first name, now uses the full form 'Gottfried', and on the pretext of political tolerance refuses to remove Nazi texts from the school library. Other members of the 'old guard' still promote nationalistic xenophobia and assiduously misrepresent the past, including the reactionary Bettenbühl who, in a perversion of the school's humanistic principles, used to make his pupils translate *Mein Kampf* into Latin, and former headteacher Wolfgang Sondermann who, though once a convinced Nazi, is still teaching at the school. Meanwhile the new headteacher reproaches Engelbert for telling his pupils about the six million Jews murdered under National Socialism, preferring the phrase 'mehrere Hunderttausend' and referring to Engelbert's correction of this historical inaccuracy as 'solche Lappalien' (32). Engelbert's attempt to provide pupils with material on concentration camps for the school newspaper is similarly thwarted.

During a visit to the company where Herbert, a former schoolfriend, now works, Engelbert is confronted with an American-inspired entrepreneurial spirit which demands exclusive focus on economic activity and has no time for reflection on the past: 'Was glaubst denn du, wie viele alte Nazis bei *uns* in führenden Stellen beschäftigt sind! Aber was macht das schon?' (160). Herbert, like Engelbert a former Communist, has become the ultimate *Tatmensch* and has acquired the superficial self-assurance of the 'new Germans', submerging his former doubts and anger at society in a brash commercial optimism. The encounter is important in dragging Engelbert back to an awareness of the importance of the past, of his responsibility to his father's memory and in confirming that he is not cut out for Herbert's world.

The prime example of the past's continuing influence over the present is seen in the figure of Paul Sondermann. He is the ultimate opportunist who under the Nazis moved his firm over to arms production at just the right time and spent a not too difficult war in Paris where he was responsible for humiliating and murdering helpless Jewish girls. He subsequently attempts to submerge this shameful past in commercial ventures but his language betrays him: National Socialism is 'verjährter Quark' (137) and its collapse a 'kleine Betriebsstörung' (123). His fascist brutality, still evident in the language he uses, is allied to a virulent anti-Communism, and he is quick to use the contacts he has cultivated in the restorative West German state to threaten Engelbert: 'Ein kleiner Druck, nur ein kleiner Dreh von meiner Hand, ... und Sie sind aus dem Schuldienst entlassen' (106–7).

Against this background of a town seeking to deny its past, Schallück gradually builds a picture of Leopold Reineke's brave defence of humane values in the face of a perverse and brutal ideology. On the one hand, his studied eccentricity and ingenious defiance of Nazi bureaucracy border on the comic – for example, he has obtained a spurious medical note certifying an inability to raise his arm to issue the Nazi salute, displays grotesquely enlarged photographs of pock-marked Nazi figures on his wall and smuggles the works of forbidden authors onto the curriculum under the transparent pretext of holding them up as models of the decadence Nazism rejects. On the other hand, through ironic implication, subversive asides and transparent analogy he pursues a humanistic education of mind and spirit in the face of crude Nazi 'Körperkultur', propaganda and pollution of language. Yet Beileibenicht's 'resistance' is also problematic. His numerous eccentricities are ultimately meaningless, and his history lessons, with their veiled critique of the present, parallel the 'Flucht in die Geschichte' of many inner emigrants under Nazism. His condemnation of colleagues' cowardice and weakness in allowing Lehmköster's wife to be denounced and Lehmköster himself to be sacked, needs to be seen in the context of his own ineffectual private protest. In death, however, he sets his pupils the ultimate moral example; despite the promptings of the headteacher he courageously shuns the easy option of joining the party: 'Einer muß dasein, ganz, ungeteilt und sichtbar, ohne Vorbehalt und Täuschung, einer muß den Jungen wenigstens zeigen, wenn er es ihnen schon nicht sagen kann, was wahr und was falsch ist' (217). It is the memory of this which finally persuades Engelbert he must stay and fight.

The 'Dialog unter der Stehlampe', Engelbert's written record of a crucial exchange with Paul and Wolfgang Sondermann, is the novel's centrepiece in which tension steadily builds as the mystery of Beileibenicht's denunciation is gradually revealed. Paul's mock trial and cynical interruptions of his brother's faltering confession (he had done nothing to stop Siegfried telephoning the Gestapo), serve as an effective vehicle for the revelation of the guilt shared by everyone present at the engagement party. The scene thus provides an intense focus for the novel's overall exploration of the theme of accepting and sharing responsibility for the past. Paul cannot muster the slightest remorse, even though his own guilt in having incited Siegfried is quite clear, while Wolfgang's defence of his inaction, a mixture of cowardly self-interest and tragic human weakness, stands for that of millions: '[Siegfried] wäre fähig gewesen, uns alle hereinzureißen ... und ich bin doch auch nur ein Mensch' (137).

While Schallück's work is thus concerned above all with memory and attitudes to the past, it is also very much about time itself, a further feature it shares with Böll's *Billard um halbzehn*.[10] As he lies dozing in bed at the start of the novel, Engelbert dreams the hands on his watch are racing alternately backwards and forwards, an image which prefigures, on the one hand, the central theme of a society uneasy with its present because it lacks a clear relationship with its past, and on the other the novel's repeated distortion of chronology through the mixing of present narrative and remembered past. The watch had been left to Engelbert by his father who had stopped winding it when the Nazis came to power – his 'Privat-Revolution gegen die Zeit' (13). This morning the watch has once again stopped and Engelbert is inclined to wind it in order to force time to move forward again and to banish his memories of the past; by leaving the school and taking the job in industry he hopes to re-enter the world of the 'Normaluhren'. However, images, scenes and figures from the past relentlessly crowd in on him and the 'goldene Sarg der toten Zeit' (20) remains unwound as he begins to suspect that his attempt is in vain, that the past cannot be ignored and will retain its relevance for the present and future regardless.

While memories flood his consciousness, the close interweaving of past and present conveys the impression of events from the Nazi years happening in the present: 'Alles war gegenwärtig. Nichts war vergangen ... Die Zeit war aufgerissen wie eine Wand. Nichts war zukünftig, alles gegenwärtig' (50). Past and present become simultaneous for Engelbert, something underpinned by the novel's employment of film-like flashback techniques, with the past repeatedly blending naturalistically, at times almost impressionistically, into the present in a series of extended interior monologues. For example, Engelbert's thoughts on the present-day citizens of Niederhagen lead on to recollection of their culpability in allowing the rise of Nazism, which in turn prompts a general reflection on people's readiness to wave flags, which leads back effortlessly into the memory of Beileibenicht's refusal to fly the Nazi flag properly for the Rosenberg procession. This simultaneity is further reinforced by the interpolation of leitmotifs, with quotes from the past appearing in the narratorial present, and vice versa.

This notion of simultaneity has a further dimension to it. As he reflects on the way his memories relentlessly pursue him, Engelbert compares them with a series of rooms in a house, all of which seem to run into each other and which he cannot separate in his mind: 'Oder waren alle Erinnerungen zugleich in mir? War ich in allen Botschaften, in allen Räumen zugleich?' (143). Ever since his father's watch has stopped he feels condemned to a type of temporal *and* spacial simultaneity ('Gleichzeitigkeit und Gleichräumigkeit') in which his memories form a labyrinth or series of 'Gedächtnis-Katakomben' (143). This intolerable burden motivates his reluctance to surrender to the past and his desire to leave the town. In a reference to the new physics, the spatial images are linked to the expression 'Zeitraum' to denote a space-time dimension in which time's arrow has been halted and past and present have merged both physically and temporally. It is no coincidence that in his response to a questionnaire in the French journal *Esprit*, in which he talks about the unexpurgated past as one of the main causes of modern man's radically diminished existence, Schallück should employ a physics metaphor to explain his concern with past, present and future during the writing of *Engelbert Reineke*: 'Depuis plus de trois ans, ma perception est dirigée sur le point où le passé, le présent et l'avenir se rencontrent pour tourner, dans une tension continuelle, autour de l'existence humaine comme les électrons autour du noyau de l'atome.'[11] The paradox of the Einsteinian singularity in space-time which underlies Engelbert's musings serves as a metaphor of modern man's urgent need to make sense of the present and seek a harmonious relationship with it by acknowledging and coming to terms with the past.

Yet, as for Adorno, it is not a question of overcoming the past but employing it constructively to shape the future. The deceptively chaotic and random series of recollections which force their way into Engelbert's consciousness constitute what has been called the novel's 'Mosaik des Schreckens'.[12] With considerable narratorial skill and precision a picture is gradually pieced together of Beileibenicht and those responsible for his death. The parallel process of Engelbert's gradual acceptance of his moral duty to stay and contribute to reforming the school is predicated on his overwhelming sense of simultaneity, the irresistible experience of past and present co-existing in time and space. Once the experiences of this day, most notably the encounter with Lehmköster, have helped him recognize what he must do, he can return to the 'Normalzeit': the decision to share the manuscript of the 'Dialog unter der Stehlampe' with his younger, reform-minded colleagues marks the resumption of normal temporal conditions and the start of a new life rooted in the lessons of the past.

*Engelbert Reineke* is undoubtedly a significant work which has not received the attention it deserves. One of the more important school novels in German literature, superior in many ways to Valentin's *Die Unberatenen* (1963), it provides a telling critique of the role of the *Gymnasium* in perpetuating authoritarian social structures and betraying its responsibility for shaping young minds in the humanist tradition. In particular, it powerfully depicts the failure of the half-hearted, the uncommitted and those many teachers under National Socialism who chose the safer path of inner emigration. It further paints a damning picture of the petty-mindedness and cowardice of small-town Germany under Hitler and the insidious and pernicious process of post-war restoration.

While acknowledging the political and moral significance of Schallück's novel, questions remain concerning its literary merit. Since Engelbert is unlikely to manage to convert his incorrigible colleagues, the decision to stay seems to be based on a private desire to prove himself. This, allied to the exclusively subjective narrative viewpoint, appears to promote an individualistic morality which fails to encompass the social and political aspects of the evil and corruption Engelbert is fighting. Furthermore, the meeting with Lehmköster, with its strongly religious overtones and its apparent influence on Engelbert's subsequent decision, might seem to imply that, in the tradition of inner emigrant writing, fascism is an evil requiring supernatural intervention rather than a human crime which is to be countered on a social and political level. In general, one has to question the excessively subjective aspects of a novel subtitled 'Die vergessene Schuld': the reader is not shown the characteristic features of National Socialism but the intricate network of circumstances leading to one man's death which is seen to be the consequence of the moral failure of a few individuals.

However, as Schallück himself was at pains to emphasize, the novel is not concerned with socio-political prescription but is a study in weakness, cowardice, forgetfulness and deceit, those all too human failings underlying Nazism and its aftermath.[13] The effortless intertwining of present and past narrative strands, which reflects Engelbert's experience of simultaneity, emphasizes the moral requirement to acknowledge the indivisible link between past and present, to accept past failings as a basis for future social and spiritual growth and to resist the temptation to submerge conscience in a sea of amoral materialism. Ultimately it is the way the notion of time thus shapes both form and content that is the most distinctive contribution of Schallück's novel to post-war *Vergangenheitsbewältigung*.

## Notes

1. See Theodor Adorno, 'Was bedeutet: Aufarbeitung der Vergangenheit', in *Eingriffe* (Frankfurt am Main, 1963), pp. 125–46.
2. This included five novels, more than a hundred short stories, small amounts of poetry and some drama.
3. Together with Martin Buber and Heinrich Böll he founded and sat on the board of the *Germania Judaica*, the Cologne library for the history of the Jews in Germany.
4. There were two modest editions in the Fischer-Bücherei of 40 000 and 6 000 respectively, but it fared much better in two East German editions and in translation (first French, then Italian, Polish, Czech, Russian and Hungarian), with the Russian edition alone selling over 800 000 copies.
5. See: 'Von deutscher Tüchtigkeit' (1954), in Paul Schallück, *Zum Beispiel. Essays* (Frankfurt am Main, 1962), pp. 7–11; 'Von deutscher Vergeßlichkeit' (1956), *ibid.*, pp. 12–16; 'Von deutscher Resignation' (1957), *ibid.*, pp. 17–22;

and 'Von deutscher Gleichgültigkeit' (1962), *Gewerkschaftliche Monatshefte*, 13 (1962), 9, pp. 525–7.

6. Alexander and Margarete Mitscherlich, *Die Unfähigkeit zu trauern* (Munich, 1967).
7. Schallück, 'Von deutscher Vergeßlichkeit', p.16.
8. Schallück, 'Von deutscher Resignation', p. 21.
9. Page references in the text are to *Engelbert Reineke*, Rotbuch Verlag (Hamburg, 1997).
10. Schallück's novel was originally to be entitled *Riß durch die Zeit*.
11. Paul Schallück, 'L'homme diminué', *Esprit*, 26, 7/8 (1958), p. 153.
12. Roland H. Wiegenstein, *Frankfurter Hefte*, 14 (1959), p. 453.
13. Paul Schallück, 'Auf den Kopf gestellt', *Geist und Tat*, 14, 9 (1959), pp. 277–8.

# 10
## Authenticity and the 'Speaking Other': Günter Wallraff's *Ganz unten* as an Industrial Fiction
*Rob Burns*

'No class can presume to become dominant in society if in the course of its struggle for emancipation it fails to gain a distinct cultural identity, by which that class establishes itself as a protagonist in the development of humanity.'[1] Thus spoke Wilfried van der Will in 1975, and a central concern of his subsequent research and publications – on which I was privileged to be able to collaborate – was with the rich cultural creativity of the German working class that reached its apogee in the worker culture movement in the Weimar Republic. The occasion at which these words were uttered, however, was a conference Wilfried had organized on 'Workers and Writers – British and German Working-Class Writing Today', which brought together what, from today's perspective, must appear a dazzling array of literary talent that included Charles Parker, David Edgar, Steve Gooch, Max von der Grün and, most notably, Günter Wallraff. Indeed, it was not the least achievement of that conference in Birmingham that it first introduced to a British audience arguably the most successful practitioner ever of one particular form of working-class literature, the reportage. Just over a year later Wallraff's already considerable notoriety in Germany was enhanced by the publication of *Der Aufmacher* (1977), based on his experience working incognito as a reporter for the *Bild-Zeitung*. Incredibly, the furore unleashed by Wallraff's revelations about the gutter press in Germany was as nothing compared to the controversies stirred up by his next undercover project, *Ganz unten* (1985), an exposé of the inhuman living and working conditions of foreign labourers in the Federal Republic.

In the long history of working-class writing in Germany a notable and persistent feature has been the role played by cultural organizations whose governing conviction has been that the lives of working people be afforded in literature the same depth and passion given to middle-class subjects. This tradition was extended in the early 1980s by the *Polynationaler Literatur- und Kunstverein* and the editorial collective *Südwind*, two organizations founded in order to co-ordinate the creative efforts of Germany's sizeable immigrant population and to facilitate the publication of what was expressly and affirmatively designated by *Südwind* as 'Gastarbeiterliteratur'. This was to be a 'Literatur der Betroffenen', in which writing was conceived as both a therapeutic process of self-discovery and an ideological one of 'building bridges with words' and which consequently gave priority to the authenticity of experience over the attainment of formal perfection.[2] Moreover, such writing laid claim to counter-cultural status – hence the insistence on using the official term for migrant labour, 'Gastarbeiter' – for, by recuperating social experiences excluded from the mainstream, minority literature was seen as mounting an ideological challenge to the dominant culture. Conceived as an instrument of 'cultural resistance' and written in German in order to be accessible to all nationalities, it was to be a polynational literature which aimed to foster solidarity between migrant workers as well as among the politically and economically oppressed in Germany generally. It is my contention that *Ganz unten* fulfilled these criteria more successfully than any other text and the main reason for this – and for the enormous controversy surrounding the book – was its precise positioning at the intersection of class and race.

Disguising himself as a Turkish worker, Wallraff assumed the identity of a real immigrant, Ali Levent Sigirlioglu, in order to penetrate Germany's illegal labour market which is largely made up of 'guest workers'. Equipped with a hidden video camera and microphone, he then for some two years recorded his experiences in a variety of dangerous, insanitary and badly paid jobs, working at McDonald's, in the Thyssen steelworks, as a human guinea pig in the pharmaceutical industry and as a chauffeur for the subcontractor Adler. He also reported on how he was treated in pubs, at the soccer match between Turkey and West Germany and at a rally in honour of the Bavarian politician Franz Josef Strauß. In a dramatic climax Ali/Wallraff cons Adler into participating in a transaction in which the subcontractor believes he will receive tax-free remuneration in exchange for providing Turkish workers to repair a nuclear reactor emitting lethal doses of radiation. Notwithstanding the book's claims to documentary status, three reasons have been variously advanced as to why *Ganz unten* should be regarded as an industrial fiction. Predictably, this was the charge immediately levelled at Wallraff by those whose heinous practices he had exposed, but the accusation that he had fabricated his material was successfully rebutted by the author, not least in the various legal actions that followed publication;[3] and apart from a few minor emendations, attempts to contest the validity of the book's revelations have yielded little result. In a rather different vein others have questioned not so much the facts themselves as the assumptions underlying Wallraff's method of surreptitious information-gathering. As Arlene Akiko Teraoka has put it, 'the uniqueness and power of [Wallraff's] text were never a matter of its discovery of any previously unknown facts, but rather its claim to be based on the direct, personal experience of the author'.[4] And yet, for all the apparent similarity with the participant observation techniques of empirical sociology, Wallraff, it is argued, merely set out to prove what he knew to be the case all along. Thus he deliberately places himself in situations with perfectly predictable outcomes, such as the Turkey–West Germany football match or the Franz Josef Strauß rally. Although Wallraff states in the book's preface that 'die Erlebnisse haben alle meine Erwartungen übertroffen. In negativer Hinsicht',[5] for Teraoka the reverse is true: his experiences are entirely predicated on his pre-conceptions, for 'Wallraff knows even before taking on the role of the Turk exactly what he will find (and this then becomes exactly what he will seek out) in West German society' (p. 115). Or, as Robert Gillett and Astrid Köhler have expressed it, 'what he sees is what he wants to see, or perhaps also what he has been conditioned by others to look for'.[6] Moreover, Teraoka argues, the bias inherent in Wallraff's approach is equally reflected in the partisanship of the writing, with the raised index-finger of an almost self-righteous social critic apparent from the outset in the pervasive editorializing (p. 115). Thus, even in the preface to *Ganz unten* the reader is already warned about 'die Borniertheit und Eiseskälte einer Gesellschaft, die sich für so gescheit, souverän, endgültig und gerecht hält' and about conditions comparable to those in the nineteenth century or to the apartheid system in South Africa (p. 12). In short, what purports to be a reportage uncovering objective truths about German society should more properly be likened to the constructed verism of fiction, for the 'truth' to which Wallraff claims to have access 'turns out to be something carefully, sometimes brutally, manipulated by Wallraff himself' (p. 114). As Gillett and Köhler acknowledge (p. 15), Wallraff has no pretensions to scientific status or objectivity. Rather, his approach may be compared with that outlined some years earlier by Peter Weiss in conjunction with another area of documentary writing, namely drama:

> Das dokumentarische Theater enthält sich jeder Erfindung, es übernimmt authentisches Materialund gibt dies, im Inhalt unverändert, in der Form bearbeitet, von der Bühne aus wieder ... Das dokumentarische Theater ist parteilich. Viele seiner Themen können zu nichts anderem als zu einer Verurteilung geführt werden. Für ein solches Theater ist Objektivität unter Umständen ein Begriff, der einer Machtgruppe zur Entschuldigung ihrer Taten dient.[7]

For Wallraff, too, the raw material he reworks into literary form must bear the stamp of authenticity in so far as it derives from his own subjective experience, and the subterfuge in which he engages in order to gain those experiences is necessary for the purpose of exposing the truth about the power elites in German society: 'Man muß sich verkleiden, um die Gesellschaft zu demaskieren, muß täuschen, um die Wahrheit herauszufinden' (p. 12). Although he was speaking in 1975 (in discussion with Wilfried van der Will), Wallraff's description of his *modus operandi* clearly still applies perfectly to *Ganz unten*:

> His method [Wallraff said] was to act as though the given power structures didn't exist and, in confronting them in the role of a simpleton, he could expose the situation by irony. This method allowed him to gather information which he would otherwise be unable to obtain. It was a method which made those in power feel insecure, dislocated their fixed assumptions and enabled him to unmask existing exploitative structures.[8]

Teraoka's criticism that, largely as a consequence of this partisan approach, *Ganz unten* in fact vouchsafes few insights into German society and amounts to little more than preaching to the converted is scarcely borne out by the book's subsequent reception, for quite apart from the intense controversy it aroused both on the left and the right, critics differed quite sharply when seeking to identify the most important issues it raised. Thus, for Simone Sitte, the essential statement of the book concerns the unscrupulous machinations of the subcontractors and its exposure of 'ein Leben jenseits der Sozialgesetzgebung, ja jenseits aller menschlichen Würde, ein Leben "ganz unten", an dem sich wenige täglich illegal bereichern';[9] whereas, for Anna Kuhn, this was of secondary importance when set beside 'the everyday manifestations of fascistic behaviour in Germany' that Wallraff had unmasked.[10] Similarly, what for Teraoka is a source of epistemological ambiguity and a literary weakness, namely the foregrounding of the author's experience – 'the figure of Ali is the only unifying principle that holds the various episodes of Wallraff's text together'[11] – becomes for Kuhn one of the text's great strengths and provides the key to the book's ideological coherence: 'What unifies the episodic structure of Wallraff's work is the xenophobia Ali experiences in virtually all his encounters with Germans in the Federal Republic.'[12]

Moreover, what surely adds to that coherence is precisely the editorializing, almost proselytizing voice in Wallraff's text to which Teraoka so strongly objects. Here comparison with the cinema version of *Ganz unten* (1986) proves instructive. For the film, which restricts itself mainly to the footage from the hidden video camera, is a somewhat pallid affair, not least because its makers, Wallraff and the director Jörg Gfrörer, evidently overestimated the impact they thought would accrue from 'letting the facts speak for themselves'. That is to say, they opted for the generic codes of direct cinema (where the director is conceived merely as an intermediary between the subject matter and the viewer) rather than the approach of the social documentary (which deploys a variety of techniques, including – significantly – a narratorial voice-over, in the service of some preconceived statement or narrative). Partly in order to remedy this omission – and partly, one suspects, in the attempt to enliven a rather dull and repetitive set of images totally lacking in any visual gratification – some sequences end with Wallraff talking direct to camera either on location or, at some unspecified time after the event, in the form of a (mock) interview. Although still dressed as 'Ali', Wallraff now speaks as himself but in a curiously detached manner, almost as if he were a mere observer of, rather than a participant in, the events on which he is commenting. While this may serve to remind the viewer, albeit somewhat needlessly, that the main actor in this documentary is indeed an investigative journalist and not a shamelessly exploited Turk, the dispassionate tone of these interview statements seems both artificial and incongruous, and thus ultimately devoid of the authenticity issuing from the rhetoric of the book's morally enraged first-person narrator. Paradoxically, the film's one great strength is at the same time its major weakness: while those who would charge Wallraff with fabricating his material could scarcely contest the recorded evidence of the subcontractor Adler repeatedly condemning himself by his own testimony, through its excessive focus on Adler the film risks demonizing him as a manifestly nefarious, but not necessarily typical, small-time entrepreneur. In contrast, Wallraff's book concludes with the following statement: 'Nichts wäre falscher, als ihn [Adler] zu dämonisieren. Er ist einer von zigtausenden Erfüllungsgehilfen und Nutznießern des Systems der grenzenlosen Ausbeutung und Menschenverachtung' (p. 254). This comment, typical of the universalizing tendency of Wallraff's editorializing interventions, encapsulates the political subtext of *Ganz unten*, namely that the oppression he exposes is not restricted to a particular ethnic grouping. Rather, Wallraff's 'Ali' functions as a cipher, 'als bloße Chiffre für absolut untergeordnete, verfügbare, subalterne Arbeitskraft',[13] just as 'Adler becomes the cipher for all oppressors ... The "Turk", in other words, is made to represent oppressed groups everywhere.'[14]

This in turn is related to a second sense in which *Ganz unten* has been held to be a fiction, namely with regard to the particular image of the Turk the book conveys. For some critics Wallraff's work represents an egregious example of what Derek Paget has designated 'cultural tourism':

> Cultural tourists ... visit unfamiliar territory over which they hold economic power, and they go for specified periods of time in order to consume 'ways of life' different from their own. Having done this, they can collect information, they can claim knowledge, they can make authoritative pronouncements about this territory.[15]

In literary terms, Wallraff's most notable antecedent is *Black Like Me* (1960) by the (white) American writer John Howard Griffin, who 'blacked up' and travelled around the United States in order to appropriate the experience of being a black in the racist Deep South. As with Griffin, Wallraff's project is to present the world through the perspective of the Other by 'speaking "through" the Turk'.[16] And yet, it could be said, by focusing so narrowly on the sphere of industrial labour, Wallraff constructs a model of the Turkish Other which, in more or less the same way as the official designation 'Gastarbeiter', defines an immigrant purely in relation to his/her social function as a worker. Devoid of both a personal history and a private sphere, Wallraff's 'Ali' has no individual identity, no life, to speak of, beyond the work-place and in that respect the text lacks the existential authenticity which, in *Südwind*'s conception, was to be an intrinsic feature of the 'Literatur der Betroffenen' (and which so crucially underpins confessional and autobiographical narratives such

as *Unter uns war Krieg* (1978), Vera Kamenko's account of her life as a
foreign worker in Germany). Teraoka goes even further to argue that
'Wallraff's work is not really about Turks at all', for 'there *are* no real Turks
in *Ganz unten*, except as symbols of victims and oppressed groups
generally'.[17] Even more seriously, Wallraff has been accused of inverted
racism.[18] This was, in effect, the charge levelled at him by Aysel Özakin,
a female Turkish writer who was at that time resident in Germany,
namely that his book presents a patronizing and clichéd portrait of the
Turk as uneducated, unskilled, if not basically ignorant, as well as naive,
credulous and ultimately pitiful.[19] Rather than destabilizing or
dismantling cultural stereotypes, *Ganz unten*, it is claimed, merely
recycles and reinforces them. Thus, in so far as 'Ali' is locked into fic-
tionalization within a stereotype, *Ganz unten* allegedly constitutes what
Michelle Mattson has called a 'destructive fiction', one that prevents a
productive confrontation of Turkish and German cultural identities.[20]

Although prone to exaggeration, Teraoka's comments on stereotypy
are genuinely helpful. On the one hand, when she concludes that in
Wallraff's text 'specific issues of race and culture become erased within
this now-universalized fight against injustice in whatever form it takes',[21]
this surely oversteps the mark. For, as Anna Kuhn has so passionately
argued, the book's most damning indictment of German society
concerns the prevalent xenophobia it uncovered and 'its documentation
of the contiguity of contemporary anti-Turkish sentiments and the anti-
Semitism of the Third Reich'.[22] Indeed, in the light of the recrudescence
of racist violence in the wake of German unification *Ganz unten* now
seems gruesomely prophetic. On the other hand, the distinction Teraoka
draws between 'stereotype' and 'prototype' is a productive one and
underpins her conclusion that 'Wallraff is not so much presenting all
Turks as downtrodden and oppressed as he is taking their experience as
paradigmatic for the experience of oppression in general.'[23]

What Aysel Özakin overlooks with her complaint about Wallraff's
perpetuation of cultural stereotypes is the actual persona of Wallraff's
'Ali'. First, those who would charge Wallraff with epistemological naivety
should already be disarmed by his confession in the prefatory remarks:
'Sicher, ich war nicht wirklich ein Türke ... Ich weiß inzwischen immer
noch nicht, *wie* ein Ausländer die täglichen Demütigungen, die
Feindseligkeiten und den Haß verarbeitet. Aber ich weiß jetzt, *was* er zu
ertragen hat und wie weit die Menschenverachtung in diesem Land
gehen kann' (p. 12). Consequently, this awareness on the author's part
that he is not identical with his assumed role is reflected in his insistence
on designating his first-person narrator throughout the text as 'ich (Ali)'.

This contrasts markedly with the basic experience Wallraff underwent in researching the material for *Der Aufmacher*, a project he subsequently described as 'eine Selbstvergewaltigung, weil ich auch nicht mehr Ich sagen konnte, sondern mich in der Rolle als *BILD*-Reporter hatte verleugnen müssen'.[24] In fact, the subtitle of that book, 'Der Mann, der bei *Bild* Hans Esser war', could more accurately have been formulated as 'Der Mann, der bei *Bild* Hans Esser wurde', for so thoroughly does Wallraff immerse himself in the role of tabloid journalist that his invented persona gradually takes possession of him to the point where he becomes alienated from his friends, from his partner and, ultimately, from himself.[25] While there is no existential (as opposed to ideological) reason why Wallraff could not in reality have been a *Bild* reporter, not only can he not become a Turk but, as the film shows, he is able to drop the mask of 'Ali' both in private and on some public occasions too.[26] Indeed, when in the presence of real Turks he has little option but to do so since he has virtually no knowledge of either the Turkish language or Turkish culture (and hence he is obliged to tell them that he was raised in Greece). Secondly, although, as Paul Peters has observed, Wallraff has become not a real Turk but rather a Turk in the eyes of his German environment,[27] crucially the reader of the text is situated outside that environment. That is to say, if Wallraff does at times play 'Ali' as a cliché of the dumb and gullible immigrant worker, then this performance is primarily for the consumption of his adversaries and it is not in this exclusive guise that the reader perceives him. On the contrary, the ostensibly naive 'Ali' is shown to outwit that most astute of politicians, Franz Josef Strauß, just as he is able to dupe the most nefarious of entrepreneurs, Adler, by casting him as the unwitting protagonist in the book's climactic drama, the nuclear reactor hoax.

This brings us to the third aspect of *Ganz unten* where the concept of fiction can be invoked, and in this instance without serious qualification: namely, those features of the text that suggest parallels with other types of writing, parallels, moreover, which extend beyond the obvious comparison with the reportage novel in the proletarian literary tradition or in the Naturalist muckraker mould epitomized by Upton Sinclair's *The Jungle*. Nor should the dismissive, almost philistine stance towards literature that Wallraff liked to assume in the earlier phase of his career as a documentarist – most famously crystallized in his expostulation in 1973, 'Kunst – das wäre das Allerletzte'[28] – deflect us from the notion that he might stoop to the conscious appropriation of literary models. Thus the book's final episode concerning the nuclear reactor scam is designated by Wallraff as 'eine Inszenierung der Wirklichkeit' (p. 217).

This oxymoronic subtitle, while clearly meant to denote how the author has himself instigated the particular events he then narrates, also illustrates Wallraff's predilection for theatrical metaphors in *Ganz unten*. At times too, as Teraoka has pointed out, Wallraff even builds into his text the literary conventions of drama, with sets, stage directions and spoken dialogue.[29] Indeed, once Wallraff assumes the position of Adler's chauffeur, the scenario carries unmistakable echoes of Brecht's *Herr Puntila und sein Knecht Matti*, with 'Ali' as the Harlequin-like subordinate who unmasks his cynical capitalist master and Puntila's ideological schizophrenia reflected in Adler, a card-carrying Social Democrat, who mouths a sentimental paternalism even as he prepares to consign his employees to a near-certain death by radioactive contamination. Since the book was published there have in fact been theatrical productions based on *Ganz unten* in Stuttgart and Munich. This all suggests that Wallraff was striving for something beyond reportage, namely a hybrid form fusing genres in a fashion akin to John Mander's conception of the documentary as a mode of writing that deals with 'the intermediate areas of human experience', located somewhere in the middle ground 'between the public political world of the historian and the private psychological world' of the artist.[30]

For example, as well as drama, the centrality of role-playing in *Ganz unten* evokes a particular type of hero in the picaresque novel. Just like Oskar Matzerath, who in Günter Grass's *Die Blechtrommel* adopts the identity of a three-year-old child, Wallraff employs the mask of an innocent for strategic purposes: 'Meine Verstellung bewirkte, daß man mir direkt und ehrlich zu verstehen gab, was man von mir hielt. Meine gespielte Torheit machte mich schlauer, eröffnete mir Einblicke ... Ich war der Narr, dem man die Wahrheit unverstellt sagt' (p. 12). In a text not otherwise rich in comic possibilities this is a source of some humour, if not to say satirical potential, as in the encounters with Catholic clergymen mortified at Ali's request to convert to Christianity and be baptized. Similarly, when 'Ali' is promoted to Adler's chauffeur and becomes the recipient of his employer's confidences, exchanges such as the following carry an exquisitely ironic charge: '[Adler to a colleague about 'Ali']: "Der ist gar nicht so dumm und versteht mehr als du meinst." "Ich sag' nich immer alles, was denk," unterschütz ich (Ali) Adler, "aber oft viel mehr mitkrieg, als ich sag'"' (p. 191).

The knowledge that in reality the master–servant relationship between Adler and 'Ali'/Wallraff is the reverse of the fictional one surely deters us from casting 'Ali' exclusively in the role of victim and invites a response from the reader that transcends the mere outrage occasioned by the quasi-scientific disclosure of social iniquities. For Wallraff's Scarlet Pimpernel approach invests his text with the fairy-tale quality of an adventure novel in which the author, like some 'postmodern Robin Hood' (Heiner Müller) or 'ein Zorro des Spätkapitalismus', triumphs, however fleetingly, over the forces of evil. Or indeed, as Peters also suggests, like 'ein James Bond der kleinen Leute',[31] for of all the literary genres perhaps the most apposite analogy is with the spy novel. Foraging behind enemy lines for vital information to which only the powerful have access, Wallraff is bent on acts of sabotage and subversion. And if ever a piece of literature could lay claim to the epithet 'subversive', then surely it is *Ganz unten*, not just for the fierce controversy it unleashed or for the practical changes that followed in the wake of its revelations, but also for the spectacular popularity of a work which made publishing history in Germany, being translated into twenty languages (including Turkish) and selling more copies in a shorter period of time than any other post-war European book, including well over three million in the Federal Republic alone. At the conference cited at the beginning of this essay Wilfried van der Will concluded his introductory paper by expressing the hope that the momentum for the organization of a proletarian public sphere would not be lost. A decade later, with an immediate impact unmatched by any other post-war text, *Ganz unten* was singularly successful in attaining a wide working-class audience and, indeed, in accordance with the ultimate aim of a 'Literatur der Betroffenen', one that transcended ethnic divisions.

## Notes

1. Wilfried van der Will, 'Contemporary Working-Class Literature in West Germany and Britain', in *Workers and Writers*, Proceedings of the Conference on Present-Day Working-Class Literature in Britain and West Germany, held in Birmingham, October 1975, ed. Wilfried van der Will (1975), p. 3.
2. 'Literatur der Betroffenen' is the title of a programmatic essay by Franco Biondi and Rafik Schami, in *Zu Hause in der Fremde*, ed. Christian Schaffernicht (Reinbek, 1984; first published in Fischerhude at Atelier im Bauernhaus, 1981), pp. 136–50; see also Franco Biondi and Rafik Schami, 'Mit Worten Brücken bauen', in *Türken raus? oder Verteidigt den sozialen Frieden*, ed. Rolf Meinhardt (Reinbek, 1984), pp. 66–77.
3. See Frank Berger, *Thyssen gegen Wallraff – oder: Bericht über den Versuch, einen Autor durch Prozesse und Rufmord zum Schweigen zu bringen* (Göttingen, 1988).
4. Arlene Akiko Teraoka, 'Talking "Turk": On Narrative Strategies and Cultural Stereotypes', *New German Critique*, 46 (Winter 1989), p. 114.
5. Günter Wallraff, *Ganz unten* (Cologne, 1985), p. 12. All page references are to this edition.

6. Robert Gillett and Astrid Köhler, 'Manipulating the Medium: Wander, Wallraff and the Concept of Documentary Literature in East and West', Paper presented at the Sixth International Colloquium on Contemporary German-Language Literature, Bradford, April 1998 (unpublished manuscript), p. 15.

7. Peter Weiss, 'Notizen zum dokumentarischen Theater', in Peter Weiss, *Rapporte 2* (Frankfurt, 1971; first published in *Theater heute*, March 1968), pp. 91–2, 99.

8. Van der Will, *Workers and Writers*, p. 65.

9. Simone Sitte, 'Die Leiden des jungen Ali – Erfolg und Wirkung von Günter Wallraff's *Ganz unten*', in *In Sachen Wallraff*, ed. Christian Linder (Cologne, 1986), pp. 361, 362.

10. Anna K. Kuhn, 'Bourgeois Ideology and the (Mis)Reading of Günter Wallraff's *Ganz unten*', *New German Critique*, 46 (Winter 1989), p. 194.

11. Teraoka, *op. cit.*, p. 113.

12. Kuhn, *op. cit.*, p. 192.

13. Paul Peters, 'Ritter von der wandelbaren Gestalt: Zu Günter Wallraffs *Ganz unten*', *Die Neue Gesellschaft/Frankfurter Hefte*, 33 (1986), p. 1008.

14. Teraoka, *op. cit.*, p. 119.

15. Derek Paget, *True Stories? Documentary Drama on Radio, Screen and Stage* (Manchester, 1990), p. 89.

16. Teraoka, *op. cit.*, p. 106.

17. *Ibid.*, pp. 117, 127.

18. Cf. Wolfgang Braun, 'Der entscheidende Kritikpunkt an Wallraff: Umgedrehter Rassismus', *Die Brücke* 38 (1987), p. 10f.

19. Aysel Özakin, 'Ali hinter den Spiegeln', *Literatur Konkret* (1986), pp. 6–9; cf. also Kuhn: 'Thus, instead of exposing a system of representations that generate and support negative images of the other, *Ganz unten* helps perpetuate them. By cloning the victim, *Ganz unten* calls for identification with the underdog. In the double sense of *Mitleid*, it allows German readers both to empathize with and feel sorry for the *Gastarbeiter* they are oppressing daily. It thereby arguably permits them to placate their consciences and to feel superior at the same time' (*op. cit.*, p. 192).

20. Michelle Mattson, 'The Function of the Cultural Stereotype in a Minor Literature: Alev Tekinay's Short Stories', *Monatshefte*, 89, 1 (1997), p. 74.

21. Teraoka, *op. cit.*, p. 119.

22. Kuhn, *op. cit.*, p. 194.

23. Teraoka, *op. cit.*, p. 119.

24. Quoted in Christian Linder, 'Ich ist ein anderer: Über einige Motive Günter Wallraffs', in *In Sachen Wallraff*, p. 15.

25. Cf. Günter Wallraff, *Der Aufmacher: Der Mann, der bei Bild Hans Esser war* (Cologne) (revised and extended edition 1982; first published 1977), pp. 211, 215.

26. This is not, of course, to underestimate the heavy toll that working as a 'Gastarbeiter' for two and a half years inevitably took on Wallraff's physical and psychological well-being and which left him suffering from suppurating gums, chronic bronchial problems and, in the wake of his experiences in the pharmaceutical industry, a whole range of side-effects such as severe migraine, dizzy spells and loss of balance.

27. Peters, *op. cit.*, p. 1008.

28. Quoted in Michael Töteberg's entry on Günter Wallraff in: *Kritisches Lexikon der deutschsprachigen Gegenwartsliteratur*, ed. Heinz Ludwig Arnold (Göttingen, 20. Nlg.), p. 6.
29. Teraoka, *op. cit.*, p. 115.
30. John Mander, *The Writer and Commitment* (London, 1961), p. 110.
31. Peters, *op. cit.*, p. 1012.

# 11

## Grass Parodied: Notes on the Reception of *Die Rättin*

*Manfred Durzak*

Almost simultaneously with the publication of Grass's *Die Rättin* in 1986 there appeared a 112-page parody with the title *Der Grass*, purportedly written by one Günter Ratte.[1] Was this merely a 'literarisches Bubenstück' – the book's subtitle – the product of an opportunistic publisher intent on cashing in on the market success of Grass's novel and thus hardly worth critical attention? The facts of the matter are more complicated than such a reaction would suggest.

To begin with, the harsh treatment meted out by the critics to *Die Rättin* on its appearance was no isolated event. The critical slating that greeted Grass's fictional attempt to thematize the complicated process of German unification, *Ein weites Feld* (1995), put the negative reception of *Die Rättin* in the shade. The history of the later novel's reception has been fully documented.[2] And the story recalls the nature of the attacks on *Die Rättin*: 'Hinrichtung eines Dichters'.[3] Against this background one can see the controversy surrounding *Die Rättin* as a case study which reveals critical mechanisms at work that also made their impact on the reception of *Ein weites Feld*. From this vantage point the media reaction is more than a mere curiosity; it also documents the permanent tension that exists between Grass and the German public. Perhaps, too, the reference to *Ein weites Feld*, far from disproving the critics' estimation of the status of *Die Rättin* in the context of contemporary German literature, will with the benefit of the passage of time confirm it.

For whatever reasons *Die Rättin* was certainly not greeted with great enthusiasm either by critics or readers on its publication.[4] Indeed, it was rejected by the majority of critics with a vehemence which confused many, including Grass's friend, Henrich Vormweg. In his Rowohlt monograph, published in the same year, he commented on the reactions *Die Rättin* provoked:

> Das umfangreiche Buch gibt wie jedes literarische Werk auch Ansatzpunkte für Kritik. Doch die aggressiven Beschimpfungen, ja Verhöhnungen, die *Die Rättin* auf sich gezogen hat, während die Leser sich auch um dieses Buch rissen, sind schwer zu begreifen.[5]

Vormweg was right on one point. In the majority of newspapers and journals which enjoy wide influence, for example, *Der Spiegel*, *Stern*, the *Frankfurter Allgemeine Zeitung* and *Konkret*, the novel was given hostile treatment. The monthly *Tempo* was typical in its summing-up: 'Es ist die Bibel für die letzten Jahre liberaler Dummheit, moraltriefend und von pastoraler Bescheuertheit ... Gebt dem Mann den Literaturnobelpreis, damit er endlich den Mund hält!'[6] At the same time, Vormweg was incorrect in his assertion that 'Leser sich auch um dieses Buch rissen'. Indeed, it was said that a considerable number of the initial print-run of 150 000 never left the warehouse. *Die Rättin* came nowhere near the phenomenal success of *Der Butt* (1977). Clearly the readers withheld their approval. To suggest that this was down to feeling bullied by the negative critical reception would be to overestimate the influence of literary critics.

There is another factor that argues against any simple dismissal of the parody as a fleeting literary phenomenon. According to the publisher, Vito von Eichborn, *Der Grass* has already sold 20 000 copies, for many authors a dream sales figure.[7] Why the parody has proved so astonishingly successful is a question that needs answering. And its significance for the history of the reception of Grass's novel should not be seen as marginal.

Parody may, as a genre, appear marginal, but it can look back on a tradition going back centuries.[8] This is not the place to trace its history; it is enough to bear in mind the function of parody as a permanent subversion of high culture literature, mocking its pretensions with its own chameleon-like reversals. At the same time, parodies attest to the canonical status of the author or work parodied, and thus Günter Ratte's *Der Grass* pays the author Grass an indirect compliment.

Or is this to pay too much respect to this particular anonymous parodist? Is *Der Grass* perhaps nothing more than the jealous sniping at a famous author by a less successful colleague? The possibility cannot be excluded, but an answer can only be found by examining the text of the parody. And indeed, *Der Grass* – quite apart from any aesthetic merit it may possess – encapsulates and summarizes themes and attitudes in Grass-criticism that appear only indirectly and in isolated form in the critical reception of Grass's work. Thus an analysis of the way the parody deals with the iconology of Grass and his literary status can prove more instructive than merely sifting through individual reviews. Just how problematic the latter process can be has been demonstrated by Heinz Ludwig Arnold in his investigation of the critical reception of *Die Rättin*. Significantly, Arnold entitled his article 'Literaturkritik: Hinrichtungs- oder Erkenntnisinstrument?'[9] He has no doubt that the result was a concerted hatchet-job. But do German literary critics in fact act as a team of literary executioners? As a general rule they present a more chaotic appearance in which the major critics attempt to outdo each other, tearing a book to pieces merely because a rival has praised it, or vice versa. Obviously, there are times when the loudest voice can determine for a while the general tone of the debate, that is, a review in the weekend edition of the *Frankfurter Allgemeine Zeitung* can be parroted by countless minor reviewers in provincial newspapers.[10] The point is made by Arnold in a reference to the baleful example of the Robespierre of the German *Feuilleton*:

> Den 'Unsinn' aber, den Reich-Ranicki nicht kommentieren möchte, hat er in seinem groben Gemisch aus Denunziatorischem und Rhetorik selber erst zusammengerührt. Dieser Methode folgt Reich-Ranickis gesamte Rezension. Sie ist typisch für die Verfertigung globaler Verrisse, die nicht nur ein Buch, sondern auch seinen Autor treffen sollen.[11]

Here – though it is not easy – I must defend Reich-Ranicki. His review of *Die Rättin* was not intended to set the trend for the reception of the novel, since it did not appear until six weeks after the book's publication and thus long after the initial reviews appeared. The picadors with their lances and banderillos were already at work. Reich-Ranicki appeared on the scene rather like a belated matador. It cannot be said that his attempt to dispatch the bull was particularly graceful. Eschewing the sword, he went about his business with a mace and flail. The aggressive solidarity of Grass's critics was indeed astonishing and could not be broken by the few contrary voices, for example, Joachim Kaiser in the *Süddeutsche Zeitung*. Since it would be naive to assume some sort of critical conspiracy behind these aggressive attacks on Grass and his novel – indeed, the way German literary criticism functions precludes the idea – the uniformly hostile reception needs to be taken seriously and not be dismissed in an attempt to defend Grass as cultural ephemera, as Arnold does when, understandably prompted by his sympathy for Grass, he tends to oversimplify the issue: 'Absicht solcher Artikel ist es offensichtlich, den Autor als politische Person zur Strecke zu bringen, ihn schweigen und mundtot zu machen.'[12]

That there is an element of truth in this assertion cannot be denied, but such black-and-white conclusions are not helpful in getting to the bottom of such widespread condemnation of *Die Rättin*. One must ask whether the reason for such a predominantly negative reception has something to do with the aesthetic concept of the novel itself. Of course, one can proceed by enumerating the criticisms raised and listing their frequency and plausibility. For example, Grass was attacked for a loss of narrative flair or for serving up a *Reader's Digest* of contemporary problems without creating a convincing epic framework. Many critics attacked the central figure of the female rat in its function as a dream-like counterpart to the narrator.

It is in fact strange that in this book, which thematically so strongly recalls *Die Blechtrommel* (1959) and *Der Butt*, Grass places his rat in a narrative position similar to the technique used in *Der Butt*, yet uses this animal image with its extensive literary and mythological connotations of disgust and destruction quite differently in *Hundejahre* (1963). I am thinking here of the expert rat-hunt organized by the soldiers, Liebenau, Matern and Störtebeker in the Kaiserhaufen battery, the nauseating nature of which is made bearable by Störtebeker disguising the events behind a protective screen of ideological jargon borrowed from his revered Heidegger. There are, of course, also the two rats, called Perle and Strich, in the play *Hochwasser* (1957), but as far as any anticipation of the rat-image in Grass is concerned, this contradictory reference to *Hundejahre* cannot be ignored. Here the image indicates a dimension of meaning which Heinrich Vormweg correctly relates to a key scene in George Orwell's dystopia *1984*: the torture of the protagonist Winston Smith during which a rat-cage containing two starving rats is placed directly before his face, ready to pounce the moment the cage-door is opened. Vormweg comments: 'Noch immer ist die Ratte zugleich ein Tier, das Urängste symbolisiert, ja in einer widersprüchlichen und komplexen Metapher bündelt.'[13] Grass's use of the rat-image in *Die*

*Rättin* contradicts this widespread view. However, rather than pursue individual criticisms of *Die Rättin*, I want to trace their basic thrust as aesthetically presented in 'Günter Ratte's parody and thus to test the plausibility of the rejection of Grass's novel. My hypothesis is that the use of the aesthetic form of parody will reveal in a more concentrated and more readily assessible manner the controversy surrounding the book. For example, Grass's aesthetic shortcomings may be better judged in the reflection of parody.

Some sixteen years ago, Günter Herburger published a 'portrait' of his colleague Günter Grass under the title 'Überlebensgroß Herr Grass'.[14] At that time Grass was deeply involved in the election campaign to support Willy Brandt, which he recorded in *Aus dem Tagebuch einer Schnecke* (1972). Herburger's portrait aroused great interest because it accentuated a critical view of his famous colleague which ended in the declaration:

> Ich, wir, wie gesagt Freunde und Feinde, wovon die insgeheimen Freunde überwiegen, was er wahrscheinlich schon nicht mehr wahrhaben will, denn Polarisation ist bequem nützlich, wir können uns nur ereifern, weil wir alle noch auf ihn hoffen. Wir glauben, daß er, der überlebensgroß gewordene Kleinbürger, noch genug Zähigkeit, Temperament, Phantasie und Selbstmitleid, schöne, dicke Selbstanklage besitzt, daß er wieder einmal zu uns gehören könnte, wenn er genügend schrumpft. Er hat, als Millionär und automatisches Auflagenroß, seine Klasse vergessen, den miesen Mittelstand der schimpfenden, nörgelnden, verzweifelten, erschöpften und eines Tages mörderischen Mehrheit.

I mention this at times clearly polemical portrait not simply because its features reappear in various guises and modifications in the parody, but also because the kind of gritted-teeth sympathy it reveals for Grass quite plainly applies to the fictive narrator of *Der Grass*, too. 'Erzählen kann er, der Grass!' (p. 27) exclaims the latter at one point. And with a reference to *Der Butt*, the narrator bursts into praise: 'Erzählte uns seine Geschichte, und erzählte sie, wie nur er erzählen kann. Erzählte sie pikaresk und verschnitt sie mit Märchenmotiven' (p. 68). And Oskar Matzerath, who appears in the parody, as he does in *Die Rättin*, as an old age pensioner, but energetic dealer in pornographic videos, made by Günter Ratte and Tulla (the girl from *Hundejahre*) in their cellar in Kreuzberg, registers his admiration for *Die Blechtrommel*: 'Hast ein prima Buch über uns und unser altes Danzig geschrieben!' (p. 20). At one point the narrator even declares: 'Eigentlich ist er ein ungemein sympathischer Dichter, der

Grass' (p. 68). It is thus not surprising that Tulla exclaims towards the end of the parody: 'Mensch, wir mögen dich doch!' (p. 94).

At first glance such expressions of sympathy contradict the initial impression that the text is a malicious attempt to condemn Grass on the lines of the critics whom Arnold attacked. Are we dealing here with one of those 'insgeheimen Freunde' mentioned by Herburger? In the parody the narrator called 'Günter Ratte', who is given Grass in a cage as a Christmas present by Tulla – *Die Rättin*, too, opens with the biographical anecdote of the gift of a tame rat[15] – is both an individualized character and equipped with a biography and distinct attitude to life. He is a writer, a 'früherer Juso', who 'seit der Demo in Wackersdorf' (p. 7) lives with Tulla in a Kreuzberg cellar. He is a drop-out who earns his living by writing 'alternative Lore-Romane und anti-autoritäre Kochbücher' (p. 8) and carouses with writers such as Robert Wolfgang Schnell and Günter Bruno Fuchs – until recently, well known figures from the literary bohemia of Berlin – in diverse Berlin bars, for example, the establishment run by the Austrian writer-turned-pub-landlord, Oswald Wiener. Of course, these are all literary counterparts to Grass. In one of the densest passages towards the end of the parody the fictive narrator caricatures this literary establishment by describing a visit to a Berlin literary café:

Als ich ins 'Café Adorno' kam, war die Spannung, wie immer eine Stunde vor Mitternacht, auf dem Höhepunkt. An fast allen Tischen saßen Autoren, die einander hochachteten, sich ständig ihre Bedeutung versicherten und dabei lächelnd kleine silberne Dolche in den Rücken stießen. (p. 85)

At one table Hans Magnus Enzensberger and Martin Walser are shown indulging in this typical activity, whereas Siegfried Lenz is portrayed sitting alone:

Nur am Tisch von Siegfried Lenz waren wie immer alle Stühle bis auf seinen frei ... Hans Christoph Buch stürzte ins Café: 'Platz da! Der Landvogt kommt!' Er bückte sich ... scheuchte mit einer Handbewegung Botho Strauß vom Tisch, eilte zurück zur Tür und warf sich dort auf den Boden, damit er einmal mehr als Fußmatte dienen konnte. Er schaffte es gerade noch rechtzeitig. Kaum lag er da, flog die Tür aus den Angeln, der Boden erzitterte und eine riesige Gestalt trat ins Café. Längst waren alle Autoren von den Tischen aufgesprungen, standen ängstlich an den Wänden, warteten ab, an welchen der Tische sich der Riese setzen würde ... 'Alle mal herhören,' schrie der Grass. 'Ich habe lange über die Situation der Menschheit nachgedacht, und ich bin endlich zu einem Ergebnis gekommen!' ... Der Grass holte ein Manuskript aus der Tasche, und als er die ersten Sätze las, wurde es noch stiller im Café ... Eine der unvergeßlichen Nächte hatte begonnen. (pp. 86–7)

The quotation is an example of how parody mutates into literary satire and indicates that this 'literarisches Bubenstück' is far more than an attack on a single book by Günter Grass. Of course, individual scenes of *Die Rättin* are parodied, for example, the scene, echoing *Der Butt*, in which five women take a motorized fishing smack, named *Der neue Ilsebill*, out into the Baltic in order to measure the increasing incidence of jellyfish and thus the pollution of the sea, but secretly on a mission to locate the vanished utopia of Vineta. In the parody this becomes an outing in a canoe with three feminists, Alice Schwarzer, Marielouise Jurreit and Antje Kunstmann, who christen their boat – purchased during the Nazi period from Anna Bronski – according to the latest ideological trends in the feminist movement: from Hilde Dohm via Brünnhilde to Penthesilea, until it drifts off into the Atlantic only to make an unexpected encounter.

Orbiting in 'seinem Knallfrosch' (p. 40) – a further parody of the science fiction episode in *Die Rättin* in which Grass's narrator circles the planet in a spacecraft – Grass splashes down right next to the canoe:

Der Grass preßt sein neues Gedicht an die Brust und rennt entsetzt zum Notausgang. 'Rettet mich!' schreit er den Frauen zum Faltboot rüber. 'Ich bin Deutschlands berühmtester Dichter!' 'Rettet mich!' ruft die Alice zurück. 'Ich bin Deutschlands berühmteste Feministin!' 'Rette sich, wer kann!' kräht Rumpelstilzchen (alias Oskar). 'Was mich betrifft, ich hab den Fahrtenschwimmer-Schein!' ... da strudelt es im Wasser. 'Der weiße Hai!' schreit Alice entsetzt. 'Schlimmer noch,' brüllt Grass, 'der Reich-Ranicki!' Schafft es der Grass, das Ungeheuer nur mit einer Dichterlesung in die Tiefen des Ozeans zurück-zuscheuchen? (p. 106)

Such minor parodic jokes occur on numerous occasions in the text. It would be hypocritical to deny that they possess a certain entertainment value. That is true also for the parodies of some formal features of *Die Rättin*, for example, the poems interwoven in Grass's novel which are neatly travestied, or the complicated mixed form of the novel whose aesthetic intention is difficult to unravel and which is revealed through the device of exaggeration as a random compilation of narrative strands. If the Günter Ratte parody were merely a sum of such details, the book would be of limited interest. But it seems to me more productive not just simply to stick to plot parallels which can be read as an argument about Grass's literary career and his position between literature and politics, but also to see the text as a counter to Grass's ideas about what the possibilities of literature are and how it can actively influence reality. From this point of view the parody clearly follows Günter Herburger's polemical Grass-portrait of 1971. Indeed, on various occasions Herburger is indirectly quoted. 'Groß und berühmt (bin ich), und jetzt weiß ich nicht mehr weiter.' '"Überlebensgroß, was?" fragte Rumpelstilzchen (Oskar)' (p. 21). Furthermore, the parodist has his fictive Grass march through Berlin like a kind of literary troll using the Brandenburg Gate as a monumental writing-desk. The fictive narrator, who speaks of himself and of his kind – the Grass characters Tulla and Oskar belong in this category – as 'wir Ratten' (p. 18), does not interpret this identity in a literary manner like Grass himself in the famous digression in *Die Rättin* which deals with the theme of rats in world literature, but rather on a moral and political level – indeed, in the same semantic context of 'rats' and 'blowflies' created by the notorious Franz Josef Strauß in his attacks on left-wing intellectuals and writers. The parody's narrator declares his membership of the anarchist opposition, revealing himself as a subversive and saboteur of all megolomania wherever it appears, whether it is in the ideological bombast of dictators or in an incalculable technology whose profileration is no longer susceptible to human control. The rat becomes a metaphor for Murphy's Law, that iron necessity which declares that whatever can go wrong will one day go wrong, irrespective of any measures taken to prevent it. Thus at a central moment in the book appears the statement:

Wir Ratten wollen das Leben! Zugegeben, einige von uns sind in eure Systeme eingedrungen. Um sie lahmzulegen, Günter. Nur um sie lahmzulegen! Wenn Napoleon an der Beresina nicht weiterkam und sein Größenwahn im Schnee erstickte – die Ratten waren daran schuld. Wir haben Frau Holle damals wachgekitzelt. Wenn Adolf Hitlers Wunderwaffe nie fertig wurde – es ist unser Verdienst. Wir haben alle Pläne in Peenemünde schlicht und einfach aufgefressen. Als das Kernkraftwerk in Harrisburg durchbrannte – wir waren es, die das Kühlsystem verstopften und die Amis zum Umdenken veranlaßten! Kein Kernkraftwerk ist in den USA danach mehr ans Netz gegangen! Und auch was deinen Größenwahn betrifft ... Was immer ihr Menschen euch ausdenkt, sagte ich, wir Ratten sind wachsam. Wir sitzen in unseren Kellern, freuen uns unseres kurzen Lebens, und wenn eure Hybris zu gefährlich wird, kommen wir aus den Löchern. Wir reden nicht. Schreiben nicht. Diskutieren nicht. Wir handeln. Wir nagen Kabel durch. Mischen Marihuana in den Tabak von GIs, die in Vietnam nichts zu suchen haben. Die berühmte Ratte McMurphy, nach der ihr Menschen sogar ein Gesetz benannt haben ... Nicht daß wir uns für irgend etwas verantwortlich fühlen. Wir wollen Spaß und wir wollen spielen. (p. 18)

I must confess that in the context of anarchic subversion the elderly figure of Oskar Matzerath, leaping about as Rumpelstilzchen – however paradoxical it may seem – seems to owe more to the spirit of *Die Blechtrommel* than to the supposed video-dealer and producer, a minor media mogul in the mould of Leo Kirch, who has himself chauffeured in a Mercedes company car back to the Kaschubei in order to present his miniature Kaschubian relatives with, among other things, comic smurfs. In this connection I remember Grass's remark in a TV interview on 1 May 1984 after the first showing of the film of *Die Blechtrommel*. When he looked back on his attitudes between the ages of thirty-five and fifty, when he had believed in certain changes for the better being brought about in society if even at a snail's pace, his basic feelings at this point in time had returned to their anarchic roots. The movement of the snail as symbol of progress had been too optimistic, as was evidenced by the present state of the world.

Yet what is the nature of Grass's hybris, his uncontrollable megolomania, which is the object of the parody's attack? It is exemplified at several points in the text, for example, in the travesty of the fairy-tale, 'Vom Fischer un syner Frau', which functions in *Der Butt* as an integrating myth, transforming the various narrative levels into a convincing epic whole. The tale encapsulates Grass's literary success. The flounder, caught in the river Seine, fulfils all Grass's dreams of fame and literary glory. He wants to become a famous writer and he does so. He wants to be the 'Königmacher' (p. 69), and he reaches his goal at the side of Willy Brandt:

Willy Brandt Kanzler und überlebensgroß der Grass. Ist endlich Königmacher und fast König. Fährt mit dem Bundeskanzler in die DDR ... Ich war es, dröhnt der Grass, den ich mir träumte, der die SPD zur Regierungspartei gemacht hat ... ICH, donnert er, habe den

Schriftstellerverband in den Deutschen Gewerkschaftsbund aufgenommen ... Riesengroß und mächtig geworden Günter Grass. Günter Groß, Günter Überlebensgroß ... 'Sag bloß, jetzt wollte er der liebe Gott werden?' entfährt es Tulla. Schlimmer, sagte der Grass. Boxweltmeister. Und da wurde der Butt echt knatschig ... schwupp, schon hat Rumpelstilzchen am Kanzlerstuhl gesägt. Tritt Willy Brandt zurück. Kommt ein neuer Kanzler, der nun seinerseits dem Dichter erklärt, wo es lang geht. Nicht zum Pißpott. Nein. Viel schlimmer. Zurück zum Schreibtisch! (pp. 70–1)

The criticism levelled at Günter Grass is that he has become a highly visible public institution, which, equipped with literary fame, offers comments on every important question of the day, comments which are thoroughly aired in the media and have turned the writer into a larger-than-life national Ombudsman. The central reproach is clearly this metamorphosis of the writer into an indefatigable public mouthpiece whose literary fame ensures that his pronouncements are attended to. This criticism runs like a political leitmotif through the parody:

Das Leben ist ein Zirkus, Günter, und wir sind die Artisten. Du reitest Hohe Schule, ich bin der Pausenclown. Unser Publikum will von uns unterhalten werden ... Wir sind Artisten, Grass, und wenn wir vergessen und größenwahnsinnig werden, sind wir verloren. (p. 79)

And alluding to Grass's essay, 'Vom mangelnden Selbstvertrauen der schreibenden Hofnarren unter Berücksichtigung nicht vorhandener Höfe' (1966), the anonymous parodist asserts: 'Jeder Hofnarr ist verloren, wenn er vergißt, wer er ist. Wenn er sich einbildet, er wäre plötzlich der König, weil der ihm aus einer Laune heraus die Krone aufsetzt und das Zepter in die Hand gibt!' (p. 45). In 1971 Herburger had written: 'Als Schriftsteller kann er (Grass) sich jedoch nur retten, wenn er wieder klein wird, nicht mehr recht haben will und untergeht. Dann würde er wieder leiden ohne Widerhall in der Presse, Film und Funk.' At the end of *Der Grass* this state of affairs appears to have been reached:

und da gerät endlich Bewegung in die Statue. Erzeugt Reibung endlich Wärme und läßt den riesigen Gletscher von Dichter schmelzen bis ein frierender, erschöpfter, einsamer Mann vor uns steht und uns unsicher ansieht. Du bist ein Dichter, Grass, sagt Rumpelstilzchen, einer der besten, den wir haben. Freu dich drüber, aber komm endlich wieder zu uns runter. Du bist ein großartiger Dichter, aber du kannst deswegen noch lange nicht alles. Du kannst zum Beispiel nicht auch nur annähernd so gut operieren, wie Sauerbruch es konnte, und bei allem Respekt, Maria Callas konnte entschieden besser singen als du ... (p. 94)

Through these words shines that clear sympathy for Günter Grass that the anonymous parodist himself analyses elsewhere in his text when he offers disappointed love as the reason for his attacks on the SPD rather than on the right-wing parties: 'wo Haß ist, war meistens mal Liebe!' (p. 67).

It is such aspects of the parody which make it difficult, indeed rash, to brush aside this slim volume as merely spiteful and malicious sniping at a major author. *Der Grass* articulates a view which is widespread not only among literary critics but also among Grass's own colleagues: namely the opinion that here is someone who improperly overplays his literary reputation as a master story-teller when it comes to commenting on social affairs. I do not know how to rebut this criticism. I merely register a critical consensus *vis-à-vis* Grass and see the parody – doubtless the work of a colleague – as a symptomatic paradigm for it. Naturally, I ask myself whether this can be the only response to the determination of a writer, as Grass himself once put it, to overturn his writing-desk and involve himself with great physical commitment in the intractable political problems of the day. This activity has not only left calluses but plainly deep scars as well. Towards the end of *Der Grass*, the narrator opines:

der Grass, den ich mir träumte, schüttelte den Kopf. Er sei müde, sagte er, ganz einfach müde. Hätte lange genug Geschichten erzählt, die nichts geändert hätten, und wollte jetzt nur noch nach Indien ... 'Vielleicht suche ich mir bloß eine Säule und meditiere auf ihrer Spitze, bis alles zuende ist.' (p. 110)

Here again the parodist reveals himself as an expert on Grass. In the second half of the 1950s Oskar Matzerath's forerunner climbed down from his column and in his new guise as a little boy caused a stir with his famous drum. It is not difficult to imagine that after *Die Rättin*, a novel which attempted in vain to attain the marvellous narrative sweep of *Die Blechtrommel* and *Der Butt*, Grass wished to test his novelistic gifts once more. The point is made by the anonymous parodist who listens to his fictive hero: 'Er redete, formulierte, artikulierte, spielte mit der Sprache, daß wir gebannt, fasziniert, begeistert lauschten' (p. 64). When one reads *Ein weites Feld*, one can only say that this turned out to be pious wishful thinking. Grass remained impervious to the didactic admonition of the parodist; with his new novel he once again mobilized his formidable ego and threw down the gauntlet to both critics and general public. As with Don Quixote and his windmills, the result is well known.

Translated by Michael Butler

## Notes

1. Published by the Eichborn Verlag, Frankfurt am Main. All page references are to this edition.
2. Oskar Negt (ed.), *Der Fall Fonty. 'Ein weites Feld' von Günter Grass im Spiegel der Kritik* (Göttingen, 1996). See also Georg Oberhammer and Georg Ostermann (eds), *Zerreißprobe. Der neue Roman von Günter Grass. 'Ein weites Feld' und die Literaturkritik. Eine Dokumentation* (Innsbruck, 1995).
3. This was the title of Manfred Bissinger's review in *Die Woche*, 25 August 1995.
4. The Luchterhand Verlag has drawn my attention to a substantial study conducted in the German Department of Zürich University which attempts to examine the critical reception of *Die Rättin* in the German-speaking countries: Walter Gilgen, 'Die Beobachtung der Rattenfänger. Günter Grass: *Die Rättin* – Eine Kritik der Kritik' (typescript). By proceeding in a purely quantitative way, the paper gives the impression that the positive and negative reactions balanced themselves out. The weakness of such a method is obvious: in terms of reception there is a qualitative difference between reviews published in the major national press and those in provincial papers; those in the leading newspapers and peridocials were uniformly negative.
5. Henrich Vormweg, *Günter Grass* (Reinbek bei Hamburg, 1986), p. 119.
6. Helmut Ziegler, 'Wort zum Sonntag', *Tempo* (March 1986), p. 102.
7. Private communication from Vito von Eichborn.
8. For a thorough historical survey, see Winfried Freund, *Die literarische Parodie* (Stuttgart, 1981).
9. In *L'80*, 39, p. 13.
10. See the revealing article 'Über Literaturkritik', *Text + Kritik*, 100 (1988).
11. Arnold, *op. cit.*, pp. 118–19.
12. *Ibid.*, p. 121.
13. Vormweg, *op. cit.*, p. 114.
14. *Die Zeit*, 4 June 1971, p. 13.
15. This is rooted in autobiographical reality. Grass was presented with a tame rat by his wife, Ute. For a while it could be seen on his writing-desk in Wewelsfleth. The creature died before the novel was finished. One can only speculate on how the superstitious Grass reacted to the event.

# 12

## East German Literature and the Cold War: The Example of Erich Loest's *Die Westmark fällt weiter*

*Martin Kane*

In the first two decades after the end of World War II, those responsible for controlling the political and ideological direction of East German culture attempted to mould literature into a vehicle of propaganda for the values, ideals and goals of the new socialist society in the making. A considerable part of the energies dedicated to this purpose was aimed, in the period which saw the Cold War at its height, at pedagogic and hostile portrayal of the West, and – in the texts with which I am dealing here – with what was perceived as the debilitating and subversive effect of American culture. This was articulated – at official instigation one suspects – by, amongst others, Bodo Uhse, a leading returning exile writer and, up until 1952, secretary to the Deutscher Schriftsteller-Verband, the East German Writers' Union. He propounded the theory that the flood of lurid pulp fiction produced in the West and which allegedly glamorized war and crime, was all part of a deliberate and concerted campaign to brutalize young people in preparation for another capitalist war:

> Wohl ohne überrascht zu sein, aber dennoch beunruhigt, erleben wir ..., wie sich gegenwärtig in den Vereinigten Staaten ein Literaturzweig entwickelt, eine eigene Literatur möchte man sagen, deren Inhalt der Schrecken ist, Angst, Greuel, Entsetzen, die sich mit

nichts anderem als mit dem kommenden Krieg beschäftigt, als sei er
nun einmal eine ebenso selbstverständliche wie unumgängliche
Notwendigkeit. Seine möglichen Formen als Atombombenkrieg, als
Krieg der Bakterien und Epidemien mit der Tötung von Millionen
glücklicher, hoffender Menschen werden in darstellenden und
erzählenden Zukunftsvisionen mit aller Ausführlichkeit beschrieben.
Das geschieht in billigen Groschenheften geschmacklosesten
Abenteuerstils sowie in teuer aufgemachten pseudowissenschaftlichen
und ästhetisierenden Büchern ... [1]

Erich Loest may, or may not, have been familiar with Bodo Uhse's
comments. What certainly would not have escaped his attention is the
document 'Der Kampf gegen den Formalismus in Kunst und Literatur,
für eine fortschrittliche deutsche Kultur', which was the fruit of the deliberations of the *Zentralkomitee* of the SED of 15–17 March 1951.[2] This
polemic mounted an excoriating attack on an art and literature described
as the 'Verherrlichung des Glaubens an die rohe Gewalt ... von Mord,
Brutalität und Pornographie', on a culture which manifested itself 'in der
massenhaften Verbreitung von pornographischen Magazinen, Kriminal-
und Kolportageromanen übelster Sorte und in der Herstellung von Kitsch-
und Verbrecherfilmen', and which was in the service of imperialist and
war-mongering American forces preparing the next world war.

The aim of this essay is to examine how official East German views on
the relationship between a Western, supposedly imperialist culture and
the Cold War found their way into the GDR literature of the day. After
touching briefly on a few examples of the representation of decadent
American influences in East German writing of the early 1950s,
particular attention will be given to the way in which Erich Loest, in his
unexpectedly absorbing novel *Die Westmark fällt weiter* of 1952,[3] adapts
the genre of crime fiction – a literary form more usually associated with
capitalist culture – to Socialist purpose, utilizes it to dramatize the
ideological battle lines between East and West from a GDR perspective,
and focuses his tale on Berlin where this confrontation was at its most
acute and immediate.

As already indicated, the partisanship of early GDR writing has to be
viewed in an international political context. The appeals which
Johannes R. Becher – erstwhile Expressionist poet who had spent the
Nazi period in exile in Moscow and returned to East Germany to
become the GDR's first Minister of Culture – had made immediately
after the war for a unified, national, cross-border German culture,
became but a distant memory as the irreconcilable political interests of

the Soviet Union and the Western allies led to the increasing tensions of the Cold War and the establishing in 1949 of two separate German states. Becher himself had used the occasion of the second German *Schriftstellerkongreß* in July 1950 not only to deliver the obligatory adulatory speech in praise of Stalin ('es lebe der Meister, der geniale Autor dieser Achthundert-Millionen-Sprache des Friedens: Stalin'), but also to launch a blistering attack on Melvin Lasky's anti-Communist *Kongress für kulturelle Freiheit* which had been held in West Berlin some weeks before. His comments were couched in Cold War vocabulary of the most intemperate kind. He described the Western writers and intellectuals who had attended this 'Spitzel- und Kriegsbrandstifter-Kongress' as 'Handlanger der Kriegshetzer' who had transformed themselves into 'eine Bande internationaler Hochstapler', into 'literarisch getarnte Gangster'. They were, furthermore, a 'kriminelle Clique' whose 'Schund und Schmutz' must not be allowed to spread to the German Democratic Republic. 'Wir wollen,' Becher concluded, turning his back on all his earlier endeavours to bring about a unified German culture, 'nichts mehr wissen von euch, euch weder sehen noch hören.'[4]

In the late 1940s and early 1950s East German writers increasingly gave fictional expression to these hostilities, insisting on political and cultural separateness, and stressing it in unambiguously didactic fashion (in the East, promise and perspective, new life, hope and peace-seeking endeavour; in the West, decadence, moral depravity, despair, and warmongering profiteering) – all in a concerted effort to demonstrate the ethical and social superiority of Socialism. This is the linking thread throughout much of an anthology such as Vilmos Korn's *Offen steht das Tor des Lebens* (1951). In a story by Rudolf Bartsch, 'Der große Übergang',[5] for instance, two young writer friends of bohemian proclivities decide to go their separate ways. Högler goes to Braunschweig – a place where one may observe a fishmonger throwing away herrings under the eyes of a 'schwindsüchtigen, ausgehungerten jungen Menschen'. Here, he not only prostitutes his talents writing sensationalist fiction for an unscrupulous publisher who regards literature as 'Ware', as a mere commodity, but leads the dissolute life of his fictional creations, 'das Leben von Säufern, Totschlägern und Verrückten'. His companion Doboschek, on the other hand, finds fulfilment on a building-site in the East while writing propagandistic reportages soggy with official slogans and clichés:

Seit langem hatte er die Gelegenheit gesucht, von dem neuen, wieder aufatmenden Leben erfaßt und mitgenommen zu werden; er hatte erkannt, daß dieses neue Leben nichts dringender brauchte als Menschen, die guten Willens waren.[6]

Interestingly enough, contemporary criticism had, it seemed, at this point not yet been brought behind the official line. It was still able to evaluate new writing according to some notion of literary quality rather than on the basis of unquestioning commitment to the new state, and it found this brand of platitudinous tendentiousness – the product of what the East German critic Leonore Krenzlin would later come to describe as the 'Steuerbarkeit des Literaturprozesses'[7] – hard to stomach. This is exemplified by reaction to another piece in the Korn anthology, Hildegard M. Rauchfuss's 'Das Gastspiel', in which a chance visit to a Russian Army Choir concert persuades a piano player in the Kansas Bar in West Berlin to abandon his aimless lifestyle and decamp to the East. The tale ends on a crassly symbolic note as he crosses the border: 'Das fahle Grün der Neonröhren reichte nicht bis zur anderen Seite hinüber. Ganz hinten am Ende der Straße war der Himmel noch hell.' The story elicited the withering judgement from Günter Caspar that it did not even begin to give an impression of the realities of divided Berlin:

'Schoko. Amis. Gold' dort und Transparente hier – das gibt nicht einmal eine Impression vom zweigeteilten Berlin. Die Studentin als Taxi-Girl, der arbeitslose Musiker als Klavierspieler in der Bar dort, hier ein Gastspiel des Alexandrow-Ensembles – das bleibt oberflächliches Symbol, weil nicht die Ursachen gestaltet werden, im Einzelnen nicht die Gesamtheit.[8]

There is a transparently propagandistic and unconvincing quality to this and those other contributions to Korn's anthology which seek to expose the lupine decadence of the West as a way of persuading the citizens of the East to stay and opt for socialism: this at a time when, as Erich Loest would note in his autobiography, people were moving in droves from East to West, not the other way round: 'Wer drüben einen Platz gefunden hatte, zog andere nach; der späte Strom begann mit seinen Bächen.'[9]

Loest made his own contribution to this highly *parti pris* literature in a series of stories written in the early 1950s, as well as the highly successful novel (it sold some 65 000 copies) *Die Westmark fällt weiter* of 1952. One may speculate, however, that the irreproachable political line he pursues in these works was prompted not only by the SED's attacks on Formalism, but was also in no small part as a consequence of the rap over the knuckles he had received as a result of his first novel *Jungen, die übrigblieben*, published two years earlier.[10] This autobiographical account of (as an adolescent) being caught up in the final stages of the war had provoked the accusation of 'Standpunktlosigkeit' – GDR critical code for failing to deliver the required (Marxist) perspective, in this case, on the origins and causes of National Socialism. As a result, he had lost a well-paid job as a journalist working on the *Leipziger Volkszeitung*, and been sent off to redeem himself 'in der Produktion'.[11]

In view of the harsh lesson Loest had learned over *Jungen, die übrigblieben*, it was unlikely that he would make the same mistake twice, and 'Standpunktlosigkeit' was certainly not something with which his second novel *Die Westmark fällt weiter* could be reproached. It was the outcome, as he himself readily admits, of the ideological schooling he had begun to receive as a trainee journalist with the *Leipziger Volkszeitung*, and which is summed up in the view, expressed in his autobiography of 1981, of the simple, unavoidable choices of the time: 'Inzwischen gab es die Alternative: Kapitalismus oder Sozialismus, Westzone oder Ostzone' (*Durch die Erde*, p. 134). While the tendentious political emphasis of *Die Westmark fällt weiter* is beyond dispute, it was nevertheless – as the sales figures indicate – very popular in its day, and is even now still worth reading. What redeems it, what lifts it above the utterly dreary, similarly propagandistic *Betriebsromane* of the time by writers such as Hans Marchwitzka or Karl Mundstock, is a lively sense of milieu and a certain panache in the creation of fast-moving incident and readily identifiable characters. These were the product, incidentally, of talents which would enable Loest, at a later and darker point in his career, to write a series of successful detective novels under the pseudonym 'Hans Walldorf'.[12]

As indicated, *Die Westmark fällt weiter* may itself be classified as a kind crime fiction, but one which locates its heroes and villains firmly in the context of East–West political relations, and brings a clear East German perspective to bear on them. Set in Berlin in 1951, it interweaves three of the events which loomed large in the divided city in that year. First, the wave of violent crime emanating from the 'Gangsterbande um Gladow', the group of young thugs who had terrorized Berlin with robberies and violent crime, until being captured, convicted, and three of them sentenced to death in spring 1951 (see *Durch die Erde*, p. 144). Second, the attempt of West Berlin industrialists to secure American capital investment – a process which entailed ensuring a labour force free of Socialist and Communist influence. And third, the *Weltfestspiele der Jugend und Studenten* held in East Berlin in the summer of the same year.

How are these events depicted in Loest's novel? The figure of Egon Kamm, the would-be 'Al Capone von Berlin' (*Westmark*, p. 476) and ringleader of the gang of young criminals is clearly modelled on Gladow. He is portrayed as the product of an American gangster and war culture and of institutions such as the 'Eagle Club' behind which stand the sinister figure of the American Clark Haydock and his 'Abteilung für "Psychologische Kriegsvorbereitung"'. Loest leaves us in little doubt as to how we are to understand Haydock and his organization:

> Der nach Berlin ausgestreckte lange Arm der Abteilung heißt Clark Haydock. Wie schon ihr Name sagt, hat diese Abteilung die Aufgabe, die Seelen der Menschen auf den Krieg vorzubereiten. Man macht das, indem man beispielsweise am 'Tag der amerikanischen Armee' deutschen Jungen dicke Panzer und schnelle Jeeps vorführt, indem man ihnen Pistolen zeigt und die besten Schnellfeuergewehre der Welt, und indem man vor ihnen kleine Gefechtsszenen mit Blitz und Knall und Bumm vorführt. Auch ist es sehr wirkungsvoll auf Jungenseelen, wenn sie mal in einen Panzerspähwagen kriechen oder hinter den Röhren einer Vierlingsflak hocken dürfen. Um all diese Wirkungen weiß Clark Haydock. Ihm ist auch bekannt, daß das ständige Wiederholen von Kriegsartikeln in Zeitungen die Menschen erst allmählich in einen Zustand der Kriegsangst, dann der Kriegsbereitschaft versetzt. Er weiß, daß nichts so sehr ein Jungenherz für das Schießen begeistert wie ein zünftiger Kriminalfilm ... Und da sich Mister Clark Haydock in all diesen Dingen hervorragend auskennt, ist er der richtige Mann, die Seelen der Berliner – in aller Stille natürlich – auf den Krieg vorzubereiten. (*Westmark*, p. 168)

The negative repercussions of this malevolent influence are not long in coming. The taste for the activities glamorized and encouraged by the American-style pulp fiction and crime films promoted by Haydock combined with the fact that, unlike their peers in East Berlin, they have neither secure employment nor a meaningful purpose to their lives, soon propels Kamm and his companions into a life of crime. From the theft of a handful of watches, they move on to relieving three West Berlin policemen of their pistols, to armed hold-ups, and eventually the murder of a taxi driver. Loest is at pains to give these criminal activities an unambivalent political and ideological twist. Scarce West Berlin police resources, for instance, are – at the prompting of businessmen politicians anxious not to jeopardize the promise of American investment – taken off the job of investigating the Kamm crimes in order to winkle out East

Berlin agitators for peace who are employed in a West Berlin factory. Furthermore, the same three officers who are revealed as cowardly and passive when being robbed of their weapons, are, at a later point in the novel, shown to be brutally energetic in the use of their truncheons against East Berliners – women and children included, who – at the invitation of the West Berlin mayor Ernst Reuter – had been allowed to stage a march through the city in protest against plans for West German rearmament.[13]

Set against all of this is the account of the productive endeavour of those involved in organizing the *Weltfestspiele* in East Berlin, the other half of an argument which Loest mounts with narrative vigour and energy, but in blissfully simplistic terms. His tale of the confrontation of East and West, of good and evil, has all the unambiguousness of a cartoon film, reminding us of Anna Seghers's gentle castigation of the simplicities of early GDR novels when she compared them to medieval mystery plays in their signposting of character and ideological location: 'Man erkennt augenblicklich, wie in den Mysterienspielen des Mittelalters, die Engel an ihren Flügeln und die Teufel an ihren Hörnern. Und die Personen handeln, wie es ihren Insignien entspricht.'[14] On the one hand, Egon Kamm and his twilight companions, the CIA, corruptible West Berlin politicians, and policeman more interested in clubbing down demonstrators engaged in peaceful protest against West German remilitarization than in pursuing criminals; on the other, model socialist lorry drivers, bright-eyed members of the *Freie Deutsche Jugend*, clean-jawed *Volkspolizisten*, and an ubiquitous mood of constructive endeavour. These clearly drawn lines of ideological battle are helped along by the novel's montage method, and the rapid, cinematic switching between a series of simultaneously narrated, parallel lives, and action which runs almost contemporaneously with the writing of the novel: 'Er abonnierte die >Berliner Zeitung< und bettete seine Handlung in den exakten Zeitablauf ein', Loest informs us, speaking of himself in the third-person singular (*Westmark*, p. 159). Even as reality, the news of the day, unfolds before him, he is engaged in giving it fictional form. The juxtaposing montage technique of the novel permits him easy comparisons. Hard-drinking and womanizing American industrialists and financiers prepare remilitarization deals with West Berlin entrepreneurs, as tenants of an East Berlin appartment block busily prepare the attic to accommodate young visitors to the *Weltfestspiele*, or as homeward-bound office workers are galvanized into helping to unload shuttering boards on the site of the Stalinallee *Sporthalle* which is under construction.

*Die Westmark fällt weiter* presents the contemporary reader with the fully-formed, ideologically seamless black-and-white world characteristic of all socialist realist writing. Its main challenge today is how to explain the conspiratorial, paranoid even, tale it tells of American policy towards Germany in the immediate post-war period. One view might be that it offers perfectly reasonable comment on the historical realities of the time. In their useful account of post-war Berlin, Helmut Peitsch and Rhys W. Williams note that in the early 1950s there were 'ninety espionage organizations working in West Berlin, a number run by Germans under CIA control', and that in 1951–2 – precisely the time in which Loest's novel is set – members of these groups 'were convicted in East Berlin courts of various acts of sabotage, such as adulterating dried milk by adding soap powder or saccharine, shutting down turbines and machines, destroying rolling stock on the railway, derailing trains and causing collisions in shunting yards', quite apart from undermining the GDR economy through the extortionate exchange rate and illegal trade.[15]

It is clear from this that a good deal of energy was being directed from the western side of the city towards damaging the GDR. What might also be argued, however, is that anti-Communist activities such these would – subsequently, and increasingly – be made the excuse for the in-built systemic failings of Socialism. The classic example here is the evidence assembled in *Befehdet seit dem ersten Tag. Über drei Jahrzehnte Attentate gegen die DDR.*[16] The authors of this volume – first published at a point (1981) when, with hindsight, the GDR was irredeemably doomed to collapse – attempt to explain away the failure (albeit that it is never expressed as such) of Socialism to truly thrive in the GDR as a product of implacable Western hostility. Given what has come to light, since unification, of the effect of the *Kommandowirtschaft* and the crippling centralized control exerted by autocratic figures such as Günter Mittag, arguments of this kind now look exceedingly threadbare.[17]

The total commitment of *Die Westmark fällt weiter* to the GDR could help neither it, nor its author, some years later when Loest would fall foul of the system. The events of the 17 June 1953, the revelations about Stalin in 1956, along with the uprisings of the same year in Poland and Hungary were to shake the ideological certainties which had inspired what he had written hitherto. The first signs of disaffection occur in articles written in the wake of the East Berlin uprising in which he argued for a more honest appraisal of the causes of the troubles.[18] In addition, the debates initiated by Hans Mayer in Leipzig, where Loest was a student at the *Johannes R. Becher Literaturinstitut* in 1955/6, about the possible liberalizing consequences for the GDR of destalinization were to lead him into even deeper water, and to his being sentenced to seven and a half years in Bautzen (of which he would serve all but six months), for 'Bildung einer Staats- und parteifeindlichen Gruppe'. As Loest himself notes of the fate of his erstwhile best seller, in the lightly ironic, distanced tone which characterizes his autobiography: 'Auch dieser Titel des Staatsfeindes L. [wurde] aus den Bibliotheken entfernt' (*Durch die Erde*, p. 169).

*Die Westmark fällt weiter*, along with the other texts discussed here, belongs to the early history of East German literature. Such works deserve our attention as curiosities, as examples of literature at the disposal of political and ideological purpose. We may wish to read them now if only to remind ourselves of Franz Fühmann's characteristically wise and courageous adhortation in his address to the Seventh Writers' Congress of 1973 – 'Wunschdenken, so gut es auch immer gemeint sei, bringt Gesellschaft wie Literatur nicht weiter.'[19]

## Notes

1. Bodo Uhse, 'Träume, Pläne, Wirklichkeit (statt eines Vorwortes)', in *Menschen und Werke. Vom Wachsen und Werden des neuen Lebens in der Deutschen Demokratischen Republik* (Berlin, 1952), pp. 11–27 (here, pp. 12–13).
2. 'Der Kampf gegen den Formalismus in Kunst und Literatur, für eine fortschrittliche deutsche Kultur', in Elimar Schubbe (ed.), *Dokumente zur Kunst-, Literatur- und Kulturpolitik der SED* (Stuttgart, 1972), pp. 178–86.
3. Erich Loest, *Die Westmark fällt weiter* (Halle/Saale 1952). Hereafter as *Westmark*.
4. Johannes R. Becher, 'Schlußwort auf einem Schriftstellerkongress', in *Publizistik III 1946–1951* (Berlin/Weimar, 1979), pp. 348–58.
5. Rudolf Bartsch, 'Der große Übergang', in Vilmos Korn, *Offen steht das Tor des Lebens. Eine Anthologie junger deutscher Prosa* (Berlin, 1951), pp. 160–95.
6. *Ibid.*, p. 160.
7. Leonore Krenzlin, 'Theoretische Diskussionen und praktisches Bemühen um die Neubestimmung der Funktion der Literatur an der Wende der fünfziger Jahre', in Ingeborg Münz-Koenen (ed.), *Literarisches Leben in der DDR 1945–1960* (Berlin, 1980), p. 156.
8. Günter Caspar, 'Junge Prosa', in *Aufbau*, 7 (1951), p. 1032. As Manfred Jäger has reminded us, this brand of sharp criticism of ideologically correct but hapless new writing would not be tolerated for long: 'Vor allem jüngere Autoren sollten nicht durch harte Kritik an der sprachlichen und psychologischen Qualität ihrer Arbeiten irritiert werden, falls sie sich parteilich den politischen Zielsetzungen öffneten.' Manfred Jäger, 'Literatur und Kulturpolitik in der Entstehungsphase der DDR (1945–1952)', in *Aus Politik und Zeitgeschichte. Beilage zur Wochenzeitung Das Parlament*, 5 October 1984, p. 43.

9. Erich Loest, *Durch die Erde ein Riß. Ein Lebenslauf* (Hamburg,1981), p. 166. Hereafter as *Durch die Erde.*

10. Erich Loest, *Jungen, die übrigblieben.* (Leipzig, 1950).

11. It was one of the unfathomable oddities of the 'Arbeiter-und-Bauernstaat' that being sent off to work in industry or on the land could be conceived of as a kind of chastisement.

12. In their bibliography of GDR crime fiction, Reinhard Hillich and Wolfgang Mittmann list fourteen titles written by Loest under the pseudonym Hans Walldorf, and one under that of Hans Falldorf. See *Die Kriminalliteratur der DDR 1949–1990. Bibliografie,* zusammengestellt von Reinhard Hillich and Wolfgang Mittmann (Berlin, 1991), pp. 129–30.

13. Loest, in his representation of these events, and of the involvement in them of some of his principal characters, is being deliberately polemical by drawing unfavourable comparisons between the tenacious commitment of his exemplary East Berlin *Volkspolizist* Karl Bornemann and the fecklessness of the West Berlin police. Nonetheless, his account does not stray too far from historical fact, as is borne out by the version of the episode in Heinz Lippmann's biography of the then head of the *Freie Deutsche Jugend,* Erich Honecker. See Heinz Lippmann, *Honecker and the New Politics of Europe* (New York, 1972), and particularly pp. 127–31. What Loest omits to mention is the damage – clearly outlined by Lippmann – that this episode did at the time to Honecker's status and reputation in the GDR. Also, incidentally, it is interesting to note that Loest, on p. 570 of *Die Westmark fällt weiter,* has the spelling of Honecker's name as 'Honnecker'. This may, of course, be due to the fact that a character in the novel is quoting here from *Der Spiegel,* and that it is the magazine which has got it wrong.

14. Anna Seghers, 'Der Anteil der Literatur an der Bewußtseinsbildung des Volkes', in *Über Kunst und Wirklichkeit,* vol. 1 (Berlin, 1970), p. 100.

15. Helmut Peitsch and Rhys W. Williams (eds), *Berlin seit dem Kriegsende* (Manchester, 1989), pp. 12–13.

16. Eberhard Heinrich and Klaus Ullrich, *Befehdet seit dem ersten Tag. Über drei Jahrzehnte Attentate gegen die DDR* (Berlin, 1981).

17. For a short account of the economic ravages wrought by Günter Mittag see, for instance, Harry Maier, 'Herrscher aller Kombinate. Nach drei Jahrzehnten an der Spitze tritt der führende SED-Wirtschaftsfunktionär Günter Mittag ab', in *Die Zeit,* 3 June 1988, pp. 25–6.

18. See Erich Loest, 'Es wurden Bücher verbrannt', in *Börsenblatt für den deutschen Buchhandel* (Leipzig), 1953, Nr. 26, p. 526, and 'Elfenbeinturm und rote Fahne', in *Börsenblatt für den deutschen Buchhandel* (Leipzig), 1953, Nr. 27, pp. 548–9.

19. Franz Fühmann, 'Literatur und Kritik', in Franz Fühmann, *Essays Gespräche Aufsätze 1964–1981* (Rostock, 1983), p. 79.

# 13

## *Was bleibt* Revisited: Christa Wolf and the Fear of Transience

*Michael Butler*

Es gibt kein richtiges Leben im falschen.

Adorno, Minima Moralia

The furore which greeted the publication of Christa Wolf's 'Erzählung' *Was bleibt* in 1990 has obscured the text itself for too long. The timing of the publication of the manuscript – dated June–July 1979/November 1989 – rapidly dominated its reception and fuelled an at times vicious controversy about the value of GDR literature in general and Christa Wolf's integrity in particular.[1] Indeed, so politicized did the debate become and so personalized the commentaries that the fact the book was presented as a piece of literature ('a story') was obscured if not totally ignored. Of course, Christa Wolf's fiction has always been characterized by its strong autobiographical emphasis, and in that sense *Was bleibt* represents no new departure. However, without wishing to deny the political and social context of this short text, I wish to offer a modest re-reading which will, I hope, help to rescue the story from the polemical morass in which it has been stuck for almost a decade.[2]

The opening sentences of *Was bleibt*, written just before the onset of spring with its promise of hope and renewal, contain *in nuce* the central themes of the story: the fear of transience, that is, the specifically human fear of running out of time before reaching a stage of honest articulation, the problem of ageing and the inadequacy of memory:

Nur keine Angst. In jener anderen Sprache, die ich im Ohr, noch nicht auf der Zunge habe, werde ich eines Tages auch darüber reden. Heute, das wußte ich, wäre es zu früh. Aber würde ich spüren, wenn es an der Zeit ist? Würde ich meine Sprache je finden? Einmal würde ich alt sein. Und wie würde ich mich dieser Tage dann erinnern?[3]

For this narrator, writing is clearly a way of controlling time or at least a way of defeating its inexorable predations by leaving clearly shaped memories as proof of having existed. The existential seriousness of her purpose is clearly articulated in the closing pages of her narrative as she wanders alone through her dark, quiet flat. She looks through her collection of records, pausing at two of her particular favourites, Mozart's *Exsultate Jubilate* and Schubert's setting of Wilhem Müller's poem-cycle, *Die Winterreise*, with its plangent opening lines, 'Fremd bin ich eingezogen, / Fremd zieh ich wieder aus'. However, neither Mozart's joyous affirmation nor the ordered desolation of Müller's text offers its customary solace. In her deadened, fragmented world art appears – momentarily at least – to have lost its vital, integrating function: 'Nichts trifft' (105). Similarly, her well-stocked bookshelves merely mock an artistic solidarity she no longer feels. A single line sums up the stark truth of her condition: 'Mit meinem Mörder Zeit bin ich allein' (105).

As in a musical composition, the final lines of the text recall that opening cadence in an elegiac coda:

Eines Tages, dachte ich, werde ich sprechen können, ganz leicht und frei. Es ist noch zu früh, aber ist es nicht immer zu früh. Sollte ich mich nicht einfach hinsetzen an diesen Tisch, unter dieser Lampe, das Papier zurechtrücken, den Stift nehmen und anfangen. Was bleibt. Was meiner Stadt zugrunde liegt und woran sie zugrunde geht. Daß es kein Unglück gibt außer dem, nicht zu leben. Und am Ende keine Verzweiflung außer der, nicht gelebt zu haben. (107f.)

Clearly, these words bear a heavy social and political weight, but the existential crisis they adumbrate is deeply rooted in the personal and the private. The ultimate despair of never having lived is surely linked to the fear of transience, to the loss of creative energy to use to the full every irretrievable moment of life. Indeed, the narrator points to this acute awareness of the remorseless nature of time as clearly distinguishing her from the Stasi watchers outside her flat:

Zeit war eines meiner Stichworte. Eines Tages war mir klar geworden, daß es vielleicht mehr als alles andere, ein gründlich anderes Verhältnis zur Zeit war, daß mich von jenen jungen Herren da draußen ... unterschied. Jenen war ihre Zeit wertlos, sie vergeudeten sie in einem unsinnigen, gewiß aber kostspieligen Müßiggang ... Mit beiden Händen, lustvoll geradezu, warfen sie ihre Zeit zum Fenster hinaus. (23)

The fact that the final sentences of the text are left as bleakly honest statements rather than questions is significant in view of narrator's faintly mocking self-admonition at the start of the story: 'Die Zeichensetzung in Zukunft gefälligst ernster nehmen, sagte ich mir' (12). The time has come to confront truth rather than skid round it via hypothesis or flight into self-deluding prevarication.

To arrive at this belated recognition – in all its painful melancholy – the narrator has to pass through a number of experiences and encounters which sharpen both her moral sense and her insight into herself. An analysis of three such encounters will suffice to illustrate the specific point and to reveal deeper, existential meanings of the text.

Without doubt, the most vivid and certainly the most significant encounter is the visit of the young woman writer to the narrator in her flat. The contrast between the recklessness of dissident youth and the circumspection of middle age could not be clearer.[4] Though the narrator recognizes the quality and searing truth of the younger woman's writing, her instinctive reaction – as much motherly as it is cowardly – is to advise her against publication. Obviously, such sentiments have everything to do with the context of the oppressive Stasi state and the tactical advisability of self-censorship, but at the same time the confrontation can be interpreted in a more general sense: the nagging feeling of the older writer that she has ducked the issues, missed her time, betrayed her vocation – 'Es ist soweit. Die Jungen schreiben es auf' (76). For her, the joy and perils of spontaneity have long since become a distant and rapidly fading memory.[5] In contrast, the young woman – by no means unaware of the danger she courts – is determined to write the truth, 'Jetzt. Hier' (78). And the word 'jetzt' rings mockingly in the narrator's ear as she watches her colleague depart in a flourish of youthful courage.

The existential sadness of this key episode is underlined by the fact that during her imprisonment the girl had been sterilized due to a mistaken diagnosis, a tragedy which cuts her off from a familial future but one which she does not allow to cloud her vision of the need to use the present with all her power. The older woman's daughters, *her* link to the future, seem suddenly small compensation for her own lack of moral courage in the fight against the strutting Lie in all its meretricious finery. Maintaining an inner integrity behind a mask of outward conformity, which may once have seemed the option of common sense – a strategem often characterized as *Zweigleisigkeit* in the former GDR – now appears merely to be a mendacious subterfuge. Youth, as it were, has no time for transience: 'Das Mädchen fragt nicht krämerisch: Was bleibt. Es fragte nicht danach, woran es sich erinnern würde, wenn es einst alt wäre' (79).

This unsettling confrontation indelibly colours the two other episodes I wish to discuss briefly: the narrator's visit to her husband in hospital and the literary reading at the *Kulturhaus*. The impact upon the narrator of the young woman's uncompromising pursuit of truth is fundamental. She suffers an alienation from her self. Indeed, it is almost as if part of her has left along with the young writer who is clearly presented as a shock reminder of her own youthful idealism: 'Mit diesem Mädchen trat etwas mir vom Ursprung her Verwandtes und zugleich ganz und gar Fremdes über meine Schwelle.' At the same time, for all her own compromises – an inevitable consequence, perhaps, of maturation and familial responsibilities – the reminder once made will not fade again: 'Mein Gefühl verdichtete sich, daß dieses Mädchen meine Wohnung nie mehr verlassen würde' (74).

With routine precision the narrator drives to the hospital to visit her husband. But her whole 'Wahrnehmungsapparat' (79) has been severely unbalanced. Indeed, she describes her state of mind in terms which strongly recall Georg Büchner's *Lenz*:

> Ich hatte weder Angst noch überhaupt ein Gefühl, auch mit mir selbst stand ich nicht mehr in Kontakt, was waren mir Mann, Kinder, Brüder und Schwestern, Größen gleicher Ordnung in einem System, das sich selbst genug war. Das blanke Grauen, ich hatte nicht gewußt, daß es sich durch Fühllosigkeit anzeigt. (80)[6]

That this alienation also strikes at the root of genuine articulation is made clear as the narrator mechanically acts out her role as hospital visitor: '[ich] machte alles ganz echt und ganz natürlich, vermied nicht einmal Wörter wie "Sorge" und "Sehnsucht", da einem ja, wenn man nichts fühlt, alle Wörter frei zur Verfügung stehen' (81). Despite the life-threatening illness of her husband, an unwillingness to face the bleak fact of transience vitiates true communication between the pair: 'Gestern hatte ich mich, einen ganzen Vormittag lang, gewaltsam der

Schreckensvorstellung eines Lebens ohne ihn erwehren müssen. Es ist alles gutgegangen, sagte ich. Es ist alles gut' (83). Fear of a most obvious kind, of course, is palpable in the *Kulturhaus*. For the organizer of the event has begun to dread the impact of the narrator's reading on the audience, especially in view of the prominent presence of the Stasi in the room. But this belongs to the surface of the tale; more interesting is the attitude of the narrator. Although her good humour is somewhat restored by the comic timidity of her hostess – a memory the narrator will store up for future use: 'Wir werden im Alter wenigstens etwas haben, wovon wir zehren können' (90)[7] – her reading itself is presented as anything but a full engagement of the senses: 'Den Text kannte ich auswendig. Die Sätze betonen sich von selbst, die Stimme hebt sich, senkt sich, wird weicher, härter. Wie es sich gehört. Alles mechanisch, keiner wird es merken' (91). Moreover, the narrator mentally addresses the Stasi in the audience with a display of suppressed bravado which underlines her own sense of current inadequacy: 'Oja. Sie werden bedient werden. Eines Tages werdet ihr bedient sein, Kolleginnen und Kollegen' (92).

In such moments, the gap that has opened up between the established writer who can fill a hall and the unknown young woman clutching the truth in her fist is brilliantly indicated with an irony that amounts to fierce self-criticism on the part of the narrator. Such self-censure is intensified by implication when a young nurse in the audience poses the key question for the younger generation: 'Auf welche Weise aus dieser Gegenwart für uns und unsere Kinder eine lebbare Zukunft her-auswachsen solle' (95). Although the narrator has acted as a catalyst for a vital discussion in the audience – 'denn nun standen die wirklichen Fragen im Raum, die von denen wir leben und durch deren Entzug wir sterben können' (95) – it is significant that it is the predominantly youthful members of the audience who debate the issues with each other, leaving the narrator a mute spectator.

The narrator's steep learning curve in this text is completed by the phone call from her daughter once she has returned home from the reading. Having heard of the disturbance outside the *Kulturhaus*, the daughter wants to know that her mother is unharmed. Her final words to her mother are: 'Was ich noch sagen wollte: sie haben recht, dir zu mißtrauen.' To which her mother replies: 'Das fange ich gerade zu begreifen an' (106). Once again, the contemporary political context is plain. However, the narrator's reply is rich in ambiguity. For the mistrust evinced by the state, it is hinted, is a mistrust now shared by the narrator herself, though naturally for very different reasons. The visit of the young writer has brought home to her the full implications of what she calls at the beginning of her story, 'mein beschämendes Bedürfnis, mich mit allen Leuten gut zu stellen' (20).[8] The interior dialogues she has with her conscience all point to the accusation that she has betrayed her calling as a writer, that is, as an individual who looks reality straight in the eye and unflinchingly sets it down.

In the final analysis, what the narrator has had to confront is not others, whether Stasi or young people seeking advice, but precisely her own conscience ('Sie soll tun, was sie tun muß, und uns unserem Gewissen überlassen'; 78). She is well aware of the privileges she enjoys as a creative writer: 'Jeden Tag sagt ich mir, ein bevorzugtes Leben wie das meine ließe sich nur durch den Versuch rechtfertigen, hin und wieder die Grenzen des Sagbaren zu überschreiten, der Tatsache eingedenk, daß Grenzverletzungen aller Art geahndet werden' (22). And this imperative applies to *all* writers, whether they are subject to state oppression or not. As T.S. Eliot put it in 'Burnt Norton': 'human kind / Cannot bear very much reality'. It is precisely the task of poets to articulate reality at whatever cost, and in a world of colliding relativities it is a melancholy fact that their efforts invariably end in failure, at least by their own standards.

In this light, *Was bleibt*, for all its undeniable political contemporaneity, can be seen as an exploration of this constant sense of defeat which goes beyond the immediate circumstances of its composition. The 'andere Sprache' which Wolf can hear but not yet articulate is not just simply a form of expression free from state or self-censorship, but also – and perhaps more importantly – the promise of ultimate clarity which encourages the writer to pursue her sisyphean task. As she put it herself in an interview given a year before she wrote the first version of *Was bleibt*:

Meine Arbeit hat kein 'Ziel', ich kann niemals ankommen. Ich wünsche mir, daß ich imstande wäre, mich in dem, was ich schreibe, ganz auszudrücken, so daß am Ende der Überhang von Ungesagtem – soweit es im Bereich des mir Sagbaren ist – gleich Null wäre. Das ist natürlich unerreichbar.[9]

Far from Christa Wolf attempting some kind of *Annäherungsversuch* in the new political climate or cheaply claiming for herself the status of victim in the aftermath of the collapse of the GDR, the text lays bare the narrator's personal but very human inadequacies. It belongs to that difficult process of drawing up 'eine erste Lebensbilanz' forced upon her by a more self-confident younger generation, unencumbered by fascism, which she spoke of in the above interview.[10] In this sense, Wolf can be seen as a moralist in the same mould as Max Frisch, a writer with whom she has considerable affinities. Thus *Was bleibt* represents a necessary step in a critical reappraisal of herself as a writer. In an interview with Günter Gaus in 1993, after the controversy had abated and she had recovered from the ferocious attacks upon her motives and person, Christa Wolf expressed her determination to renew the search for genuine expression: 'Auf irgend ein hohes Roß werde ich mich bestimmt nicht setzen. Aber härter gegen mich werde ich sein, rücksichtsloser.'[11] The test of this new fearlessness will not be seen in how the writer adapts – yet again! – to the radically changed circumstances of her society, but in how she comes to terms with the existential problem of transience. In particular, she has to cope with the fear, shared overtly or subliminally by all writers, that one day she may lose her most precious gift, her creative imagination. If the latter disintegrates, whether through the ravages of time or through sheer loss of moral courage, so will her ability to orientate herself in the world and by doing so store up stories – 'Wegzehrung' – to help sustain future generations.

## Notes

1. The so-called 'Literatur-Debatte', unleashed by *Was bleibt*, is fully documented in Thomas Anz (ed.), *'Es geht nicht um Christa Wolf'. Der Literaturstreit im vereinten Deutschland* (Munich, 1991). See also Hermann Vinke (ed.), *Akteneinsicht Christa Wolf. Zerrspiegel und Dialog. Eine Dokumentation* (Hamburg, 1993). For an up-to-date analysis of the central issues, see Thomas Anz, 'Der Streit um Christa Wolf und die Intellektuellen im vereinten Deutschland', *German Monitor*, 38 (1996), pp. 1–17.
2. Georgina Paul has attempted to look at the formal aspects of the story and place it in the context of Christa Wolf's subsequent development; see 'Text and Context. *Was bleibt* 1979–1989', in Axel Goodbody and Dennis Tate (eds), *Geist und Macht. Writers and the State in the GDR* (Amsterdam and Atlanta, GA, 1992), pp. 117–28. Christopher Colton, too, has tried to see the book as a work of literature against the distortions of the polemic. See *'Was bleibt* – eine neue Sprache?', in Ian Wallace (ed.), *Christa Wolf in Perspective* (Amsterdam and Atlanta, GA, 1994), pp. 207–26. Closer to my argument is Judith M. Sallis, 'The Search for Permanence in a Disintegrating World: Christa Wolf's *Was bleibt*', *German Monitor*, 38 (1996), pp. 109–23. My existential emphasis, however, differs from her more socio-political approach.
3. *Was bleibt* (Frankfurt am Main, 1990), p. 7. All future references are to this edition. The fragility of memory, of course, is a major theme of Wolf's mature fiction, *Nachdenken über Christa T.* and *Kindheitsmuster*. But it first occurs in a characteristically elegiac moment in her early story, 'Juninachmittag' (1965) where the narrator observes her small daughter playing and muses on the nature of time and memory: 'Der Garten wird längst versunken sein, über

ein altes Foto von mir wird es verlegen den Kopf schütteln, und von sich selbst wird es fast nichts mehr wissen.' Christa Wolf, *Neue Lebensansichten eines Katers. Juninachmittag. Erzählungen* (Stuttgart, 1981), p. 44.

4. It is known that this episode was based on Gabriele Kachold whose outspoken dissidence in the former GDR brought her a harsh prison sentence and considerable ill-health. See Graham Jackman, '"Wann, wenn nicht jetzt?" Conceptions of Time and Narrative in Christa Wolf's *Was bleibt* and *Nachdenken über Christa T.*', *German Life and Letters*, XL, 4 (October 1992), pp. 358–75, here p. 361.

5. This painful recognition of lost spontaneity – and its risks – is not new. Christa Wolf recalls how the notion of 'subjektive Authentizität' freed her once before from a sterile rigidity: 'Aber der Durchbruch einer neuen, fast schon für immer verloren geglaubten Spontaneität war ein derart realer und befreiender Vorgang, daß ich wohl schlecht beraten wäre, wenn ich ihn geringschätzen oder gar ängstlich zurücknehmen würde.' 'Subjektive Authentizität. Gespräch mit Hans Kaufmann', in Christa Wolf, *Die Dimension des Autors. Essays und Aufsätze, Reden und Gespräche 1959–1985* (Darmstadt/Neuwied, 1987), p. 778.

6. The importance of Büchner's story for East German writers is well known. See Dennis Tate, *The East German Novel. Identity, Community, Continuity* (Bath, 1984), pp. 177–226. See, too, Christa Wolf's comment on the impact of the story on her own sensibility: 'Das ist mein Ur-Erlebnis in der deutschen Literatur. Bei mir setzt die deutsche Prosa mit Büchners Lenz-Novelle ein.' 'Unruhe und Betroffenheit. Gespräch mit Joachim Walther', in *Die Dimension des Autors*, p. 758. This example of intertextuality – a narrator apparently unaware of 'quoting' a literary source - reveals that a simple equation of narrator = Wolf will not do. Despite the obvious autobiographical detail, *Was bleibt* remains on an essential level an 'Erzählung', a work of imaginative fiction.

7. The notion of lighter moments saved up as a permanent source of 'Wegzehrung' for a dark future is introduced at the beginning of the story: 'Morgenlicht, das ich liebe, und von dem ich mir einen gehörigen Vorrat anlegen wollte, um in finsteren Zeiten davon zu zehren' and 'Ich fürchte ja, alle diese wüsten Tage würden nichts beisteuern zu dieser dauerhaften Wegzehrung und deshalb unaufhaltbar im Strom des Vergessens abtreiben' (9). Once again, though such passages bear an obvious political relevance, at the same time they are resonant of the more profound theme of transience and the concomitant problems of memory and ageing.

8. The phrase anticipates Günter Grass's comment in his article defending Christa Wolf against her detractors: 'Man erfährt [in ihren Büchern] ihr Bedürfnis, es allen recht zu machen. Eine gewisse biedere Wohlerzogenheit und Konfliktscheu spricht aus ihren Texten.' 'Nötige Kritik oder Hinrichtung? Spiegel-Gespräch mit Günter Grass über die Debatte um Christa Wolf und die DDR-Literatur', *Der Spiegel*, 16 July 1990. Reprinted in Anz (*op. cit.*), pp. 122–34.

9. 'Arbeitsbedingungen. Interview mit Richard A. Zipser' [April 1978] in *Die Dimension des Autors*, p. 864. Christa Wolf's most famous fictive forebear is Gustav von Aschenbach who was similarly haunted by 'seine Künstlerfurcht, nicht fertig zu werden – diese Besorgnis, die Uhr möchte abgelaufen sein,

bevor er das Seine getan und völlig sich selbst gegeben'. *Der Tod in Venedig,* edited by T.J. Reed (Oxford, 1971), p. 65.

10. 'Eine junge Generation, nicht mehr belastet durch unsere Vergangenheit, kündigt sich an, in ihr Talente von einer erfreulichen Unbedingtheit. Die Autoren der mittleren Generation, zu denen ich gehöre, stellen sich teilweise und nicht ohne große Schwierigkeit einer ersten Lebensbilanz, und die Leserschaft hat sehr deutliche Forderungen an uns, denen wir uns nicht entziehen können: Die Forderung, die Widersprüche des Lebens in der Literatur zu finden, sich auch mit Hilfe der Literatur zu erkennen und sich ihrer bewußt zu werden.' 'Arbeitsbedingungen. Interview mit Richard A. Zipser', *op. cit.* p. 862.

11. 'Auf mir bestehen. Christa Wolf im Gespräch mit Günter Gaus', in Vinke (*op. cit.*), p. 258. This determination recalls the advice Gottfried Benn gave to younger artists in a lecture, 'Altern als Problem für Künstler': 'Härte ist das größte Geschenk für den Künstler, Härte gegen sich selbst und gegen sein Werk. Wie sagte Thomas Mann? "Lieber ein Werk verderben und weltunbrauchbar machen, als nicht an jeder Stelle bis zum Äußersten gehen."' *Gesammelte Werke in acht Bänden. Band 4: Reden und Vorträge,* edited by Dieter Wellershoff (Wiesbaden, 1968), p. 1144.

# 14
## High and Low Literature and the German Reading Public

*Keith Bullivant*

Whilst it has to be conceded that 'high' and 'low' forms of love-poetry emerge in Middle High German and that a similar divide exists between the Latin texts of the educated classes and the 'Volksbücher' of the sixteenth century, the international debate about high and low culture, 'Kultur' and 'Massenkultur', 'hohe' and 'niedere Literatur', 'Trivial-literatur' or 'Kitsch', whatever terms we may use, is closely linked to social and political developments in the eighteenth century. Changes in the nature and pattern of work, the increasing professionalization and bureaucratization of society, led to the emergence in England, then later in other countries, of that 'bürgerliche Öffentlichkeit' analysed so perceptively in Jürgen Habermas's *Habilitationsschrift*.[1] The emergence of a wider educated reading public, quickly reflected in the number of journals and newspapers published, brought to an end the arbitrary system of patronage and led to the emergence of the independent publisher, to the subscription and later to more speculative forms of publishing and the establishment of commercial lending libraries in the towns, which were of particular importance in breaking down the homogeneity of the audience.

The size of the reading public in Germany around 1800 was still relatively small: only some 0.1 per cent of the population could read, it is estimated, but nevertheless around 10 per cent of those in the towns and cities were readers, and there were already 2 000 lending libraries by this time. Things were really to gather pace in the nineteenth century, but the reading market had widened and diversified sufficiently by the late eighteenth century to force Schiller, in his review of Bürger's poetry, to recognize that there was no longer a homogeneous reading public, and that the poet had to choose between writing for an 'Auswahl' or for the 'Masse'. Increasingly, Levin Schücking claims, the writer as self-styled 'Dichter' was guided only by his own sense of artistic taste and his conviction as to the quality of his work. It was at this point, where the social role of literature becomes for the first time problematical, that the view of it as a binary system starts to emerge. The debate about the key differences between 'Dichtung' and popular literature in the late eighteenth century was provoked in particular by strong disapproval of the 'verschlepptes Empfindsamkeitsfieber' of the time. The theories of Sulzer, Bährens, of even Goethe, Schiller and the Schlegels are typical of oversensitive reactions by German aestheticians to the intentions of what Schiller called 'Schundskribenten'. Whereas the true poet, in the words of August Wilhelm Schlegel, was 'seinem Zeitalter voraus', the popular writer, according to Eichendorff, was engaged in a dubious 'Liebäugeln zwischen Dichterpöbel und Leserpöbel'. Here are the origins of a distinction between 'high' and 'low' art that run through to Hermann Broch's notions of the key differences between 'Kunst' and 'Kitsch'. Closely linked to this, and which also fed into contemporary wisdoms about the nature of 'Kitsch', were Goethe and Schiller's ideas on dilettantism, which they saw as having an uncreative reliance on literary clichés. The concomitant of these debates is the increasingly rarified notion of the writer that we find in the early Romantics and which continues on through Stefan George to, most recently, Peter Handke and Botho Strauß. In *Phantasien der Wiederholung* (1983) Handke expands at length on his concept of the poet as 'Götter-Bote', which is then demonstrated in the novel *Die Wiederholung* (1986) and in a number of other prose works written since. Some of Botho Strauß's pronouncements on the figure of the writer go even further than Handke. In his speech in acceptance of the Büchner Prize in 1989 he claimed that the 'Dichter ... spricht am liebsten zu Entfernten, zu seinesgleichen ... Strahler und Kristallsucher über die Zeiten und Länder hin.'[2] In *Fragmente der Undeutlichkeit*, published in the same year, he characterizes the poet as a mediator between God and those denied visionary powers; his function in this over-rationalized world is to translate all experience 'in die Undeutlichkeit ... Zurück ins Nicht-Verstehen'.[3]

In the period after 1830, as literacy increased rapidly, the reading public and the market offering grew commensurately: the number of lending libraries doubled and sales of sensational novels were by 1850 regularly reaching 50 000. To this should be added the success of magazines like *Die Gartenlaube*, which by 1876 had reached an imprint of 400 000 per issue, and which regularly featured serialized popular novels: it was here that Marlitt's romantic novels were first published. Over and above that, we have to take note of the 'Hefte' and 'Broschüren' being hawked around the rural communities by the 'Kolporteure'. It has been estimated that by 1850 the sales of this 'Kolportageliteratur' (a term which added another pejorative barb to the weaponry of proponents of high literature) were in the order of one million items. It was at this time that a true mass culture was established that continued to grow and in the twentieth century led logically on to the post-war paperback boom, having been diversified on the way by developments in the cinema, the record player, radio, TV, video and all those other aspects of contemporary popular culture.

This scenario was and is in no way peculiar to Germany and all developed societies generated their own debates about 'high' and 'low' culture, with the former being associated with timeless values and artistic achievement, the latter with the ephemeral and the sensational. I would argue, however, that such debates in, for example, England and the United States, especially where literature is concerned, have never had the vehemence and the rigidity that they have frequently had in Germany, because of a more flexible – or, some might argue, more tolerant – view of things. Let just a few examples here suffice. The status of Charles Dickens is now more or less unchallenged within the English canon, yet here is an essentially 'popular' writer whose livelihood was dependent on the serialization of his novels and for whom there is no German equivalent, merely a series of dismal imitations, especially of the *Pickwick Papers*. The so-called 'Condition of England' novels of the 1840s are accorded, thanks to the efforts of Queenie and F.R. Leavis, an important place within the history of the English novel, yet similar novels of the time by Ernst Willkomm, Johannes Scherr and Robert Prutz, for example, are more or less forgotten, long consigned to the ranks of 'Trivialliteratur'. If we think of such diverse writers as Arnold Bennett, John Galsworthy, John Steinbeck, John Updike, Joyce Carol Oates and David Lodge, it is clear that their highly accessible – yes, 'popular' – work is accepted by the academy and by critics as 'good' literature; it is difficult to think of German equivalents, despite recent attempts to claim Johannes Mario Simmel for the ranks of good writers. Indeed, the success of so many Anglo-Saxon writers in Germany seems to point to a sense of lack in German literature on the part of many readers: every second novel published in Germany is a translation and the best-seller lists are dominated by Anglo-Saxon writers.

There has long been, Arnold Hauser and Helmut Heissenbüttel have argued, an implicit equation in the mind of Germany's cultural elite between lack of commercial success and quality. Hauser maintains:

> Die Entfremdung der Künstlerschaft von der Gegenwart und ihr Verzicht auf jede Gemeinschaft mit dem Publikum geht so weit, daß sie die Erfolglosigkeit nicht nur als etwas durchaus Selbstverständliches hinnimmt, sondern den Erfolg als ein Zeichen der künstlerischen Minderwertigkeit betrachtet und im Verkanntsein durch die Zeitgenossen geradezu eine Vorbedingung der Unsterblichkeit erblickt.[4]

This attitude, I would argue, can be traced back to Goethe's essay 'Literarischer Sansculottismus' of 1795, in which he argued that, unlike his French counterpart, the German writer tended not to write for a wide public, but was self-centred, essentially concerned therefore with his own existential problems. In the course of the nineteenth century this inwardness, with its concomitant social marginalization of the writer, was to be at the core of both theory and practice of the German novel. The aesthetic theories of Hegel, Fr. Th. Fischer, Schopenhauer and Otto Ludwig, in particular, effectively canonized a view of writing according to which, in the words of Otto Ludwig, 'wahre Poesie' had to 'sich ganz von der äußern Gegenwart loslösen, sozusagen von der wirklichen Wirklichkeit'.[5] Such a step was necessary, Fritz Martini explained, in order 'das dichterische Sprechen zu retten'.[6] This aesthetic of alienation remained the prominent discourse on into the twentieth century, and as late as 1939 Thomas Mann, in his Princeton Lecture 'Die Kunst des Romans', quoted with approval a view put forward a century earlier by Schopenhauer. In his 'Zur Metaphysik des Schönen und der Aesthetik' the latter had claimed that 'die Aufgabe des Romanschreibers ... besteht darin, daß man mit dem möglichst geringen Aufwand von äußerm Leben das innere in die stärkste Bewegung bringe'. Moreover, for Schopenhauer a novel would 'desto höherer und edlerer Art seyn, je mehr *inneres* und je weniger *äußeres* Leben er darstellt'.[7] This discourse was later compounded by the increased alienation of the individual in this century, as the full impact of the transition to life in modern society was felt. It is a measure of Kafka's genius that, coming from a different tradition, he was able to thematize the new problems of the individual in such a readable way, one that contrasts with the heaviness of many of the post-1945 novels dealing with alienation. There are notable exceptions, such as Grass's *Die Blechtrommel*, Martin Walser's *Ehen in Philippsburg* and the novels of Wolfgang Koeppen, but student response to Walser's Anselm Kristlein trilogy, Max Frisch's novels of the 1950s and 1960s, those of Dieter Wellershoff and Günter Steffens and others, is testimony to the fact that there are more readable works. Moreover, even the relative commercial success of those writers who have managed to leave the sacred grove of the 'Bestenliste' for the occasional appearance on the 'Bestsellerliste' has to be put in its true context of the economic weakness of many of the so-called quality publishers. I shall return to this point in my conclusion.

There have been, it has to be conceded, numerous attempts over the past century and a half to promote a different discourse. As early as 1831, Heine, in his famous remarks anticipating the death of Goethe, was complaining of the dominance of 'überwiegende Geistigkeit' and the 'kümmerliche Privatbegeisterung' in German literature; and a decade later Robert Prutz was saying in a similar vein: 'Was gut ist in der deutschen Literatur, das ist langweilig, und das kurzweilige ist schlecht, was die Ästhetik billigt, das degoutiert das Publikum, und umgekehrt, was dem Publikum behagt, davor bekreuzt sich die Ästhetik.'[8] Jungdeutschland and the Vormärz were clearly in part about a change in the aesthetic agenda, as the conversion of Ferdinand Freiligrath to the aesthetics of political activism in the early 1840s demonstrates. It could, indeed, be argued that things might have been different if the revolutions of 1848–9 had ultimately succeeded, but they did not, and their failure ushered in one of the least memorable periods in German literature. Essays in *Kritische Waffengänge, Die Gesellschaft* and other Naturalist publications towards the end of the nineteenth century seemed to make the point forcefully that a reappraisal of accepted aesthetic criteria was being demanded, but a closer reading of important statements by the brothers Hart, by Wilhelm Bölsche and Fritz Lienhard, amongst others, exposes this as essentially rhetorical; their actual position is fully in accord with that of Vischer, Ludwig and others. The period of the Weimar Republic was in many ways the time of real breakthrough: the 'Amerikanismus' of the era, the emergence of new popular media, the theatre and cabaret, together with that complex we call 'Neue Sachlichkeit', all seemed to indicate that a decisive change in cultural values was taking place, a change marked in particular by Brecht's review of Thomas Mann's *Der Zauberberg*, in which he advised those looking for a good read to try thrillers instead.

Whatever change had in fact been made was, of course, nullified in March 1933. After 1945 the restoration that marked the Federal Republic of Konrad Adenauer generally was also true of the literary scene, as can be seen by the pattern in the award of prestigious literary prizes or in the vigorous propagation of the superiority of high culture by such conservative commentators as Friedrich Sieburg, Hans Egon Holthusen, Günter Blöcker and other leading critics of the period. It was, as in so many other areas of West German life, not until the 1960s that well established notions as to what constituted 'high' literature were challenged. An early combatant was Martin Walser, who – in a way that constituted self-criticism by the author of *Halbzeit* and *Das Einhorn* – was increasingly critical of what he termed the 'pures Sprachspiel' of contemporary West German literature of that time. He began to publish the real life stories of the socially disadvantaged and took a sabbatical from imaginative writing. A louder challenge came from Herbert Marcuse, who – putting aside for once the usual suspicion of the Frankfurt School about the manipulation of the masses exercised by popular culture – ascribed a revolutionary potential, a 'Neue Sensibilität', to the new subculture of the decade. A final and important complementary voice was that of Leslie Fiedler, who in 1968 gave a lecture at the University of Freiburg with the prophetic subtitle 'The case for post-modernism'. In this seminal lecture, which was quickly translated into German and unleashed a heated controversy, he called for literature to be radically subversive and, by drawing on the alternative agenda of pop culture, to undermine dominant social and cultural values. Fiedler received vigorous support from Rolf Dieter Brinkmann, whose poems 'Vanille' and 'Flickermaschine' were clearly written in the spirit of Fiedler and who in 1969 introduced German readers to the new scene in the United States through his anthologies *ACID* and *Silver-Screen*. Apart from the work of Brinkmann, the late 1960s and early 1970s saw a veritable boom in literature from serious publishing houses that corresponded to that critical assimilation of pop culture demanded by Marcuse and Fiedler. A few names and titles, perhaps now forgotten, if ever known, would have to include: *Trivialmythen*, *Supergarde*, the comic strips of Karl Alfred von Meysenbug ('Mini-Faust', 'Glamour-Girl' and 'Supermädchen'), the 'Foto-Roman' *Oh Muvie*; the 'Texte' of Wolf Wondratschek, the early prose and poetry of Jürgen Theobaldy, as well as the general popularity of so-called 'Parlando-Lyrik' of the 1970s. Not unrelated here, though coming from a different philosophical position, was Uwe Timm's argument that left-wing writers could learn much from the narrative strategies of 'Trivialliteratur', an argument which resulted in the establishment of the

*Autoren-Edition* in the early 1970s and which has recently been advanced again by Uwe Wittstock and Wolfram Schütte as a way of addressing current problems of German publishers. Wittstock argues that 'Literatur gilt hier zulande als harte Bildungsaufgabe, als intellektueller Leistungsnachweis, und sobald ein Buch bei der Lektüre spürbar Genuß bereiten will, keimt gleich der Verdacht auf, es müsse trivial sein.' Noting the absence of commercial success of so much German literature, he now claimed it to be 'gegenwärtig legitim, an traditionelle Erzähltechniken anzuknüpfen ... Was spricht dagegen, die Erzählmuster routinierter Unterhaltungsautoren (sie beruhen auf jenen traditionellen Techniken) zu übernehmen, um etwas Besseres daraus zu machen?'[9] Reactions to such a view were predictably outraged.

Much of this overtly 'popular' literature proved to be ephemeral, in some cases rightly so. Looking back, it is clear, despite Marcel Reich-Ranicki's absurd claim that the Student Revolt had ruined German literature,[10] that the West German literary scene reverted very largely to what it had been before, and I will come back to that in my conclusion. There are those who would argue this case by reference to the one or the other so-called 'Tendenzwende' – that of 1973 or that of 1982. I would prefer to illustrate my claim that the general literary scene reverts back to received ideas of high and low culture with reference to the critical perception of the work of two writers: Heinrich Böll and Martin Walser. The case of Böll is the more straightforward. Very early on he was pigeonholed as a decent chap, but a somewhat old-fashioned and limited sort of writer: this is present, for example, in reviews by Friedrich Sieburg. Indeed, in 1961 *Der Spiegel* labelled him 'ein katholischer Fallada'.[11] The different perception of him in other countries, however, led to the award of the Nobel Prize for Literature in 1972 and a period of subsequent critical discretion, but the tone of reviews of his *Fürsorgliche Belagerung* and the whole range of obituaries in 1985 make clear that little had changed over the years as to the evaluation of his abilities as a writer. The late J.P. Stern, who had considered justifiable the omission of Böll from the overview of German literature in Martin Seymour-Smith's *Guide to Modern World Literature*, published some weeks before Böll's death, then went on in his own obituary notice two weeks later to damn with faint praise the style of 'the most important writer of traditional humanist prose' as being 'a little old-fashioned and unsmart'.[12] The other case, that of Walser, is more complex. While the first two volumes of his Anselm Kristlein tragedy were quickly absorbed into, and still constitute, part of the critical canon of post-war German novels, Walser himself – as I have indicated – became increasingly uneasy about the way in which in 'bürgerliche Literatur' those story-telling qualities that had marked it in earlier times had come to disappear. After his sabbatical from writing, Walser experimented somewhat with *Fiction* and *Die Gallistlsche Krankheit* and completed his trilogy, before publishing in 1976 the novel *Jenseits der Liebe*, the first of a series of prose works in a then new, more accessible style that is still continuing. While Walser's thematic concerns have remained much the same throughout his career, here the human story interest was placed in the foreground and, instead of the linguistic opacity of his work of the 1960s, the novel was written in the traditonal form of the preterite, with flowing, rounded sentences and the liberal use of free indirect speech revealing the presence of a caring, more or less traditional narrator. It was roundly condemned by Marcel Reich-Ranicki as constituting the low point of German literature. One year later came the publication of *Ein fliehendes Pferd*, clearly thematically and stylistically closely related to *Jenseits der Liebe*, but which was fulsomely praised for its 'Klassizität' by Reich-Ranicki and became an enormous commercial success. Was it praised, I wonder, because Walser here had recourse to the form of the 'Novelle' which has such a central place in the German canon of the past two centuries? Be that as it may, in the course of the next few years Walser quickly acquired an enthusiastic and large reading public that was unusual for an author of 'Belletristik' (as opposed to 'Unterhaltungsliteratur'). It was precisely at that point that the equation between commercial success and quality (or lack of it) kicked in. Martin Lüdke, now one of the better known literary critics, commenting on what he called the 'stetig steigende[r] Unterhaltungswert' of Walser's prose writings, compared Walser's 'Bodensee' writings unfavourably with the 'gran teatro del mundo' depicted by Faulkner's Mississippi and Marquez's Colombia; Walser's work represents for him 'tiefe deutsche Provinz. Da leben Leute, die den Kopf in den Sand stecken – und sich nun liebevoll/ironisch karikiert in Walsers Bodensee-Büchern wiederfinden.' This, together with Walser's writing his novels 'wie vor zwanzig, dreißig Jahren', means, for Lüdke, Walser 'bewegt sich auf die fließende Grenze zu, die "Literatur" von "Unterhaltung" trennt'.[13] Others have subsequently argued that he has long since crossed that border, and much the same sort of thing is said of the eminently readable work of Uwe Timm, damned with faint praise by Heinrich Vormweg as 'ein richtiger Erfolgsautor'.[14]

    An interesting footnote to this and related to the current market situation of literature in Germany is provided by three articles in *Der Spiegel* in recent years. The first, published in the spring of 1992, noted that every second novel published in Germany came from abroad, and set out to establish from publishers why this was so. The head of the Fischer-Verlag had an instant explanation: 'Deutsche Leser schätzen den erzählerischen Schwung der Briten und Amerikaner.' The work of German authors, on the other hand, consisted, in the words of another publisher, of 'langweilige Nabelschau, Innerlichkeit und Ichbesessenheit'.[15] In an unsigned article from 1994 on the financial difficulties of small, quality publishers, the writer claimed that these problems stemmed from the way in which 'über Jahrzehnte hin viel theoretischer Sachverstand aufgewendet wurde, um mit deutscher Gründlichkeit allem Unterhaltlichen, leichthin Erzählten, vor allem Roman mit farbigen Figuren und handfester Handlung den Garaus zu machen'.[16] And Reinhold Neven Du Mont, whose Kiepenheuer & Witsch house admirably uses the sales of more popular works to subsidize publication of the less commercial, stated quite firmly that the problems of publishers stemmed from the way in which 'der Literaturbetrieb in Deutschland allzulange die hermetische Darstellung, die selbstverliebte Innenspiegelung, die Beschreibung stillstehender Binnenwelten ... gefeiert hat'. If we think back to the enthusiastic reviews of Peter Handke's work in the last fifteen years or so, or to the adulatory championing of the more controversial Botho Strauß by leading critics, then we – or at least I – would have to accept the substance of Neven Du Mont's remarks. There are, it is true, rare notable exceptions like Patrick Süskind's *Das Parfum* and Josef Haslinger's *Opernball* that have achieved both commercial success and critical acclaim, but the binary system of 'high' and 'low' literary culture that emerged in the late eighteenth century still pertains today and is, according to Sibylle Knauss, responsible for the persistent 'deutsche Erzählmisere'.[17] Moreover, it impacts now not only on the internal market, but also on the international one as well, in which 'langweiliges Zeugs' – a term used by a distinguished British publisher to characterize recent German writing[18] – has produced a situation around the world in which '[d]eutsche Autoren liegen wie Blei'.

## Notes

1. Jürgen Habermas, *Der Strukturwandel der Öffentlichkeit. Untersuchungen zu einer Kategorie der bürgerlichen Gesellschaft* (Neuwied, 1962).
2. Botho Strauß, 'Der Erde ein Kopf', *Die Zeit*, 27 October 1989, pp. 65–6.
3. Botho Strauß, *Fragmente der Undeutlichkeit* (Munich, 1989), p. 50.
4. Arnold Hauser, *Sozialgeschichte der Kunst und Literatur*, vol. 2 (Munich, 1953), p. 313.
5. Otto Ludwig, *Gesammelte Schriften*, vol. 5 (Leipzig, 1891), p. 75.

6. Fritz Martini, 'Zur Theorie des Romans im deutschen "Realismus"', *Festgabe für Eduard Behrend* (Weimar, 1959), p. 296.
7. August Schopenhauer, *Sämtliche Werke*, vol. 6 (Leipzig, 1908), pp. 473–4.
8. Quoted in C.P. Magill, 'The German author and his public in the nineteenth century', *Modern Language Review*, 43 (1948), p. 496.
9. Uwe Wittstock, 'Autoren in der Sackgasse. Warum die deutsche Literatur weitgehend langweilig geworden ist', *Süddeutsche Zeitung*, 26 February 1994.
10. Marcel Reich-Ranicki, *Entgegnung* (Stuttgart, 1979), p. 21.
11. *Der Spiegel*, 50 (1961), p. 72.
12. J.P. Stern, 'The literature of catastrophe', *Sunday Times*, 7 July 1985; and 'Germany's conscience', *ibid.*, 21 July 1985.
13. Martin W. Lüdke, 'Der stetig steigende Unterhaltungswert der späten Prosa Martin Walsers', in K. Bullivant and H.J. Althof (eds), *Subjektivität – Innerlichkeit – Abkehr vom Politischen?* (Bonn, 1986), pp. 288–307, here pp. 304–7.
14. Vormweg in several conversations with me.
15. 'Gedankenschwere Nabelschau', *Der Spiegel*, 12 (1992), pp. 258–63.
16. 'Erzähler müssen her', *Der Spiegel*, 3 (1994), pp. 146–8. All subsequent quotations are from this article. It would have to be conceded that recent writing, for example, by Ingo Schulze and Jens Sparschuh is far from boring; whether it succeeds in overseas markets is another matter.
17. 'Lesen muß ein Laster sein', interview with Sibylle Knuss, *Der Spiegel*, 30 (1998), pp. 154–6.
18. *Der Spiegel*, 12 (1992), p. 258.

# 15
# Reflections on Jewish Culture in Germany since 1945

*Eva Kolinsky*

Before the National Socialists seized control, Germany possessed a rich Jewish culture and German Jewry bore 'the hallmarks of modernity'.[1] Although political emancipation in Germany had remained incomplete and social participation not so much a right as a precarious privilege which could be renounced,[2] manifestations of Jewish culture reached imposing heights as German Jews advanced the agendas of German, European and Jewish culture.[3] When the National Socialists staged a public Burning of the Books on 10 May 1933 in order to subjugate culture to state ideology, the list of writers whose works were thrown into the flames read like a roll-call of modern literature.[4] Two-thirds of Germany's Jewish population were forced into exile. The exiles included so many prominent scientists, politicians, professionals, painters, journalists, composers, musicians, actors, religious leaders and university teachers as to amount to an exile culture and the destruction of the Jewish culture that had flourished in Germany. More than a decade of persecution in National Socialist Germany destroyed Jewish communities, depriving Jews first of their livelihood and then of their lives. Inside the Third Reich, some Jews were precariously shielded by mixed marriages and Nazi regulations on their special treatment.[5] They were the exception. From 1942 onwards, Jews who remained in Germany were deported to ghettos and concentration camps from which very few survived.[6] After liberation, the victorious Allies aided the physical survival of Jews found in camps, labour compounds and on death trains[7] and restored – with differences between the zones of occupation – the human and civic rights of which the Nazis had deprived Jews so completely and for so many years. Given this physical and cultural destruction of German Jewry between 1933 and 1945, there could be no continuity of Jewish life and Jewish culture with the pre-Nazi era. Could there be a new beginning?

In 1946, the former editor of the *Jüdische Rundschau* who had sought refuge in Palestine in the 1930s, Robert Weltsch, visited Germany in order to see for himself what had remained of German Jewish culture after the Holocaust. He found close to 200 000 'displaced persons', most of them Jews from Eastern Europe, who had been liberated from camps inside Germany or who had fled there from renewed anti-Semitism in their home towns. These Jews were cared for – in the American and British zones of occupation at least – in special camps administered by the Allies in conjunction with UNRRA, the relief organization of the United Nations. Dubbed 'displaced persons', they had begun to rebuild their lives, publish Yiddish newspapers and create an orthodox Jewish religious culture while waiting for resettlement elsewhere. Most were trapped in Germany as in a 'waiting room'[8] for three to four years until the creation of the State of Israel and amendments to immigration legislation in the United States allowed them to leave.

Weltsch also found Jewish communities set up by German Jews on the ruins of synagogues and other Jewish institutions of yesteryear. For him and for many Jews world-wide, the prospect of a Jewish presence inside post-Holocaust German society was altogether unpalatable:

> We cannot assume that there are Jews who are attracted to living in Germany. Here, the stench of corpses, of gas chambers and of torture cells remains all-pervasive. But several thousand Jews are still living in Germany ... This remnant of Jewish settlement should be liquidated as soon as possible. Germany is no place (*kein Boden*) for Jews.[9]

On his appointment as 'Jewish Advisor' to the Military Governor in the US zone of occupation, the last holder of this post, Harry Greenstein, estimated that after resettlement no more than 2700 Jews would remain in Germany: so-called hard-core cases who were too old or too ill to settle in Israel.[10] In his first full report after arriving in Germany, he admitted that this low estimate had been based on 'hope rather than an analysis',[11] while the actual number of Jews who 'would remain to form the nucleus of a new Jewish community'[12] was closer to 25 000.[13] Greenstein's assistants, Abraham Hyman and Louis Baruch, took a less charitable view of the individuals who opted to stay despite opportunities to leave: in their view, displaced persons generally besmirched the image of Jews in Germany through black-market activities, and those deciding to stay there were the worst offenders:

It is discouraging that these people who have built their little empires on the fringe of the German economy, delude themselves that they are, in fact, living *in* the German economy and are postponing plans for the ultimate resettlement. In our opinion this element will constitute a large part of the non-medical hard core.[14]

On 1 September 1949, a conference took place in Heidelberg under the auspices of the Jewish Advisor to take stock of resettlement, review Jewish community development in Germany and create an organization which could act as a Jewish voice in the nascent West German state. One year later, the Central Council of Jews in Germany began its work. Despite the Heidelberg conference's pragmatic agenda, there was no consensus about the presence of Jews in Germany and their future. Given the small number of Jews in Germany in 1949, the shortage of rabbis and religious teachers in so decimated and dislocated a population, on the high percentage of intermarriage, one speaker concluded: 'the future of these communities is not bright. Assimilation and peripheral Jewish living rather than an integrated Jewish life are the prospects'.[15] These doubts about post-Holocaust Jewish communities in Germany were widely shared and included doubts whether anybody choosing to live in Germany could be accepted as Jewish by communities in other countries. At the Heidelberg conference, a representative of the World Jewish Congress indicated a way forward when he acknowledged that misgivings about a Jewish presence in Germany would continue to exist, but also pledged not to sever links:

The premise upon which ... this conference was based was the reality of today – a fact that there are Jews who live in this land. This fact and not the question as to whether or not these Jews ought to leave or ought to stay here is our starting point. ... As long as there are and will be Jews in Germany, we shall serve them in whatever capacity they wish us. We shall be at their disposal and help them to live a life of pride, self-respect and dignity, to the extent that such a life is possible in a country torn asunder by so many problems and conflictions.[16]

Unease about the presence of Jews in Germany and reservations whether what developed in the shadow of the Holocaust among Jews in Germany constitutes Jewish culture are less acute today than fifty years ago, but have not disappeared. Paradoxically, the Jewish population in Germany has been one of the few in Western Europe to stabilize through migration gains from Eastern Europe, Iran and even Israel, and, more recently, to grow rapidly as Jews from the former Soviet Union opted to settle there.[17] Yet, during his state visit to Germany in 1996, the Israeli President Ezer Weizmann declared himself unable to comprehend that Jews should still wish to live there. Ignatz Bubis, as President of the Central Council of Jews in Germany and also their official spokesman, declared on behalf of all Jewish inhabitants: 'I have no cause to leave Germany.'[18]

In his reply to Weizmann, Daniel Cohn-Bendit, a member of the European Parliament and former protagonist of the Student Movement who had grown up in France, linked the choice of place with his perception of Jewish identity: 'I live in Germany today on the basis of my own free decision, and without any guilty feelings.'[19] Moritz Neumann, a member of the Central Council of Jews in Germany Executive, adopted a less neutral tone, but challenged the implication in Weizmann's statement that Jews in Germany helped to whitewash the Holocaust and Germany's anti-Semitic legacy and that it was impossible to live in Germany as a Jew. Both allegations date back to the beginnings of Jewish community organization in Germany after the Holocaust:

> As far as Jewish religious and Jewish traditional awareness are concerned, Jewish communities in Germany are more secure than many a Jewish community throughout the world, including in Israel. We Jews in Germany are, certainly, no fount of deep religiosity and we are, as far as I am concerned, even nowhere near enough to securing a stable, traditional, religious life. But compared with many Israelis who stay in Germany for a visit or more permanently, we can virtually claim to be a stronghold of lived and practised Jewish tradition.[20]

In the past, community leaders had remained defensive in the face of doubts about their choice of country and function in it, stressing the role of communities in providing welfare support for needy Jews, in fighting for individual and collective restitution and in making sure that Hitler's aim to cleanse Germany of Jews would not be fulfilled. They had not portrayed their culture as a model for others with its bipolarity of secular German-Jewish and orthodox Eastern European Jewish traits, which had been diversified further by Jewish migration gains and their impact on religious observance and the articulation of culture. Until the mid 1960s, German Jewish culture acted as if it was a staging post for a Jewish identity outside Germany with a strong Zionist commitment and the practice of expecting young people to settle in Israel. This no longer applies; Jews in Germany, and young Jews in particular, have begun to articulate a personal sense of identity, including their own answers about what it means to live in Germany as a Jew. This is what Cohn-Bendit meant when he declared he had no guilty feelings. Jews in Germany no longer accept accusations of complicity with the Holocaust or the failure of post-war Germany to confront it. Although living in Germany, their sense of identity as Jews also includes, as a core component, a distance from Germany, its people and its history.

A young interviewee from Berlin addressed these difficulties by separating his Jewish from his German self: 'I have a very divided relationship with Germany. I believe everyone of us has lived through his own identity-crisis of who he is – a German Jew, a Jew in Germany or an Israeli, despite holding a German passport and being born here. I have decided for myself that I am a Jew who lives in Germany. In the first instance, I am a Jew, because this I can be anywhere in the world.'[21] Like others of his generation, this young Jew took pride in expressing his Jewishness – one of his friends even wanted to wear a skullcap in the street but was prevented from doing so by his parents who dreaded this kind of visibility. Visibility remains indeed hazardous: in the summer of 1998, an orthodox Jew visiting Berlin from Israel and wearing his customary traditional dress of black *caftan*, fur hat and earlocks was stared at, ridiculed and beaten up in the street.[22]

The survivor generation who remained or returned to Germany preferred to remain invisible, hide outward signs of their Jewishness and live 'out of packed suitcases' just in case anti-Semitism rose again. In the 1980s, Jews in Germany began to unpack their suitcases. In particular, members of the second and third generation who had grown up in the post-war era had developed a new confidence in admitting to their Jewishness in public in an increasingly diverse and multicultural environment. Even these younger Jews, however, perceived as part of their identity the need for a refuge should such be needed and Germany became too hostile a place for Jews to live in. Recasting Jewish culture after the Holocaust established a Jewish presence and Jewish communities in Germany, not a German-Jewish culture but a – newly diverse and different – Jewish culture in Germany. Has Germany, therefore, become a 'place for Jews'?

In December 1946, a leader in the *Jüdisches Gemeindeblatt*, the forerunner of the *Allgemeine Jüdische Wochenzeitung*, focused on a common experience of Jews in Germany – whether Jewish members of the Allied forces, residents of displaced persons camps or Jews living in German society at the time: the collective amnesia among Germans about persecution, concentration camps – even those in their immediate vicinity – and the Holocaust generally. Giving his name as 'X', the author wrote:

> About six months ago, I returned to Germany. I came back from exile since I belonged to those who believe they have a duty, as German Jews, to contribute to building a really democratic Germany ... When I decided to return, I assumed there would be many people in Germany who, immediately after the collapse of National Socialism, would have the courage to admit that Jews were treated badly and declare publicly: 'We have a solemn obligation to somehow make up for this in our treatment of the Jewish remnants.' I returned to Germany and was bitterly disappointed. During my first months here I have been unable to find – despite many hundreds of conversations – a single National Socialist ... To this day, I have only found Germans who told me that they had known nothing about what happened to the Jews, that on 9 November 1938 they chanced to notice that something was wrong and, deep down, did not like what they saw.[23]

Indeed, the unspoken consensus among Germans that nobody except a tiny circle of top-level leaders and perpetrators knew about the Holocaust or that Jews were driven to their death and not resettled in the east as Nazi propaganda claimed, translated in the harsh years of post-war shortages and dislocation into hostility towards survivors as an unfairly privileged group. In a speech to the American Jewish Conference, Judge Simon Rifkind, the first civilian to serve as 'Jewish Advisor' to General Lucius D. Clay in the US Zone recalled: 'I shall never forget that one of the first requests of the so-called de-nazified civil government of Germany to the Allied Control Council was that the rations of the displaced persons be reduced. That is a measure of the German confession of guilt; that is an index to the level of character that today prevails among the Germans.'[24] Most displaced persons camps were located on or near the site of former concentration and labour camps where the survivors had been liberated. Yet, local populations resented their presence, local burgomasters only agreed to supply clothing, milk or fresh vegetables if ordered to do so by the military, and if those orders were enforced. Nazi-style raids by German police on displaced persons camps in Stuttgart and elsewhere provoked an outcry among Jewish survivors and resulted in a decree placing Jews under Military Police protection.[25] In Buchenwald, Dachau and Bergen-Belsen, Allied commanders forced the German population who lived near these camps to witness the suffering inflicted on survivors and to help dispose of the many unburied bodies. While the Germans complied, they did not develop the sense of guilt and personal accountability that had been intended.[26] The same holds true for the Nuremberg trials and for trials of concentration camp commanders and guards: Germans remained impassive, preoccupied with their own plight and unwilling to take an interest either in the Holocaust or in the Jews who survived it. Travelling in Germany in the 1960s, the Israeli writer Amos Elon noted that Germans had constructed their own Holocaust and pointed their finger at the Allies as perpetrators: 'It has become common to compare – even equate – the extermination camps of Auschwitz and Treblinka with the destruction of Dresden by Allied bombers a few weeks before the end of the war, or with the expulsion of the German population from East Prussia, Silesia or Czechoslovakia in 1945. Some people demand trials against "Allied War Criminals".'[27]

Yet, the Germany that emerged from the rubble of World War II seemed sufficiently transformed to offer a political and social environment in which the Jews who lived there could at least feel physically secure and accepted, in general terms, as equal citizens. The division of Germany produced two divergent models. In the east, the German Democratic Republic adopted Soviet-style state Socialism. Jewish Holocaust survivors were allocated the special status of 'victims of fascism', entitling them to housing and a small supplementary pension, but they were also downgraded compared to Communist 'fighters against fascism'. Similarly, Holocaust memory was incorporated into the anti-fascist image of the GDR, but it extended only to communists and excluded Jews. With National Socialism explained as a product of capitalism and Jews classified as capitalists, they seemed strangely implicated in the rise of the system that set out to destroy them. In the late 1940s, the efforts of Jewish aid organizations to assist survivors with food and clothing, laid East Germany's Jews (and Jews generally) open to the charge of 'internationalism' designed to undermine the socialist consensus. In the early 1950s, demands by East German Jews that their state should pay restitution and undo Nazi injustices by returning property to its Jewish owners, contributed to a state-orchestrated anti-Semitic campaign which drove most of East Germany's Jewish inhabitants to seek refuge in the West. Until its collapse, the GDR pursued a bipolar strategy: inside the country, Jewish religious communities were permitted to function, albeit subjected to state interference and prevented from developing a distinctive Jewish voice. From the mid 1950s onwards, anti-Zionism became state policy in the GDR. While Jews could secure integration if they renounced their Jewish culture and embraced the prescribed Socialist ideology, anyone living as a Jew in the GDR was always suspected, openly or covertly, of being an enemy of the East German state.

Compared with East Germany, West Germany offered a favourable environment for Jews. The Basic Law of 1948/9 proved an effective shield against Weimar-type anti-democratic tendencies and political polarization, laying the foundations for a stable polity and a democratic political culture. Moreover, the guarantee in the Basic Law of human and civil rights of individuals and groups, including minority cultures, created a legal framework in which cultural diversity, individualism and, in principle at least, the acceptance of difference could develop. In this recast polity, Jews, it seemed, had nothing to fear. This was the message when Konrad Adenauer, the first Chancellor of the FRG, declared in the *Bundestag* on 27 September 1951:

> The attitudes of the Federal Republic to its Jewish citizens has been unambiguously defined in the Basic Law. Article 3 of the Basic law stipulated that all human beings are equal before the law and that nobody may be disadvantaged or advantaged on account of gender, origin, race, language, country of origin or background, belief, religious or political views ... These legal norms ... obligate every German citizen, and in particular every civil servant, to refrain from any form of racial discrimination.[28]

Yet, when a draft version of the Basic Law was published in 1948, Jews objected to the use of 'race' as a classification of an individual's status and to the implication that democracy ruled out the possibility of any group receiving special considerations. Writing in the *Jüdisches Gemeindeblatt*, Ralph Giordano asked:

> Will not German civil servants tell persons who are seeking restitution: 'We are now living in a democracy. You are no longer discriminated against but you are also not receiving preferential treatment' ... Who can tell us, us Jews of all people, that an admittedly democratically

worded constitution will suffice to drain the undemocratic bog in the interior and exterior life of Germany?[29]

Giordano's contention that the *Grundgesetz* remained too vague to protect Jews from a denial of their rights and his fear that democracy was less well rooted in society than in the constitution, have been at the core of Jewish self-perception in post-war Germany. On the one hand, the democratic political order and its elected representatives are seen as guarantors of civic rights. One of the key purposes of Jewish community leaders from the local to the national level – and one which has drawn criticism from inside and outside the Jewish community[30] – has been to monitor public policy and bring their perspective to bear on public authorities and policy makers.[31] On the other hand, German democracy never met the expectation that Jews could live without fear, that anti-Semitism had been erased and the memory of the Holocaust incorporated into an understanding of democracy.[32] In his first address as *Rektor* of Frankfurt University, Max Horkheimer, who had earlier returned to Germany from exile in the United States, took heart from the fact that German intellectuals seemed committed to reconciliation with Jews in Germany.[33] Some ten years later, German intellectuals on the left distanced themselves from Germany's Jews and advocated anti-Zionism.[34] Their acceptance of Jews was increasingly narrowed to pitying Jews as victims of the Holocaust, not viewing them as a minority inside Germany with their own culture, sense of identity, community organizations and socio-political interests.

At the opposite end of the political spectrum, matters were more complex and hostilities more evident. Intellectuals to the right of centre propagated post-war Germany as a new and altogether different world from that which had masterminded and implemented the Holocaust. For them, the presence of Jews and their community organizations was evidence of this renewal and reason enough to demand that a *Schlußstrich* be drawn under regarding Germany as the 'land of the murderers' (Leo Baeck). The majority of Germans of all generations as well as successive governments have concurred with this view. In addition, anti-Semitism, right-wing extremism and neo-Nazis have always constituted significant, albeit not dominant facets of the political culture – even in eastern Germany where young people expressed their distaste for the prescribed anti-fascism by adopting those segments of Nazi ideology which glorified Germans, vilified 'others' and justified violent action against their chosen targets.

Unification brought a short-lived surge of German nationalist sentiment which soon lost its glow when the social and economic consequences of unity left a trail of disappointment and unmet expectations. While national fervour withered after unification, hostility against 'others' surged. Xenophobic violence was not specifically aimed at Jews, but included Jews among its victims. After reaching record numbers in 1992 – at least half the incidents occurred in the east – right-wing extremist violence subsided somewhat, only to flare up again in 1997.[35] Unification, therefore, did little to make Germany a more hospitable place or to address the two key themes of identity for the Jews living there: the legacy of anti-Semitism and Holocaust memory.

## Notes

1. David Sorkin, *The Transformation of German Jewry 1780–1840* (Oxford, 1990), p. 3.
2. Peter Pulzer, *Jews and the German State. The Political History of a Minority, 1848–1933* (Oxford, 1992), esp. Chapter 1.
3. For a comprehensive analysis of German-Jewish cultural and social history, see the four volumes *Deutsch-jüdische Geschichte in der Neuzeit*, 1600–1780; 1780–1871; 1871–1918; 1918–1945, edited by the Leo Baeck Institute (Munich, 1996/1997) and published in English by Columbia University Press (New York, 1998).
4. Eva Kolinsky and Wilfried van der Will, 'In Search of German Culture', in Eva Kolinsky and Wilfried van der Will (eds), *The Cambridge Companion to Modern German Culture* (Cambridge, 1998), pp. 1–2.
5. In May 1945, 15 000 individuals were liberated who had been categorized as Jews by the Nazis (although many had converted to Christianity before the National Socialists applied their racist definitions of status) and who were married to a non-Jewish partner. They had been conscripted to forced labour but most escaped deportation and survived inside the Third Reich.
6. Details in Erica Burgauer, *Zwischen Erinnerung und Verdrängung. Juden in Deutschland nach 1945* (Reinbek, 1993), pp. 14–18 and p. 356.
7. A report compiled by the Displaced Persons, Refugee and Welfare Division at the Supreme Headquarters of the Allied Expeditionary Force (SHAEF) recorded that a total of seventy-seven concentration camps had been discovered by Allied troops. Fifty-four camps had 'populations' and 334 956 individuals were liberated, although records seized at the camps showed that 1.5 million had been imprisoned there. In line with Allied policy at this stage (June 1945), Jews were not regarded as a group with special needs but subsumed under their respective nationalities. Reports on Concentration Camps. Shaef/G-5/DP/2711/7. 29 June 1945, signed A.H. Moffitt Jr., Colonel, G.S.C. Executive Officer. United States National Archive, Suitland, MD. RG 331–50. G-5/2711/7.
8. Angelika Königseder and Juliane Wetzel, *Leben im Wartesaal. Die Jüdischen DPs im Nachkriegsdeutschland* (Frankfurt am Main, 1994).

9. Quoted in Monika Richarz, 'Juden in der BRD und der DDR seit 1945', in Micha Brumlik (ed.), *Jüdisches Leben in Deutschland seit 1945* (Frankfurt am Main, 1988), p. 14.
10. Harry Greenstein, Statement to the Press, in United States National Archive, Suitland, MD. RG 260, Box 138 Folder 156.
11. Harry Greenstein, Report No. 429, dated 22 March 1949. Library of Congress Manuscript Collection. Emmanuel Celler Papers, Box 17.
12. *Ibid.*, p. 6.
13. Maor estimated that of the 15 000 who survived in mixed marriages inside the Third Reich, 9000 became founder members of a Jewish community in 1945 or 1946; at least 12 000 so-called 'displaced persons' decided to remain in Germany. German-Jewish Holocaust survivors who were forced to live in German society without the special protection of a camp until resettlement opportunities arose (one camp, Deggendorf, accommodated about 700 German-Jewish survivors intending to settle in the United States) constituted the smallest part of the post-Holocaust community membership. Details in Harry Maor, 'Über den Wiederaufbau der jüdischen Gemeinden in Deutschland seit 1945'. PhD, University of Mainz (Mainz, 1961), p. 3ff.
14. Abraham Hyman and Louis Baruch, Report covering the period 15 January 1949 to 15 February 1949. Library of Congress Manuscript Collection. Emmanuel Celler Papers, Box 17, p. 7. Hyman and Baruch acted as Jewish Advisors in the interim between the departure of the previous holder (Dr Haber) and the arrival of Harry Greenstein. Abraham Hyman remained in Germany between September and December 1949 to wind up the office of the Jewish Advisor.
15. *The Future of Jews in Germany*. Conference held in Heidelberg, 1 September 1949. Minutes. Archive of the Central Institute for Research into Anti-Semitism, Technical University Berlin, p. 18.
16. Dr Prinz in *The Future*, p. 46. The term 'conflictions' is used in the Minutes.
17. Julius Carlebach, 'Jewish Identity in the Germany of a New Europe', in Jonathan Webber (ed.), *Jewish Identities in the New Europe* (London/ Washington, 1994), p. 205ff.
18. Rudolf Augstein, 'Der Solo Flieger', *Der Spiegel*, 4 (1996), p. 34.
19. Daniel Cohn-Bendit, 'Ein Widerwort an Israels Präsidenten Eser Weizmann', *Die Zeit*, 4 (1996), p. 1.
20. Moritz Neumann, 'Wir, die deutschen Juden', *Allgemeine jüdische Wochenzeitung*. Sonderausgabe 25 April 1996. Chronik 1946–1996, p. 67.
21. ' "Alle sind ziemlich nervös" Jüdische Schüler über ihr Leben unter Polizeischutz in Berlin', *Der Spiegel*, 41 (1994), p. 112.
22. *Jewish Chronicle*, 28 August 1998, p. 2.
23. 'X', 'Das kurze Gedächtnis der Deutschen', *Jüdisches Gemeindeblatt*, 10 December 1946.
24. Speech by Judge Simon H. Rifkind, delivered at the Hotel Biltmore on 2 April 1946, United States National Archives, RG 165 (Papers of Col. Frost), Box 150, File 4, Folder 'Rifkind'.
25. For details see the material in the United States National Archive, Suitland, MD. RG 260, Box 275, Folder 26 (DPs and German Police); RG 260/320/7 (Stuttgart Raid); RG 260/320/10 (Raid at Frankfurt Station).

26. Statement by eighteen American editors and publishers who toured German concentration camps at the invitation of General Eisenhower, *New York Times*, 6 May 1945, p. 8.

27. Amos Elon, *Journey Through a Haunted Land. The New Germany* (London, 1967), p. 22.

28. Reprinted as 'Das Bekennntnis der Bundesregierung', *Allgemeine Jüdische Wochenzeitung*, 28 September 1951.

29. Ralph Giordano, 'Wir fordern Garantien. Verfassungsanspruch und Verfassungswirklichkeit: Zum Entwurf des neuen bundesdeutschen Grundgesetzes', *Jüdisches Gemeindeblatt*, 15 October 1948.

30. Michal Bodemann and Henryk M. Broder have been particularly outspoken in their attacks on Jewish community representatives, arguing that the presence of Jews in Germany and the collaboration of their community leaders with the public authorities creates the impression that Germany has overcome anti-Semitism and faced up to its Holocaust legacy. See Michal Bodemann (ed.), *Jews, Germany, Memory* (Ann Arbor, 1996); Henryk M. Broder and Michel R. Lang, *Fremd im eigenen Land. Juden in der BRD* (Frankfurt am Main, 1979).

31. Leo Katcher, *Post Mortem. The Jews in Germany – Now* (London, 1968) includes profiles of community leaders and their sense of mission. For a more recent discussion, see Ignatz Bubis, *Juden in Deutschland* (Berlin, 1996).

32. For an excellent survey, see Werner Bergmann and Rainer Erb (eds), *Antisemitismus in der politischen Kultur nach 1945* (Opladen, 1990).

33. 'Horkheimer: Der jüdische Rektor und seine deutsche Universität', *Allgemeine jüdische Wochenzeitung*, 1 August 1952.

34. For a more detailed discussion see Andrei S. Markovits *et al.*, 'Jews in German society', in Eva Kolinsky and Wilfried van der Will (eds), *The Cambridge Companion to Modern German Culture*, p. 98ff.

35. Bundesamt für Verfassungsschutz, 'Verfassungsschutzbericht 1997'. Unpublished Report, Cologne 1997, p. 77.

# 16
## Reflections on German History and Anglo-Saxon Liberalism

*Günter Minnerup*

In 1989, the year the fall of the Berlin Wall sealed the fate of Soviet Communism, Francis Fukuyama of the Rand Corporation and US State Department published his now famous essay 'The End of History?': 'What we may be witnessing is not just the end of the Cold War, or the passing of a particular period of post-war history, but the end of history as such: that is, the end point of mankind's ideological evolution and the universalization of Western liberal democracy as the final form of human government.'[1] Fukuyama's thesis became the received wisdom of the early 1990s as articulated in countless newspaper articles, television programmes, university lectures and dinner table conversations. There seemed to be no longer any credible alternative to the brave new world of globalization, deregulated markets, transnational capital movements and the autonomous consumer. Life chances now depended on private provision and individual entrepreneurial risk-taking rather than the old outdated collectivist ethos of a welfare-providing, interfering 'nanny state'.

Although the substance of Fukuyama's ideas and the ideological content of the 'globalization' propaganda of the 1990s were far from new – and indeed somewhat older than the much-derided 'nineteenth-century ideologies' they claimed to have rendered redundant – the uninhibited triumphalism with which they were articulated certainly was. For much of the century, after all, 'Western liberal democracy' had been on the defensive, locked in deadly struggles against a succession of dangerous enemies – German imperialism and fascism, Soviet Communism, Japanese imperialism, Third World liberationism, social democratic welfarism – and occasionally even forced to make concessions to, and pacts with, one against the other to ensure its own survival. Throughout this darker era, Germany had somehow always loomed large among Western liberalism's foes: as the immediate enemy in two world wars or as the progenitor of anti-liberal ideologies of worldwide appeal, chief among them Marxism. In a sense, therefore, the history of the twentieth century could be seen as the history of a long struggle between Western liberalism and Germany or German-inspired illiberal ideologies, with the triumph of Western liberalism taking two stages: the defeat and successful 'Westernization' of Germany in and after 1945, and the defeat of Marxism – symbolically sealed on German soil – in 1989.

It is therefore hardly surprising that 1945 came to be treated by liberal historians as the 'end of German history' in much the same sense as Fukuyama was to treat the collapse of Communism some forty years later. Even before victory over Hitler was assured, Anglo-Saxon opinion had already come to see the war as the culmination of a broader struggle between liberal individualism and statist tyranny, as crystallized in the Anglo-American and German traditions of thought. In a volume published in 1945 but based on a series of wartime lectures on the theme of 'The German Mind and Outlook', G.P. Gooch asserted that, 'broadly speaking modern Germany has thought primarily in terms of the might and majesty of the state, modern England primarily in terms of the rights and liberties of the citizen'.[2]

After the war, such juxtapositions of the traditions of Western liberalism and German illiberalism became the staple fare of the liberal historiography of modern Germany. The arguments are too familiar to be repeated here in detail except to emphasize that the real targets were not so much the National Socialists, their intellectual precursors and hangers-on, or even their ultraconservative and ultranationalist allies. After all, racism, militarism and irrationalism as intellectual currents could be found everywhere – Gobineau was French, Houston Stewart Chamberlain English – but it was only in Germany that liberalism had failed to take root in the intellectual mainstream of a 'civilized', modern industrial society.

The deeper problem therefore lay with those who, while their moral and intellectual standing was beyond suspicion of fascist or proto-fascist sympathies, had shaped that mainstream in such a way as to drive a lasting wedge between German thought and Western liberalism: thinkers like Hegel, Fichte, Herder, Marx, List, Ranke, Tönnies; even Ferdinand Lassalle, Max Weber and Thomas Mann. Each of these had made their own contribution to alienating Germany from the West, by extolling the state over civil society, *Gemeinschaft* over *Gesellschaft*, the collective over the individual, culture over civilization, the nation over the citizen, speculative theory over empirical reality.

Originally the 'history written by the victors', this pattern of inter-pretation has since been adopted by many (West) German historians, though often supplemented by sociological arguments about the weaknesses and failures of the German middle class, especially during the Bismarckian and Wilhelmine eras. From the 'Fischer controversy' to the 1980s *Historikerstreit*, left-liberal historians and social scientists (Bracher, Dahrendorf) have equated the eventual victory of democracy in the Federal Republic with the adoption of Anglo-American liberal values. As Wolfgang Mommsen put it, 'a free [political] order in the west of Germany has only been possible by means of a break with essential elements of the German tradition and a free adoption of Western European and American examples'.[3] The incorporation of East Germany into the Federal Republic in 1990 as part of Fukuyama's global 'end of history' only seemed to complete the end of German history already sub-stantially accomplished four decades earlier.

The moment of Western liberalism's historic triumph, however, would also become its greatest test. Proclaiming it to be the 'final form of human government', as Fukuyama had done, was the easy part, but proving its ability to solve the world's problems was another matter. As the newly 'liberated' Russia and Eastern Europe descended into destitution, political chaos and civil war; as the Third World, now no longer of strategic significance, became ever poorer; and as the globalized casino economy accelerated its slide into financial turmoil and economic destabilization, even some of those who had been staunch believers in the liberal creed during the Cold War confrontation with Communism now expressed their doubts. The Oxford social philosopher John Gray, for example, once an ideologist of Thatcherism, turned against the 'delusions of global capitalism' and observed that the free market 'was feasible in nineteenth-century England only because, and for so long as, functioning democratic institutions were lacking. The implications of these truths for the project of constructing a worldwide free market in an age of democratic government are profound. They are that the rules of the game of the market must be insulated from democratic deliberation and political amendment. Democracy and the free market are rivals, not allies.'[4] He continued:

A global free market belongs to a world in which western hegemony seemed assured. Like all other variants of the Enlightenment Utopia of a universal civilization it presupposes western supremacy ... A global free market works to set sovereign states against one another in geopolitical struggles for dwindling natural resources. The effect of a *laissez-faire* philosophy which condemns state intervention in the economy is to impel states to become rivals for control of resources that no institution has any responsibility for conserving.[5]

If Gray is right, then the core creed of Western liberalism, the 'invisible hand' of market forces, works not only against democracy but also against world peace and the long-term ecological survival of the human race – hardly a reassuring thought if it is to be the 'final form of human government'. However, any rejection of the 'grand narrative' of Western *laissez-faire* liberalism as the inexorable march of progress must also have implications for a reassessment of the past, a past which we know chiefly through the work of historians dedicated to the liberal world view, and above all for a reappraisal of the conventional Anglo-Saxon liberal interpretation of German history.

The following brief historiographical sketch is little more than a tentative reconnaissance mission in the direction of reappraising some aspects of the German 'anti-liberal' tradition, an exploration of some of the territory in modern German history that might yield fresh insights if viewed without the distorting prism of the Anglo-Saxon liberal world view.

## The 'Prussianization' of Germany

The economist Friedrich List has been a favourite target of those seeking to identify the roots of Germany's deviation from the Anglo-Saxon path of liberal virtue. List was undoubtedly a highly influential figure and it is probably no exaggeration to call him the single most important nineteenth-century liberal critic of Adam Smith's school of free-trade liberalism. His insistence that free trade served the British interest and that 'infant industries' like Germany's could only catch up with Britain if the nation was united under Prussian leadership to create a large home market and, led by a strong state and the mobilization of all national resources, expanded its interests and markets world-wide as Britain and others had already done before it, provided the intellectual foundation for the National Liberals and their alliance with Bismarck. In Rohan Butler's *Roots of National Socialism*, List shares pride of place with Moeller van den Bruck, Bernhardi, Naumann and Ratzel as a precursor of the Nazi demand for 'living space'.[6] For Dahrendorf, List is an intellectual source of totalitarianism: 'Smith's theory of political economy is market rational; but List's theory of national economy is plan rational. The political theory and practice of liberalism imply an attitude of market rationality; the authoritarian and, more recently, the totalitarian state are based on an attitude of plan rationality.'[7]

Yet despite these ideological denunciations nobody has actually been able to specify a plausible alternative path for the development of German capitalism to that of Prussianization. Austria, with its economic backwardness and far-flung imperial interests in the Balkans, was in no position to assume national leadership. Without the benefit of an already existing, centralized national state to take over (as was the case in Britain and France), the German liberal middle classes – deeply divided along regional and denominational lines – were incapable of acting in a revolutionary fashion against the might of Prussia and the dynasties of the other states. What Friedrich List had grasped, and after him Marx and Engels, was that capitalist industry and commerce did not spread evenly, that those who controlled the markets could keep others in dependence and underdevelopment, and that national economic development was not just a matter of markets but always required – as it had in eighteenth-century England and Colbert's France – a symbiotic partnership with a strong state.

Indeed, Friedrich Engels, during the famous Prussian constitutional conflict over army reform, criticized the bourgeois liberals in the Prussian *Landtag* not for being insufficiently radical in their opposition but for opposing the army reform at all:

> Day in day out, from morning till night the bourgeoisie talks of Prussia's glory, Prussia's greatness and the development of Prussian power; but it *refuses* to grant Prussia an increase in the size of its army … The bourgeoisie should have seized the opportunity with both hands, for such a chance could not be expected again in a hundred years. Detailed concessions should have been wrung from this government if the Progressives had approached the matter, not in a niggardly spirit, but as great speculators![8]

As is well known, Marx and Engels supported the Prussian war against France, as long as it did not lead to annexations, for very similar reasons – to speed German unification which, under the given circumstances, could only be brought about by Prussia. This did not mean abandoning the democratic critique of the Prussian regime but to accept that there was no other developmental path for Germany. As recent studies of Bismarckian and Wilhelmine Germany have shown, neither the industrial and commercial nor the cultural interests of the bourgeoisie suffered unduly under the Imperial regime, and talk of its alleged 'feudalization' simply does not fit the empirical facts of what was, on the contrary, a rapid *Verbürgerlichung* of the Imperial state, army and bureaucracy.

It cannot be denied, of course, that German liberalism, and above all the National Liberals – although the Progressives and even the Catholic Centre Party were also affected by this – became infatuated with the state, state power, and nationalism. This may be deemed to have constituted a German 'peculiarity', as could the reluctance of German liberalism to press determinedly for constitutional reform. However, far from constituting an irrational pathology afflicting the German middle-class mind, this was entirely rational behaviour given the economic and political conditions of its existence and its dependence on the state for protection against perceived external and internal threats. To attribute these 'peculiarities' to the lingering philosophical influences of Hegel, Fichte or Herder and Germany's problematic relationship with the eighteenth-century Enlightenment is to put the cart before the horse: it was surely the realities of the second half of the century that created an intellectual climate in which the statist strands in German thought could flourish, in all their variants – from the mainstream bourgeois culture of the Treitschkes, Bassermanns and Lamprechts, to the wilder shores of irrationalism of Langbehn and Lagarde, to the oppositional left of Lassalle, Bebel and Kautsky. Imperial Germany, it is true, offered an inhospitable climate for Anglo-Saxon liberal individualism: but this was a distinction shared by Germany with the rest of the world outside Britain and the USA.

## Germany's imperialist ambitions

Perhaps no single historiographical controversy connected with modern German history has generated as much heat and as little light as the debate over Germany's responsibility for World War I. The relevant facts have been pretty well known for a long time, and even Fritz Fischer in his celebrated *Griff nach der Weltmacht* (1961) actually added little that was really new. The shock for the conservative German historical profession was that one of their own had openly embraced the Anglo-Saxon view that it was Germany's expansionist plans for a new, German-dominated

European order that lay behind the Imperial government's readiness to go to war – war aims which Fischer saw largely echoed, albeit in a more radicalized form, in the war aims of the Third Reich.

The important distinction, however, and one which Fischer himself acknowledges but is not often made clearly enough by others, is between the very different natures of the two German regimes in the two world wars. Imperial Germany may not have been a liberal democracy but neither was it a totalitarian regime guided by a racist ideology. It was very conscious of the fact that it could not sustain a war effort without the domestic support of the socialists and the liberals. It did not even wish to break completely with internationally accepted norms of great power conduct – such as they were – as its attempts to reassure international opinion over the violation of Belgian neutrality showed. It certainly did not aim at the genocidal extermination of entire ethnic groups, and even its annexationist aims were (at least initially) moderate, the main aims being the decisive weakening of France and Russia and the consolidation of German economic and military supremacy in continental Europe, coupled with some colonial expansion. In other words, there was nothing in Imperial Germany's war aims that represented a fundamental break with the imperialist spirit of the era, except of course in that two of the main targets were themselves major imperialist powers and that the intended recipients of the blessings of a German-controlled Customs Union were white Europeans rather than dark-skinned, far-away 'savages'.

By contrast, Nazi Germany had already eliminated all domestic opposition and begun the systematic persecution of Jews well before World War II began. The Nazi war aims involved not only the direct annexation of far greater territories but also a systematic policy of large-scale genocide, ethnic and racial cleansing to prepare vast territories in the East for resettlement by Germans and other so-called Aryans. The difference between Germany's aims in the two world wars was clearly as much a qualitative one as that between the two regimes, and one should not conceal this behind the undoubted continuities in interest and outlook of the economic, social and political elites between the two periods.

There can be little disagreement that a German victory in World War II would have constituted a fundamental break in European civilization, with catastrophic consequences not only for the Jews and the Slavonic peoples of Eastern Europe but for the cause of democracy in Europe more generally. But can the same be said of a German victory in World War I? Since it is generally acknowledged that Germany had probably lost the war the moment it failed in its attempts to keep Britain out of it, and certainly the moment the USA entered it on Britain's side, it may be best to rephrase this as, 'What if Britain (and the US) had kept out of the war, and Germany had won it?' It is precisely this question which Niall Ferguson, in his recent collection of counterfactual essays *Virtual History*, answers as follows:

> A fresh assessment of Germany's pre-war war aims reveals that, had Britain stood aside ... continental Europe would have been transformed into something not unlike the European Union we know today – but without the massive contraction in British overseas power entailed by the fighting of two world wars ... And there certainly would not have been that great incursion of American financial and military power into European affairs which effectively marked the end of British financial predominance in the world. True, there might still have been fascism in Europe in the 1920s; but it would have been in France rather than Germany that radical nationalists would have sounded most persuasive. It may even be that, in the absence of a world war's stresses and strains, the inflations and deflations of the early 1920s and early 1930s would not have been so severe. With the Kaiser triumphant, Hitler could have lived out his life as a failed artist and a fulfilled soldier in a German-dominated Central Europe about which he could have found little to complain.[9]

One may disagree with Ferguson's assessment that the replacement of Britain by America as the leading power of the Anglo-Saxon world would have been significantly delayed, if not averted, by a decision to stay out of the continental war. But it is hard to resist his conclusion that it was the defeat of German imperialist ambitions which prepared the ground for the subsequent European catastrophes, and that a German victory then might, on balance, have been better for the world. It might even have accelerated the evolution of the *Reich* towards a British-style constitutional monarchy, much like British liberal democracy had itself evolved out of successful imperial expansion.

## The fate of the Weimar Republic

So far, we have sketched a German bourgeoisie which had little option but to look towards Prussia for its industrial and commercial development, national unification and the promotion of its interests in the outside world. Its peculiar brand of statist liberalism, its predilection for authoritarian law and order, bureaucratic efficiency and Hegelian philosophy, for romantic nationalism and an inward-looking, apolitical cultural life, as well as its reluctance to press for constitutional democracy are explained in terms of this dependency on the Prusso-German state and its fear of proletarian revolution – that is, as largely rational responses to the conditions of its existence. It has even been suggested that its imperialist aspirations were nothing out of the ordinary in an era of intense imperialist rivalry, and that on balance the defeat of these aspirations did more damage than their successful realization in World War I might have done.

But what about the Weimar Republic? The fate of the first German republic is often cited as definitive proof of the fundamentally illiberal nature of German society before its eventual 'Westernization' after 1945: here the Germans had, at last, a liberal democratic constitution and they rejected it. Accordingly, the historiography of this 'democracy without democrats' is generally of a highly teleological nature, portraying the Republic as the antechamber of the Third Reich and the eventual Nazi *Machtergreifung* as essentially inevitable. It is indeed difficult to make a case for the possibility of a stable liberal democracy under the conditions of the 1920s and early 1930s in Germany: any counterfactual construction of this kind would have to write out of history too many of the key ingredients – the revanchist preoccupation of the nationalist elites with the defeat of its imperialist ambitions, the civil-war-like intensity of the class struggle; above all the devastating effects of the Wall Street crash and Great Depression on an export- and credit-dependent economy – to remain within the realm of plausibility. But to accept that, under those conditions, a stable liberal democracy was difficult to envisage does not mean that there was no alternative to Hitler. There was, and there had been since the beginning.

For the fundamental dilemma of the Weimar Republic was not that of a liberal-democratic 'Weimar Coalition' fighting a losing struggle against anti-republican enemies on the extreme right and left, as it is so often portrayed. The reality was that the Weimar coalition itself was not unambiguously committed to a liberal capitalist democracy of the Anglo-Saxon type, with a good part of the liberal and Catholic element still yearning for a restoration of monarchy and empire, and much of the SPD rank-and-file considering the republic as merely a stepping stone to full-blown Socialism ('Republik, das ist nicht viel – Sozialismus ist das Ziel'). In effect, the Weimar Republic was a latent civil war between two irreconcilable conceptions of society in which the parties of the Weimar coalition did not represent a truly liberal alternative to, but rather the moderate wings of, the respective civil war camps, in that they found themselves temporarily able to agree on the formal rules under which politics should be conducted – as *Vernunftrepublikaner* of the left and the right – but not on a substantial shared vision of a liberal society. The economic collapse after 1929 destroyed whatever common ground there was and the civil war was inexorably pushing towards a resolution: either an authoritarian regime of the right (fascist or otherwise), or a completion of the unfinished socialist revolution of 1918–19.

It is not, of course, the fault of the liberal historians that the former alternative prevailed over the latter, but that of the leaderships of the Social Democrats and the Communists who each preferred to fiddle their own separate tunes while the *Reichstag* was burning. Yet by equating 'extremism' of the right and the left, liberal historiography is not only refusing to acknowledge that there was indeed an alternative to Hitler, but also tacitly implying a moral equivalence between the two types of extremism, as if the radical left represented at least as deadly a threat to the basic values of European civilization as the Nazis.

## Germany, Europe and Anglo-Saxon liberalism today

Finally, to the 'new Germany'. Ferguson's view, already cited, that Germany's position in Europe today is essentially not dissimilar from what German imperialist planners were aiming at before World War I, is echoed by an author entirely above any suspicion of British Euroscepticism, the liberal German historian Volker Berghahn:

> Following the collapse of communism in Eastern Europe and after German reunification, it has become increasingly clear that Germany, which twice in the first half of the twentieth century vainly attempted to establish by force a formal empire stretching from the Atlantic coast to the Ural Mountains and beyond, now at the end of this century finds herself on the verge of acquiring an informal empire of similar dimensions without having fired a single shot.[10]

Berghahn calls this 'a major irony of modern history' but one might equally consider it a major tragedy that Europe (and the world) had to pay such a horrendous price to get from where it might have been in 1916 to where it is today. If there is an irony, it is surely that, having spent the first half of the century resisting the imperialist ambitions of Germany and eventually defeating them in 1945, the powers of the West proceeded to lay the foundations for a long-term recovery of not entirely dissimilar ambitions. But then the Cold War era was a highly exceptional era, characterized by the sharp decline of Britain and France and the undisputed supremacy of the United States, and above all overshadowed by the confrontation with that other arch-enemy of Western liberalism, Soviet Communism. West Germany's industrial and military potential was needed to stabilize Western Europe against the East, but the expectation was that it could be contained through the mechanisms of supranational integration.

That exceptional era is now in the past. Germany is united again and no longer confined to the narrow straightjacket of Cold War Western Europe but free once again to spread its wings into the vast expanses of Eastern Europe where, to quote Berghahn again, 'German industry and banking ... have no rival in the construction of capitalism that is currently and painfully going on in the former Soviet bloc countries.'[11] For better or for worse, Germany will be able to shape the future of Europe, East and West, in the twenty-first century to an even larger extent than at any time during the twentieth outside the years of its wartime military expansion. It is therefore important to note that even the 'new Germany', after four decades of post-war integration into the West, continues to represent an alternative, more 'statist', model of capitalism to that of the Anglo-Saxon liberal, *laissez-faire*, free-trade, individualistic tradition.

Dahrendorf, that most Anglophile of German liberals, noted with despair the extent to which the post-war reconstruction of German capitalism was a restoration in the sense that the old statist and bureaucratic structures and attitudes had survived into Ludwig Erhard's ordo-liberal 'economic miracle'. Today, authors like Michel Albert, Will Hutton and John Gray[12] cast admiring glances at what they call the 'Rhineland model' of capitalism and contrast it favourably with the Anglo-Saxon variety. Nobody who follows closely the debates about European integration today can fail to note the ideological battle between those who seek to extend the German model of state-interventionist, corporatist, 'social market' capitalism over the European Union, thus effectively turning the EU into a fortress against the US-led drive towards deregulated world markets, and the pro-US, pro-globalization, Blairite deregulators. Beyond the European Union, in Russia and the major countries of Asia, forces instinctively and by tradition of an equally illiberal, statist-bureaucratic persuasion as Germany are mobilizing to offer increasing resistance to the US project of a 'new world order' based on unfettered capital mobility. Quite unmistakeably, with the closing of the twentieth century, history is not quite finished yet.

The Cold War may be over, but the real struggle between politics and economics, the state and the market, Friedrich List and Adam Smith, democracy and liberalism continues unabated.

Perhaps future generations will consider Anglo-Saxon liberalism as the real *Sonderweg*, and Adam Smith, Herbert Spencer and Milton Friedmann as ideological oddities reflecting peculiar British and American conditions and a past age when the Anglo-Saxon powers controlled the world. If they do, they will also rehabilitate Hegel, List and Marx, and with them much of the German tradition of 'statist anti-liberalism' as pioneers of the eminently sensible principle that in human affairs, the welfare of the whole is the precondition for the welfare of each individual.

## Notes

1. The original essay was published in *The National Interest*, 16 (Summer 1989), pp. 3–18, followed later by an expanded book version: *The End of History and the Last Man* (London, 1992).
2. G.P. Gooch, E.M. Butler *et al.*, *The German Mind and Outlook* (London, 1945), p. viii.
3. Quoted in Dirk Verheyen, *The German Question. A Cultural, Historical and Geopolitical Exploration* (Boulder/San Francisco/Oxford, 1991), p. 29.
4. John Gray, *False Dawn. The Delusions of Global Capitalism* (London, 1999), p. 17.
5. *Ibid.*, p. 20.
6. Rohan D'O. Butler, *The Roots of National Socialism 1783–1933* (London, 1941), p. 277.
7. Ralf Dahrendorf, *Society and Democracy in Germany* (London, 1968), p. 58.
8. Friedrich Engels, 'The Prussian Military Question and the German Workers' Party', in Karl Marx, *The First International and After. Political Writings: Volume 3*, edited and introduced by David Fernbach (Harmondsworth, 1974), p. 127.
9. Niall Ferguson, 'The Kaiser's European Union: What if Britain had "stood aside" in August 1914?', in Niall Ferguson (ed.), *Virtual History. Alternatives and Counterfactuals* (London, 1998), pp. 278–9.
10. Volker R. Berghahn, 'German Big Business and the Quest for a European Economic Empire in the Twentieth Century', in Volker R. Berghahn (ed.), *Quest for Economic Empire. European Strategies of German Big Business in the Twentieth Century* (Providence and Oxford, 1996), p. 1.
11. *Ibid.*
12. Michel Albert, *Capitalism against capitalism* (London, 1993); Will Hutton, *The State We're In* (London, 1995); John Gray, *op. cit.*

# 17
# The Social Dynamics of Dictatorship: Re-evaluating the Third Reich and the GDR 'From the Bottom Up'

*Jonathan Grix* and *Charlie Jeffery*

## I
## Introduction: There was Such a Thing as Society

The earliest research into twentieth-century dictatorships both in Germany and elsewhere provided unwitting confirmation of Mrs Thatcher's claim that 'there is no such thing as society'. Research focused typically on two features of dictatorial rule. First, there were the mechanisms of control exercised by the state over its citizens, in particular the combination of mass indoctrination through state propaganda and mass intimidation by the organizations of state internal security. And second, there were the heroic opponents of dictatorship, persecuted and – depending on the period of dictatorship concerned – variously discriminated against, imprisoned, tortured, exiled or murdered for their beliefs. The composite vision was one of rigid social control imposed by a tightly hierarchical state structure, which only those sufficiently invigorated by conscience or conviction could, against all the odds and with often terrible consequences, resist.

The process of researching and writing history is, of course, embedded in, and a reflection of, the prevalent social norms and needs surrounding the writer. The focus on social control – 'propaganda and terror' – can largely be understood as Cold War history, shaped by theories of totalitarianism[1] which equated Hitler's Reich with the new, post-war Soviet Empire and which helped galvanize the West for a new period of struggle to defend market capitalism and (in some parts of the world at least) liberal democracy. It was also a useful tool in the West German context in establishing the Federal Republic's moral superiority over the 'totalitarian' GDR.

The focus on opposition – 'persecution and resistance' – reflected, in West Germany in particular, a need to demonstrate that there had been 'another Germany' in the Third Reich which, however badly mauled and suppressed, had lived on. This 'andere Deutschland' was, in the era of post-war reconstruction, a necessary link back to an enlightened, progressive, humanist, largely pre-nineteenth-century Germany which could now be resuscitated and mobilized to provide historically sound building blocks for establishing a functioning and stable democracy. It also sharpened the West German perspective on the GDR: the 1953 workers' uprising and the subsequent controversies surrounding East German dissidents proved that even under Communist rule 'another Germany' lived on.

What seemingly had not lived on through the Third Reich nor in the GDR was a German 'society'. In much of post-war historical writing, 'society' (looking beyond the numerically negligible resisters and dissidents) had lost its autonomy from the state. Subsumed into a new *Volksgemeinschaft* or the Workers' and Peasants' State, society's inherent pluralism – the expression of individual will, the coalescence of individuals into groups with shared identities and conflicting interests, the operation of structures and processes of intermediation between rulers and ruled – had, it seemed, been wiped out. Or, more precisely, it had been wiped out of consideration by the perspective historical research had used. This perspective was focused, for the reasons outlined above, 'from the top down' on structures of control radiating out from the centre and on 'the few', the leading personalities running the state and the relatively small number of dissidents persecuted by the state. No one was really looking for the persistence of 'society', for the fabric of social interactions which always provide an interface between individual and state – even if the state is run as a heinous dictatorship.

However, perspectives change. This became especially evident in research on the Third Reich. Growing historical distance from the Third Reich, together with the stabilization of East–West divisions in the Cold War and the consolidation of West German democracy, facilitated a more critical reflection on the nature of the Nazi dictatorship and its interrelationships with the German people. Growing methodological promiscuity, in particular a new openness to the social sciences, also opened up new lines of enquiry less focused on key individuals and more on the 'structural' and social contexts in which they operated. Finally, new source materials were opened up, in particular denazification records revealing the social structure of Nazi Party membership and the fragmentary but extraordinarily rich *Stimmungsberichte* assiduously composed at all levels of state authority by the various internal security bodies reporting ultimately to the Reich Security Headquarters. Changing perspectives, methods and sources reversed the emphasis in studying the Third Reich; increasingly, history began to be viewed 'from the bottom up' and began to focus on 'the many', the mass of 'ordinary' people, rather than the few who led or resisted the dictatorship. The result was a much more nuanced understanding of dictatorship, revealing new complexities in the relationships between rulers and ruled, but also a perhaps unexpected 'normality' as individuals and social groups pursued their everyday lives. There was, after all, such a thing as society and its relationship with the state was increasingly viewed as crucial in understanding the dynamics of dictatorial rule in the Third Reich. This is the subject of section II of this essay.

Research on the GDR did not develop quite so radically. Broadly speaking, until 1989 scholars of the second German dictatorship were either highly critical of the GDR regime, condemning it in order to prove the superiority of the FRG, or critical of the FRG and therefore looking for and finding the good in East Germany. In the first two post-war decades, rigid totalitarian typologies restricted the view to the foreground of official ideology, terror, the leading mass party, its monopoly of media, and so on.[2] This totalitarian society was seen to have uprooted cultural and historical traditions; citizen–state relations did not, as a result, feature as a focal point of analysis. By the 1970s, however, this approach had become discredited as an analytical tool.[3] Much GDR-research now fell into line with the new rapprochement of Willy Brandt's *Ostpolitik*. It also, unfortunately, at the same time all too often lost critical distance to its object of study amid the wider atmosphere of moves to secure the *de facto* recognition of the GDR as a sovereign state.[4] The result was a tendency in particular to view the 'social achievements' of the GDR in employment, welfare and equality policies with an uncritical eye which both skewed attention away from the less savoury aspects of the GDR dictatorship and, once again, away from the detailed dynamics of the relations between rulers and ruled.

Only in the 1980s were new lines of enquiry about the social constitution of the GDR dictatorship opened up as overt non-conformism in the form of (small) peace and ecology movements grew and caught the attention of Western observers.

This, however, was again a concentration on the few who were seen to openly oppose, rather than the many who did not. This was of course hardly surprising. Researchers of the GDR before its collapse had no access to the source materials required for a more widely grounded history 'from the bottom up'. Instead they had to rely on either personal contacts or officially organized and monitored trips and visits. Contacts with 'ordinary' people were mostly controlled and only very few academics managed to gain useful insights into the fabric of socialist society.[5] On the contrary, the rich and comprehensive range of sources which have emerged since the fall of the Berlin Wall (discussed in section III) is nothing less than a veritable Aladdin's cave, offering the researcher the chance to begin to understand the peculiar social conditions which both sustained the GDR dictatorship and hastened its collapse in 1989.

As a result, a new generation of researchers has now been able to approach the study of the GDR and more fully capture the nature of the GDR dictatorship by employing the methods adopted in the 'bottom up' study of Nazi Germany.[6] These researchers have shown that the complex symbiotic relationship between the citizens and power-wielding elites can only be understood by studying citizens' reactions to the state's aims and measures *alongside* simultaneous analysis of the state's reactions to citizens' demands. Just how citizens came to terms as part of this relationship with the parameters of the system, often aware of a room to manoeuvre not revealed in earlier accounts of 'Communist regimes', is introduced in section III below.

## II
## Consent and Dissent in the Third Reich

Over the last twenty years or so, research on the Third Reich has focused strongly on the study of popular attitudes, mentalities and behaviour, or 'popular opinion' in the phrase favoured by Ian Kershaw.[7] The approach taken has often been dubbed *Alltagsgeschichte*, the history of everyday life. It reversed the emphasis of more traditional historical methods by turning the focus away from the key personalities, structures of authority and decision-making processes at the political centre. Instead, the emphasis is not on these macro-level 'big' politics as such, but on the impact of 'big' politics on the everyday lives and experience of 'small' people at the micro-level. The aim has been to assess the social impact of Nazism from below, by exploring and reconstructing subjective experiences at the grass roots of society.

The *Alltagsgeschichte* approach is not uncontested. Concern has been expressed that a narrow research focus on everyday life can produce descriptive accounts of trivial details which neglect the broader political context. *Alltagsgeschichte* can thus run the danger of becoming a 'history with the politics left out'.[8] Applied to the Third Reich, this danger is especially potent given the nature of the politics which might be 'left out'. The uniquely criminal barbaric and ultimately genocidal politics of the Third Reich are of such world-historical importance that we should not risk losing sight of them as a result of changing trends in historical research.[9]

Although such criticisms might well apply to the shortcomings of individual studies, it is doubtful that they can be applied to the approach as a whole. A focus on the history of everyday life need not deflect from or downplay the world-historical significance of National Socialism. On the contrary, the products of *Alltagsgeschichte*[10] have helped to reveal that there is a crucial link between 'everyday life and barbarity', that there can be a social context in so-called civilized society in which barbarity becomes acceptable and genocide possible.[11] Such work has, in this way, clearly shown that one can hardly seek to understand the development of Nazi policies without considering fully the relationship between people and regime, how individuals and social groups experienced and responded to Nazi rule.

The first step in examining this relationship is, of course, to ask what the people were responding to. What sort of society did the Nazis aim to create? Their social aims were, in Kershaw's words, 'extraordinarily ambitious'; encapsulated in the concept of *Volksgemeinschaft*, the aim was to achieve unconditional, all-out mobilization of the German people in the cause of the *Volk* by replacing all class, religious, regional and other sectional allegiances by a 'massively intensified national self-awareness'.[12] A follow-up question has to be whether such aims were achievable. The answer is a twofold 'no'. Firstly, even if one does assume achievability, it is highly unlikely that there was sufficient capacity for enforcement in the Third Reich. The internal structures of the Nazi state patently lacked the coherence and clear lines of authority, let alone the organizational resources, necessary to achieve the level of social control and manipulation which was desired. Secondly, serious doubt has to be cast on the extent to which a regime which lasted just twelve years could eradicate long-standing pluralist traditions in society in favour of the all-encompassing loyalty to the *Volk* it aspired to.[13] Probably the most vivid finding of *Alltagsgeschichte* studies of the Third Reich is the persistence of established social cleavages through to the collapse of 1945. Even under Nazi dictatorship, different individuals and social groups retained different political perspectives and priorities which shaped a broad and heterogeneous palette of attitudes towards the state. Weimar Germany was a deeply divided society in which ordered politics was overwhelmed by a cacophony of sectional interests pressing the claims of often narrowly defined social groups. While the cacophony was eventually drowned out by the Nazis, the social groups lived on, often forming relatively closed communities with a broadly homogeneous 'environmental' background comprising shared socio-economic interests, party-political and/or religious traditions, and particularistic forms of popular culture.

The particularistic interests, values and traditions inherent in what had been an overtly riven society continued to be expressed, albeit typically in a subterranean way, in the Third Reich. Informal social networks persisted long after formal social organizations had been banned: within the family and the neighbourhood, among circles of friends, at the *Stammtisch*, in the workplace, and so on. In addition, in the special case of the Church, even the organization remained intact, albeit with a much reduced autonomy. The maintenance in these ways of a shared identity among social groups was reflected in a certain 'immunity', or 'Resistenz'[14] to the aspirations of the regime. Responses to Nazi rule were thus mediated and differentiated by the type and level of resistance different social groups could maintain. In these circumstances, the much-vaunted *Volksgemeinschaft* always remained little more than a myth, dusted down and trotted out regularly, but never with very much effect, by Nazi propagandists.

The use of the term 'Resistenz' to capture this subterranean social pluralism is, however, problematic. It is loaded towards the identification of dissenting opinion and implicitly presupposes that members of tight-knit social groups were somehow, because of their 'immunity', predestined to respond in some kind of negative way to Nazi rule. Surely the interests, values and identities of previously Social Democratic workers, God-fearing Bavarian farmers or aristocratic conservatives were incompatible with and therefore 'immune' to the social claims of Nazism? Surely this created points of friction with and, in some cases, dissent towards the regime? This is of course true, but only in part. Aspects of Nazism could also appeal to, and secure positive and consensual responses from workers, farmers, Christians, or aristocrats:

job-creation, house-building, autarchical protectionism, government contracts, anti-Communism, anti-Semitism, national self-assertion in foreign policy, and so on. Others had a wider, cross-group appeal, not least the charismatic leadership of Hitler (or, better, of the 'myth'[15] surrounding Hitler's leadership). Indeed, as analyses of the social structure of the NSDAP (before and after taking power) have shown,[16] Nazism was a genuinely popular movement; the NSDAP was arguably the party with the biggest claim to the status of *Volkspartei* in German history.

Inherent in even tight-knit social groups with their own enduring value systems were, therefore, not just points of conflict with the regime but also points of consensus. Popular responses to Nazism were not just plural, but also inconsistent and equivocal, encompassing both alienation, dissatisfaction and dissent as well as adaptation, approval and consent. Moreover, consent and dissent were not two neatly demarcated aspects of popular opinion. By and large they overlapped and were expressed simultaneously with one another.

What does this imply for an understanding of the Third Reich? Does an approach 'from the bottom up' and focused on the 'ordinary' person really add to our understanding of the Nazi dictatorship and its crimes? Or does a focus on everyday life deflect from or even trivialize the unprecedented barbarity of Nazism? Notwithstanding the 'Goldhagen controversy' of the mid 1990s,[17] there is little hard evidence of direct, active, popular participation in the execution of Nazi crimes. But there was an important indirect nexus between the people and those crimes. Most people in Nazi Germany simply got on with their lives after 1933. Most people were not moved to extreme views in support of or against the regime. Most people slipped into a new 'normality' in their relationship with their rulers: grumbling about some things the Nazis did, approving of others. Between the isolated heroics of individual resisters and the murderous criminality of Nazi leaders and their active supporters there was a vast middle ground of equivocal normality in which, alongside all the manifestations of dissent, there were sufficient points of consensus between the one or the other section of the population and the regime for the Nazis to carry the great majority of the Germans with them to the very end.

## III
## Internal Social Dynamics of the GDR

The cobwebs were blown out of the GDR research landscape, to paraphrase Stefan Heym's remark on the *Wende*, with the collapse of the regime and the barriers which had hitherto prevented people from studying it. Thankfully, the GDR authorities were especially efficient in the collation of data, information and reports, which are all extremely detailed and comprehensive in their scope. They also became available quickly to researchers after the GDR's collapse as part of the official policy of allowing access to the inner workings of the GDR dictatorship. Such sources can provide the necessary basis for a detailed reconstruction of GDR social history, if read carefully with an eye to what they do and do not say.[18] Most useful are *Stimmungsberichte* from a wide variety of official channels and organizations. These range from district Party reports sent to *Bezirk* level and from the *Bezirk* to the central committee in Berlin on the mood of the workforce in urban and rural factories, hospitals, offices and so on throughout the country. Masses of verbal and written reports were gathered by the local Stasi at the *Bezirk* level, summarized and then sent on to the centre. Information reports from the Church, Police reports on the population's mood[19] and civil non-participation, and *Freier Deutscher Gewerkschaftsbund* (the largest mass organization in the GDR) reports on workers' opinions reveal to a great extent the inner workings of the system and more importantly the interaction between rulers and ruled. They have revealed a mutual dependency between the two which eluded previous generations of researchers on the GDR. Yet, as the study of everyday life in the Third Reich has shown, dictatorial rule is always based on state–society interaction and can only endure over the long-term on that basis.[20]

Work undertaken in this vein has gradually come to balance the early post-dictatorship interest which focused on the external shock of Gorbachev's reforms, the structural dilapidation of the GDR economy and (intellectual) opposition as the immediate reasons for the GDR's collapse.[21] (Interestingly, the reverse factors were previously said to be behind the state's stability: the *'Bestandsgarantie für die DDR durch die USSR'*, the relative power of the GDR economy and the lack of any intellectual opposition or *'Gegenelite'* as in Czechoslovakia and Poland.) More recently, however, GDR research has turned to the *internal social dynamics* of a dictatorship which lasted longer than both the Nazi period and the Weimar Republic put together.

In contrast to the Nazi dictatorship, the GDR was enclosed by fortified borders from 1961 onwards and its citizens were rapidly forced to come to terms with their situation. The spawning of informal social networks in the private sphere had come to replace civil society which had been gradually eroded by the SED state. This can be seen as a direct reaction to the GDR's attempt to create a socialist society and socialist personalities governed by the doctrines of Marxism-Leninism. Indoctrination began with children's books, the Free German Youth (FDJ), mass organizations and endless celebrations and jubilees of socialist achievements. Forty years of GDR socialization did come to have an affect on citizens' 'patterns of behaviour, especially the generation of the *Hineingeborenen* who had never experienced anything else. Previous societal cleavages were affected by SED policies, educational opportunities, the type of housing available and family planning, resulting in a uniformity of way of life for citizens and an increased dependency on the state.[22] Yet, it is fair to say that the GDR state never enjoyed the full support of a majority of its citizens at any point in its history, which contributed to what may be termed a latent legitimacy crisis, held in check by 'conditional' loyalty, embedded in a tacit understanding between the state and its citizens. This form of *Anpassung* of the masses, 'a preparedness to go through the motions',[23] was externally enforced on them and did not result in absolute conformity to the regime, but in the appearance of such. At the heart of the understanding of this pragmatic co-existence between the ruled and the rulers lay the oft cited but little analysed *Sozialvertrag*. In essence this unspoken contract demanded of citizens outward conformity, lip service to ideology (rituals and flag waving) and the recognition of the leading role of the SED. In return citizens could expect guaranteed social welfare and employment, subsidized foodstuffs and to be allowed to retreat from state life into what was termed the 'Nischengesellschaft'.[24] It is important to point out that the 'Nischengesellschaft' was diverse and very fragmented and did not in any way constitute opposition to the regime. Rather there existed a 'collective of individuals'[25] within the inner spaces created by external 'top down' pressure to conform. More to the point, these internal social dynamics hold the key to both the stability of the regime through to the late 1980s, and the massive instability which led to its collapse in 1989.

Of equal importance in explaining the shift from equilibrium to disequilibrium in the GDR is the complex interrelationships between social actors, and in particular that between the so-called 'opposition' and the masses. Whilst the majority of citizens reluctantly accepted their lot until the mid 1980s and retreated from the over-politicization of daily life, a great number of tiny and fragmented grass roots groups championing human rights, peace, and so on, had emerged in East German society. Until the mid 1980s these groups found little resonance among the wider populace and they lacked any sense of social embeddedness. This was to rapidly change, however, from the mid 1980s onwards, as the increasing dissatisfaction of the masses – as a result of internal problems of supplies and the external stimulus of Gorbachev and the reforms associated with him – drew them towards the churches. During 1989, groups such as *New Forum* acted as a focal point for citizens who sought change in society and an alternative public sphere. The forum of the Church bridged the divide between the masses and the so-called 'opposition'. Grassroots groups were thus able to catalyse the widespread dissatisfaction, acting as a *public* conduit through which citizens could vent their frustration after years of grumbling acquiescence in their *private* niches. The result was the cancelling of the 'social contract' and the rapid demise of the state.

## IV
## Conclusion

The application of history 'from below' can help shed considerable light on the intrinsic nature of dictatorship, its social dynamics – in particular the relationship between rulers and ruled – and offer insights into just how they were sustained and legitimated. This approach is complementary to the huge literature on power-wielding elites and opposition; it highlights 'the real situation of ordinary people, in which confusion, dilemmas of choice, and uneasy compromises were commonplace'.[26]

With the aid of *Alltagsgeschichte* researchers have been able to begin to understand how a dictatorship functions. The Nazi dictatorship was sustained and legitimated in part by sufficient points of consensus between the population and regime. The Nazis found ways of appealing either to individual groups *or* to the wider population, effectively transcending class boundaries and other societal cleavages. The imperfect social control imposed by the Nazis, which relied to a great extent on denunciation and fear, and the points of consensus between the authorities and its subjects, meant that many traditional social groups, their beliefs and in part their practices, continued under Nazi rule. The retention of group identities helped mediate between society and state and as such were essential for the domestic stability of the Nazi regime.

The relative longevity and rapid demise of the GDR state, on the other hand, can be explained in part by the society–state relationship, that is the niche society compromise within the framework of a wider social contract between citizens with little choice and the paternalist regime. On the micro-level this compromise consisted of a plethora of nonconformist actions, too minor, too private and too individual to threaten the regime, until circumstances changed and minor turned to major, private to public and individual to collective. It is history from the 'bottom up' which has uncovered these social dynamics. Rather than deflecting from the barbarity of Nazism and the repressiveness of the GDR, this approach, if placed in the wider perspective and compared with other sources, can help us understand the complex interrelationships between, and specific behaviour of, social actors in dictatorship. Without it, research, with its focus on and preoccupation with elites, opposition, security apparatus and 'big politics', runs the danger of becoming history with society left out.

## Notes

1. See for example Carl Friedrich and Zbigniew Brzezinski, *Totalitarian Dictatorship and Autocracy* (Cambridge, MA, 1956).
2. These are some of the components making up Friedrich's and Brzezinski's typology of totalitarianism. See note 1 above.
3. Klaus Schroeder and Jochen Staadt, 'Der diskrete Charme des Status Quo. DDR-Forschung in der Ära der Entspannungspolitik', in Klaus Schroeder (ed.) *Geschichte und Transformation des SED-Staates, Beiträge und Analysen* (Berlin, 1994), p. 315.
4. Edition Deutschland Archiv, *35 Jahre SED-Politik, Versuch einer Bilanz* (Köln, 1981), p. 9.
5. See for example Lutz Niethammer's (*et al.*) study beginning in 1987: *Die volkseigene Erfahrung, Eine Archäologie des Lebens in der Industrieprovinz der DDR* (Berlin, 1991).
6. There are some exceptions, however, with a few continuing to discuss GDR society as having been under the 'totalitarian grip' of the 'Stalinist SED' whose 'totalitarian SED regime' controlled every nook and cranny of society. See Andreas Staab, *National Identity in Eastern Germany, Inner Unification or Continued Separation* (Westport, CT/London, 1998), esp. p. 78.
7. Ian Kershaw, *Popular Opinion and Political Dissent in the Third Reich. Bavaria 1933–1945* (Oxford, 1983), pp. 1–10.
8. Richard J. Evans, 'Introduction: Wilhelm II's Germany and the Historians', in Richard J. Evans (ed.), *Society and Politics in Wilhelmine Germany* (London, 1978), p. 24.
9. This was a key element of the debates on the 'historicization' of National Socialism in the 1980s. See Ian Kershaw, *The Nazi Dictatorship* (London, 1989), pp. 150–67.
10. Among which the 'Bayern-Projekt' led back in the 1970s by Martin Broszat remains outstanding both for pioneering the approach and for the quality and richness of its results. See Martin Broszat *et al.* (eds), *Bayern in der NS-Zeit*, 6 volumes (Munich, 1977–83).
11. Cf. Kershaw, *The Nazi Dictatorship*, pp. 166–7.
12. Kershaw, *Popular Opinion and Political Dissent*, p. 1.
13. The GDR, of course, had a rather fuller opportunity to implement its project of social engineering. See subsequent sections of this essay.
14. This was a key concept guiding the 'Bayern-Projekt'. See Martin Broszat, 'Resistenz und Widerstand. Eine Zwischenbilanz des Forschungsprojekts', in

Martin Broszat, Elke Fröhlich and Anton Grossmann (eds), *Bayern in der NS-Zeit IV. Herrschaft und Gesellschaft in Konflikt* (Munich, 1981).

15. See Ian Kershaw's increasingly impressive works on the nature of Hitler's leadership: *The Hitler Myth. Image and Reality in the Third Reich* (Oxford, 1987); *Hitler. A Profile in Power* (London, 1991); *Hitler 1889–1936. Hubris* (London, 1998).

16. See for example Thomas Childers, *The Nazi Voter* (Chapel Hill, 1983); Detlev Mühlberger, *Hitler's Followers: Studies in the Sociology of the Nazi Movement* (London, 1991).

17. Daniel Jonah Goldhagen, *Hitler's Willing Executioners* (London, 1996).

18. In addition to the sources discussed here, there is of course 'oral history', as the vast majority of people who lived in the GDR are still alive.

19. The so-called 'Lageberichte' made by the German People's Police offer a fascinating chronicle of everyday life in the GDR. In particular, they will become an essential source for tracing the roots and course of the *Wende* in the under researched regions *outside* of Dresden, Leipzig and East Berlin. For a good example see Georg Herbstritt, *Die Lageberichte der Deutschen Volkspolizei im Herbst 1989. Eine Chronik der Wende in Neubrandenburg* (Schwerin, 1998).

20. Thomas Lindenberger, 'Alltagsgeschichte und Gesellschaftsgeschichte', in *Die Grenzen der Diktatur* (Göttingen, 1996), p. 315.

21. For a fuller account of the approaches to the GDR's collapse see Jonathan Grix, 'Competing Approaches to the Collapse of the GDR: "Top-Down" vs "Bottom-Up"', *Journal of Area Studies, Revolution(s)*, special issue 13 (Autumn 1998),pp. 121–42.

22. Sigrid Meuschel, *Legitimation und Parteiherrschaft in der DDR* (Frankfurt am Main, 1992), p. 12.

23. Mary Fulbrook, *Anatomy of a Dictatorship* (Oxford, 1995), p. 273.

24. See Günter Gaus, *Wo Deutschland liegt* (Hamburg, 1983).

25. Stefan Wolle, *Die heile Welt der Diktatur* (Berlin, 1998).

26. Ian Kershaw, *The Nazi Dictatorship*, p. 156.

# 18
## Back to the Future: 1968 and the Red–Green Government

*William E. Paterson*

The analysis of the long-term effects of 1968 on German political culture is one of the central strands in Wilfried van der Will's recent work, and his monograph with Rob Burns, *Protest and Democracy in West Germany* (1988) remains the most incisive and influential account of the protest movement in the pre-*Wende* Federal Republic.[1] The literature on '1968' in West Germany focuses to a very large extent on the Student Movement and its role in the Extra-Parliamentary Opposition. This focus was sharpened by the emergence of urban terrorism in West Germany in the early 1970s which led to a spate of books and articles attempting to locate the genesis of the terrorist movement in the events of 1968. However, the interaction between the events of 1968 and the SPD, the overwhelmingly dominant party of the left, has been relatively neglected. The advent of a Red–Green government in 1998, many of whose members had been active participants in 1968, suggests that the time for a re-examination is overdue.

To understand the 1968 experience, it is necessary to sketch in some historical background. The SPD was reformed after 1945 on broadly the same lines as the party which had been defeated in the Weimar Republic.[2] Indeed, its programme remained substantially the one agreed in 1925 in Heidelberg. For the party leadership thought any wide-ranging discussion of aims and strategy would open up divisions which would prevent it attaining power in the first impatiently awaited democratic elections. As so often in the history of the SPD, the values invoked were the defensive ones of *Geschlossenheit* and the *Schulterschluß*.

In the early years of the Federal Republic, the SPD's attempt to provide an alternative to the policies of the CDU-led government proved very difficult. The major obstacle was created by the sustained economic boom, initiated by Erhard's Currency Reform of 1948. The constraining effect of prosperity on the articulation of alternatives was heightened, of course, by the negative impact of the existence of the German Democratic Republic. Liberal capitalism thus quickly became a central pillar of the Federal Republic's *Staatsverständnis*, a key defining characteristic in antithesis to the Communism of the widely reviled Republic next door. It was therefore hardly surprising that a consensus in the economic field began to develop fairly early in the history of the Federal Republic. After the twin electoral defeats of 1953 and 1957 and after the banning of the Communist Party in 1956 which removed the final vestiges of competition on the left, efforts to change the party accelerated, culminating in the adoption of a new party programme against very little opposition at the special conference held in 1959 in Bad Godesberg.

The Bad Godesberg programme dropped the Marxist heritage of the SPD and embraced the principle of private ownership in so far as it was compatible with a just social order. The strategy was henceforth to be one of improving and reforming capitalism rather than abolishing it. Six months later, in a famous speech on 30 June 1960 in the Bundestag, Herbert Wehner indicated the readiness of the SPD to join with other German parties to defend the FRG against Communist threats by fully accepting NATO and the exigencies of its foreign and security policy. These changes underlined the SPD's decision to become a *Volkspartei*, explicitly appealing to as wide a spectrum of social groups as possible.

Nevertheless, left-wing positions were not entirely abandoned in some areas after 1959. Hessen-Süd and Schleswig-Holstein, for example, continued to represent the heartland of the old left, and for their pains were dubbed by contemporary party insiders 'Albania' and 'China'. There was also a 'New Left' position in the party centred on the *Sozialistischer Deutscher Studentenbund* (SDS) and the ideas of Professor Wolfgang Abendroth. The SDS had been soundly defeated at Bad Godesberg, and in July 1960 the SPD executive withdrew financial support from the organization, founding in its place the *Sozialdemokratischer Hochschulbund* (SDB) which it intended as a vehicle for recruiting academics into the SPD in sharp contrast to the SDS's preferred activity as a faction primarily concerned with developing critiques of official party policy.

Subsequently, in November 1961, the leaders of the SDS and some of their prominent supporters, including Wolfgang Abendroth, were expelled from the SPD.[3] Cast out of the mainstream of West German politics, the SDS nevertheless remained influential in student politics. In the years between 1961 and 1965, this was largely a matter of providing an audience for, and disseminating the ideas of, the Frankfurt School and the recently published *Frühschriften* of Karl Marx. Things began to change from the mid 1960s when Herbert Wehner succeeded in taking the party in an unexpected direction. The most influential strategist in the SPD, Wehner had long been convinced that whilst the Bad Godesberg programme was a necessary condition, it was not sufficient in itself to ensure the SPD's return to power. In his view, the SPD would have to enter a coalition with one of the governing parties in order to demonstrate to the voter that it was *regierungsfähig* at federal level. This strategy was accepted by the party leadership after 1961, and the SPD became, in the phrase coined at the time, a *Regierungspartei im Wartesaal*. Nevertheless, sharp differences of view persisted as to whom the SPD should consider as a suitable coalition partner. Wehner favoured the CDU/CSU, while Brandt favoured the FDP. When the CDU/CSU government of Ludwig Erhard faltered in 1966, this coalition strategy was put to the test and Wehner's analysis prevailed: the Grand Coalition of CDU/CSU and SPD was formed in November 1966.

The decision of the SPD leadership to enter the Grand Coalition served to undermine the party's legitimacy in the eyes of many of its younger and more active supporters, alienating also many potential supporters in the process. In this sense, '1968' in Germany can be said to have begun in 1966, just as the seeds of what was to become the *Außerparlamentarische Opposition* (APO) were sown well before the formation of the Grand Coalition. Leading figures in the SDS had long been associated with critiques of representative democracy, but the formation of the Grand Coalition brought them support from some of the most fervent adherents of representative democracy inside the SPD itself. For the latter were outraged by what they perceived as the manipulation and betrayal of social democratic principles. An emerging alliance between the SDS and disaffected members of the SPD was strengthened by what was felt to be a climate of growing authoritarianism in the country at large. This phenomenon had already been evident in the hostile response to Ludwig Erhard's concept of the 'formierte Gesellschaft', but it was the violent events surrounding the visit of the

Shah of Iran to West Berlin in early June 1967, together with the decision of the Grand Coalition to grasp the nettle of introducing the controversial *Notstandsgesetze*, that led to the creation of a more coherent form of protest in the shape of the so-called APO. This mass protest movement incorporated at least four kinds of left-wing dissenters which have been well categorized by Kurt Shell:

1. Radical socialist democrats who wished to preserve and defend the achievements of the 'Rechtsstaat' and who saw no alternative to working for reform in and through the SPD. The APO clearly meant to them a means of applying pressure on the parties, parliament, and government. Though highly critical of German foreign policy toward the East (and generally favouring the recognition of the GDR), they opposed co-operation with the SED or any groups tainted with Stalinism.
2. Socialists, hostile to or despairing of the SPD, moderately critical or friendly toward the SED and the GDR, eager to form action. The constitutional framework remained imperative, either out of conviction or because of fear of legal prosecution.
3. Revolutionary Marxists, Trotzkyites, and Maoists hostile to the 'bureaucratic' socialist regimes of the Soviet Union and Eastern Europe, but affirming the need for organizational centralization and discipline. A socialist party was seen as useful only if it were determinedly revolutionary, 'the way the KPD (Communist Party of Germany) was till the middle of the twenties'. They rejected all forms of 'hippie' politics and 'political happenings' as lacking the necessary revolutionary seriousness.
4. The 'Anti-Authoritarian' Marxist-anarchist left, anti-parliamentary on ideological grounds, emphasizing direct action, cultivating spontaneity and libidinal liberation, aiming at a mass base not through formal organization but through joint commitment to action and revolutionary work 'at the base'. It was hostile to established Communist parties and to all organizational tendencies with bureaucratic implications.[4]

For the leadership of the SPD parliamentary party the gulf between the APO and social democratic policy was greater than that between the SPD and CDU/CSU. The strategy of the parliamentary party was to achieve power through the orthodox political system of the Bonn Republic; in contrast, the APO represented the German version of a transnational New Left which emphasized generational and participatory politics.

There were five main areas of disagreement between the APO and the SPD leadership which were expressed in divergent attitudes towards (a) the Grand Coalition, (b) US foreign policy, (c) the Emergency Laws, (d) representative government, and (e) political violence. These must be looked at in turn.

If the decision to enter the Grand Coalition in November 1966 was a severe shock to many party members, it was an even greater source of provocation to those further to the left of the SPD who normally voted for the Social Democrats. The party leadership attempted to deflect opposition by calling two special conferences in December 1966 and November 1967 to debate the issue. This strategy proved inadequate as neither of these conferences had any power to take decisions. The party leadership was consequently put under considerable pressure to bring forward the date of the biennial conference and to have a retrospective vote on the question as to whether or not it had been right to enter the Grand Coalition. At the subsequent conference in Nuremberg in March 1968 a resolution critical of the decision was rejected by a mere four votes (147 to 143) and the Party Executive resolution in favour was only adopted by 173 votes to 129. Such a narrow majority, especially in the year before a Federal Election, was almost unheard of in the SPD and it indicated the strength of feeling in the party against the Grand Coalition, a feeling intensified by the fact that the West German government was radically changed without reference to the people. Though the formation of the Coalition was clearly in accordance with the FRG's *Grundgesetz*, many argued that such political manoeuvrings were illegitimate and undemocratic. The antagonism towards the new government was very much stronger amongst ordinary party members and was universal in groups and individuals to the left of the SPD. Although the decision to enter into the Grand Coalition in fact paid off electorally for the SPD in the 1969 election, the furore surrounding it represented for a significant section of young, educated West Germans the first test of the legitimacy of the country's political institutions.

On the question of foreign policy, there was a deep gulf between the SPD leadership and the APO over American policy in Vietnam. In general, public trust in the United States had remained high in the Federal Republic and had been reinforced, especially for many younger West Germans, by the Presidency of John F. Kennedy. Indeed, as part of its strategy of demonstrating its fitness to govern, the SPD needed to be seen as a reliable partner by the United States. This was particularly true for Willy Brandt who, as Foreign Minister in the Grand Coalition, was taking his first cautious steps in developing a radically new *Ostpolitik*.

These considerations meant that the SPD leadership refused to condemn American policy in Vietnam and attempted to keep the topic off the SPD's agenda. The APO, on the other hand, was morally outraged both by the Vietnam War and by the SPD's failure to condemn it.

A precondition of the formation of the Grand Coalition had been an undertaking by the SPD to accept a set of Emergency Laws after having vigorously opposed all previous drafts. The APO was opposed in principle to the Emergency Laws which they took to be a symptom of growing authoritarianism. The laws were also opposed by the West German Trade Union Federation (DGB). The latter's opposition was led by IG Metall and its charismatic leader, Otto Brenner, who was principally worried by the impact of the Emergency Laws on the right to strike. Continuous demonstrations took place in 1968 against the proposed legislation, culminating in the *Sternmarsch* on Bonn of 11 May 1968. A major weakness of the APO's stance, however, was its inability to join forces with the trade unions who themselves objected to some of the groups involved in the organization of demonstrations like the *Sternmarsch*. Nevertheless, despite the noisy opposition and an often impassioned debate in the Bundestag, the Emergency Laws were successfully passed on the 30 May 1968 with fifty-three members of the SPD voting against the party line.

The SPD leadership and the bulk of SPD supporters were totally committed to the notion of representative government. This commitment was a direct product of their experience in the fatally fragmented Weimar Republic and the subsequent horrors of the Third Reich. Such constitutional loyalty had been further strengthened by the failure of earlier manifestations of extra-parliamentary protest such as the Paulskirche Movement and the anti-nuclear movement *Kampf dem Atomtod*.[5] In sharp contrast, there was widespread scepticism in the APO about the primacy of representative government. This was hardly surprising given the method by which the Grand Coalition had come about and the subsequent loss of all effective opposition in the Bundestag. There was thus much more enthusiasm among many members of the APO for strategies of confrontation and direct action. As the movement developed, however, disagreements surfaced about the utility of such a policy, with critical intellectuals like Günter Grass and Kurt Sontheimer in one camp and militant left-wing students in the other. The limitations of direct action were perhaps most succinctly outlined by Jürgen Habermas in a famous lecture at the so-called *Widerstandskongreß*, held in Hannover in June 1968, in which he pointed out how easily violence against property can turn into violence against people and warned against the dangers of 'linker Faschismus' – a provocative term which brought him the instant hostility of the SDS.[6] The disagreement between the APO and the main body of the SPD on what were acceptable means of political action could not have been deeper. The party's sensitivity on the issue was particularly underlined by its shocked reaction to the comparatively harmless revival of *Sprechchöre* by student adherents of the APO, for they reminded older members of similar tactics employed by Communists and Nazis in the traumatic past. Ironically, what was often seen as anti-authoritarian by the APO looked extremely authoritarian to those with long memories. The tactics developed in Berkeley and elsewhere had a quite different resonance when transplanted to a German historical and cultural setting. In this context, Willy Brandt, in general the most sympathetic of the SPD leadership to the goals of 1968, was appalled by a confrontation with young demonstrators at the 1968 Nuremberg Party Conference. 'Ich meine nicht, Ruhe sei die erste Bürgerpflicht', he declared, 'aber es ist doch wohl so, daß von der Freiheit der Meinungsäußerung einige Leute Gebrauch machen, um Intoleranz und Terror zu etablieren. Das muß man sehen, und das darf man nicht hinnehmen. Pöbel bleibt Pöbel, auch wenn junge Gesichter darunter sind.'[7] Such profound disagreements were particularly obvious in relation to the Springer Press. Although the SPD disliked the policies of Cäsar Axel Springer's newspapers with their strident right-wing ideology and, in the case of the gutter press such as *Bild-Zeitung*, their witch-hunt mentality, it did not feel able to endorse the violent blockades of Springer's publishing houses, initiated as a reaction to the attempted assassination of the student leader, Rudi Dutschke. There was also a difference of view on how to respond to the nascent right in the shape of the so-called *Nationaldemokratische Partei Deutschlands* (NPD). The SPD's tactic was to ignore the NPD as much as possible and defeat it electorally. The APO, on the other hand, wanted to confront the right and defeat it on the streets.

The background to these major areas of difference between the SPD and the APO was the SPD's preoccupation with marginalizing or neutralizing, both ideologically and in terms of organization, groups that stood to its left. This was the reason why the Party Executive had decided to expel the SDS in the first place. The tactic caused continual problems throughout this period. For example, it led to the expulsion from the SPD of Harry Ristock, Berlin's most prominent left-winger, in February 1968 for taking part in an anti-Vietnam demonstration in which non-SPD left-wing groups played a leading role. Similarly, the party leadership objected to the participation of SPD members in the *Sternmarsch* on Bonn precisely because of the involvement in its organization of such groups well to the left of the party. Many SPD members who nevertheless participated against party advice carried placards around their necks proclaiming 'Ich bin SPD-Mitglied' in order to emphasize the fact that they were breaking a party taboo. This was one of the aspects of unorthodox left-wing politics that, together with an increasing propensity to employ violence, most disturbed the leadership of the SPD. The pushing through of the controversial *Radikalenerlaß* in January 1972 can plausibly be seen as the party leadership's panicky reaction.

The emergence and development of the APO had one immediate, if short-lived, impact on the SPD: it harmed the party electorally. The party leadership had expected the economic recovery, initiated by the Grand Coalition and identified with the new Economics Minister, Karl Schiller, to benefit the SPD. The party was accordingly deeply disappointed by the unexpectedly poor result of the Land election in Baden-Württemberg in April 1968 in which the SPD vote declined from 37.3 per cent to 29 per cent. Baden-Württemberg is a Land with a markedly high percentage of students, and one lesson the party leadership drew from the result was that the SPD should attempt to absorb as many youthful members of the APO as possible. This policy was identified with Willy Brandt. Brandt's attitude was in tune with his long-term role of integrator and reconciler within the SPD. In this particular case, his strategy was also a product both of reflection on his own pre-war experiences and of dialogue with his radical sons who were both involved in the Student Movement. Brandt signalled his policy of opening the party to the APO during the debate on the Emergency Laws.[8] It was a policy which had fairly wide support in the Party Executive. Even the conservative Karl Schiller was moved to declare: 'Come in – mit allen Euren Methoden.'[9]

That such a rapprochement was necessary was clear when the impact of the APO on the SPD's Youth Organization (JUSO) is considered. For here the generational character of the APO was particularly significant. The JUSO has the status of an *Arbeitsgemeinschaft* within the SPD and all SPD members under the age of thirty-five can participate, though many choose not to do so. The reconstruction of the party after 1945, largely on the basis of an ageing pre-war membership, meant that there was a permanent need to recruit younger and more active cadres. The task of the JUSO thus became 'Nachwuchs zu suchen, heranzubilden und fit zu machen.'[10] It was astonishingly successful in fulfilling these aims. Indeed, every member of the Federal Executive of the Young Socialists between 1946 and 1967 later became a Member of the Bundestag.

In line with its role as a recruiting agency for the party, the JUSO had traditionally been fairly quiescent. Gert Börnsen provides an illuminating insight into the prevailing atmosphere in a faintly comic quotation from the Yearbook of the JUSO Unterbezirk of Obertaunus near Frankfurt: 'Im Januar 1965 fuhren Vertreter des Kreises mit dem Siegertanzpaar unserer letztjährigen Tanzveranstaltung nach Bonn. Der Genosse Kurt Gscheidle hat uns durchs Bundeshaus geführt. Als Zuhörer konnten wir an einer Bundestagssitzung teilnehmen. Bei Kaffee und Kuchen – nachdem wir vorher das Erich-Ollenhauer-Haus besuchten – klang dieser schöne Tag aus.'[11] Other activities during the year included an extended study of Molière's *Le Malade imaginaire* (with a visit to the theatre), a discussion about water supplies to the Obertaunus and a visit to the building site of the new Frankfurt metro. This benign picture changed rapidly with the SPD's decision to join the Grand Coalition against which a number of JUSO branches spontaneously demonstrated. In particular, feelings against the Emergency Laws ran very high, and at the JUSO Congress in Frankfurt in May 1968, which coincided with the last stages of the legislative progress of the Laws, the delegates put Helmut Schmidt, as parliamentary party leader and representative of the Party Executive, under considerable pressure – an experience that Schmidt, himself a former JUSO leader, neither liked nor ever forgot.

The Young Socialists also began to change at the local level. For although many supporters of the APO were not members of the SPD, they nevertheless took part in JUSO activities and exerted considerable influence. Indeed, a survey carried out by the JUSO itself at the end of 1968 indicated that in two-thirds of the branches, a quarter of the JUSO were not party members. The change in JUSO activity was particularly visible in Frankfurt and Berlin. In Frankfurt local Members of the Bundestag were visited by groups of Young Socialists in trucks with searchlights in the middle of the night in the weeks before the decision was to be taken on the Emergency Laws and asked to explain how they intended to vote. Young Socialists started to contest the candidacies of sitting Members. For example, Karsten Voigt stood against Georg Leber, and at its Federal Conference in Munich in December 1969, Peter Corterier, the JUSO Chairman and a supporter of the Party Executive, was voted out of office. Hans-Jürgen Wischnewski, the *Bundesgeschäftsführer*, was not even allowed to deliver his speech setting out the position of the Party Executive.

However, if the high point of the APO movement came in the early summer of 1968, the invasion of Czechoslovakia by Warsaw Pact troops in August, which put a violent end to the 'Prague Spring', exposed fundamental divisions within the APO in its attitude towards the Soviet Union. In this context and in pursuit of Brandt's policy of reconciliation, the SPD held a special conference for its Youth Organization in January 1969. The conference revealed a fair degree of misunderstanding and suspicion between the representatives of the youth wing and the party leadership which was not surprising given the latter's ruthless treatment of the SDS earlier in the decade. Nevertheless, with the APO running out of steam and beginning to disintegrate under the weight of its internal contradictions, it was perhaps not surprising that the majority of its members responded to Willy Brandt's invitation to support the SPD, particularly once it had become clear that the Grand Coalition would not be reconstituted after the 1969 election. A small minority around Ulrike Meinhof and Andreas Baader, however, became so pessimistic about the prospects for change in the Federal Republic that they went on to embrace a widespread campaign of urban terrorism, a discussion of which would go beyond the confines of this essay.

The long-term impact of the APO and of the radicalized JUSO on the SPD is a much more complex phenomenon to judge and its ramifications are still being worked out. But as far as the JUSO was concerned, its influence on the SPD in the early 1970s was mixed. For example, its attempt to introduce more participatory mechanisms, like the imperative mandate, whereby representatives would be tied to the views of the grassroots membership, failed. On the other hand, the JUSO's declared attempt to undertake, in Rudi Dutschke's words, 'den langen Marsch durch die Institutionen' led to a marked increase in factionalism within the SPD itself as the right wing organized itself to counter the challenge. The JUSO also scored significant victories at the municipal level, for example, in Munich and Frankfurt, but failed in the short term at the federal level, while still creating considerable difficulties for the party leadership. In the longer term, the Young Socialists of 1968, despite their radicalism, proved almost as successful as their more conformist predecessors in gaining seats in the Bundestag.

With the loss of Brandt's conciliatory presence as Chancellor and the arrival of Helmut Schmidt as Chancellor, the ideas of 1968 appeared to be initially defeated. Schmidt, for example, did not deign to disguise his contempt for the representatives of such ideas. For him the 1968 generation was composed of no more than 'Spinner'. Willy Brandt remained as Party Chairman and in this role continued to foster the careers of his 'Enkel', Gerhard Schröder and Oskar Lafontaine, both of whom had emerged from the 1968/JUSO milieu. The brusque rejection of their arguments for more participation and for improving the quality of the environment impelled a number of SPD members to leave the party altogether, and these disillusioned individuals went on to play a leading role in establishing the Greens. And it was the Greens who took forward many of the issues that define the notion of '1968': they were against hierarchy and bureaucracy; they were for spontaneity and grassroots democracy. Their emergence as a coherent political force and their clearance of the 5 per cent hurdle to enter the Bundestag in 1983 had, and continues to have, a pervasive impact on the SPD.

For much of the time between 1982 and 1998 the existence of the Greens robbed the SPD of considerable sections of their natural support and thus heightened the SPD's strategic dilemma. The ensuing frustration led a number of the most prominent '68ers', including Norbert Gansel, Volker Hauff, Wolfgang Roth and Karsten Voigt, to leave federal politics altogether. In Gerhard Schröder's new government, however, other individuals shaped by the experience of 1968, now occupy some of the most prominent positions. Gerhard Schröder himself, Joschka Fischer, Oskar Lafontaine (until his abrupt departure) and Herta Däubler-Gmelin, for example, were all youthful participants in the debates of 1968. Indeed, Otto Schily, the Interior Minister, was closely identified with radical tendencies in 1968 and later defended Baader and Meinhof. During the 'long march through the institutions' these younger politicians have shed much of the ideological baggage associated with 1968, but some distinct generic factors remain. For example, they do not have the same intimate relationship with the United States as their predecessors in previous Bonn governments. They also possess a strong belief in the possibilities of change. In part, this readiness to contemplate change reflects their attitude towards historical experience. For the characteristic '68ers' belong to a post-war generation which escaped the traumatic effects of the defeat of 1945 and the debilitating shame of the Holocaust. This makes them impatient with the constraining effects of history and partly explains Chancellor Schröder's readiness to talk in terms of German rather than European interests. Paradoxically, the '68ers', who were originally part of a world-wide post-national movement of the left, may thus be perceived – from the outside at least – as helping to shape the most *German* of post-war governments. This process is taking place in a unified German state that many of them did not in fact welcome. The 1968 generation had little first-hand knowledge of, or interest in, the German Democratic Republic. Twenty-one years later, opinions were sharply divided: some disliked the GDR's rigidly bureaucratic character and detested the Stasi that underpinned it; others wanted the East German state preserved as a socialist alternative to the Federal Republic. Very few shared the impassioned enthusiasm of Willy Brandt and his generation for a united Germany which could face the world with a newly discovered self-confidence. Ironically enough, their critical distance to the emergence of a unified Germany was shared by Günter Grass, their most articulate opponent in 1968.

The tensions about goals and methods of political action, which were so characteristic of the APO in 1968 and made a major contribution to its early demise, have also played a striking role in the new government. The positions and values taken by themselves cannot, however, be simply read off from the views the members of the new governing coalition held in 1968. Otto Schily, for example, has proved firm on law and order and Joschka Fischer has strongly supported continuity in German European policy and has fully backed NATO's intervention in Kosovo. His only concession to radicalism has been his advocacy of 'no first use' in NATO nuclear policy, a stance which, given the known views of other Alliance members, comes close to a symbolic gesture. There have, however, been two noticeable fault lines, with the first running through the SPD.

Chancellor Schröder, who achieved prominence in national politics in 1968 as Chairman of the JUSO, was by the time of his entry into government in 1998 convinced of the need to develop social democracy in a more business-friendly direction. This created sharp tensions with Oskar Lafontaine, himself a former JUSO leader in the Saarland, who wished to pursue a more orthodox social democratic policy which assumed a much greater role for political as against economic forces, that is, the continuation of social protection and fewer concessions to business. Lafontaine's resignation as Finance Minister and Party Chairman on 11 March 1999 and Schröder's decision to run for the party chairmanship himself allow him to move the Party in a more Blairite direction. This course is likely to provoke dissension in the Party where most office-holders have retained more of the ideas of 1968 than the Chancellor. Only two-thirds of the *Präsidium* voted in favour of the Chancellor's decision to seek the Chairmanship and his adoption at the Extra-Ordinary Party Meeting on 12 April was less than overwhelming.

The second fault line, of course, involves the Greens. Very many of the original Greens had personal biographies which led from '1968' into the SPD where they then became disillusioned with the Party's bureaucratic policies and methods. This impatience was widely felt even during the Helmut Schmidt government and was most brutally expressed by Oskar Lafontaine, who suggested that Schmidt possessed merely 'sekundäre Tugenden' such as might have been shared by a concentration camp guard. Only a minority, however, left to form the Greens, and the Greens who entered the new government were much closer to the norms and values of the established political class in Bonn than the 'anti-party' party of 1983, led by Petra Kelly. Nevertheless, considerable differences of policy and *Parteiverständnis* remained. The Greens continue to bear more obviously the imprint of 1968 than the SPD. The post-national and cosmopolitan legacy of 1968 is, for instance, reflected in the Greens' proposals for a massive extension of German citizenship. The other distinctive Green policy position – on nuclear energy – though an issue that came to the fore well after 1968, is in its rejection of expert scientific authority and the use of mass protest demonstrations, a technique which built on characteristic 1968 foundations.

The massive rejection of the Greens' ideas on citizenship in the Hessen Land elections of February 1999, and the failure of the Greens' policy of instant exit from nuclear energy and an end to nuclear reprocessing, which culminated in a disavowal by the Chancellor, have left the Greens with little chance of realizing their most cherished policies. These defeats were recognized by the Environment Minister, Jürgen Trittin, who, in March 1999, talked of 'the end of the Red–Green reform project'. He accompanied this remark with the suggestion that the Greens should contemplate in the long run a coalition with the CDU/CSU. This would tend to indicate that the legacy of 1968 in the Greens at governmental level is now significantly reduced. It remains to be seen whether this is true of their supporters who are still much more able to express grassroots opinion than the SPD which operates on a principle of upward delegation, a form of organization precisely designed to contain the grass roots. The result of the ill-tempered Bielefeld Conference of the Greens in May 1999 – which was called to debate the Kosovo crisis and at which the policy line of the Foreign Minister, Joschka Fischer, was supported – indicates that even here the legacy of 1968 is wearing thin.

The record of the first few months of the Schröder government has uncanny echoes of 1968. A number of its most prominent members, like Oskar Lafontaine and Jürgen Trittin, vastly underestimated the constraining effect on their political freedom of manoeuvre by established political and economic structures. There was also a noticeable lack of willingness to accept the necessary disciplines of government and to keep in line with other colleagues. Both Lafontaine and Trittin had significant experience of government, but their limitations were cruelly exposed when they moved from the provincial to the national stage.

Internationally, the legacy of 1968 is probably more of a handicap than an advantage in the wider world of the centre left. The experience of 1968 radicalism followed by a political career in the SPD is without obvious parallel elsewhere in Western Europe. 1968 scarcely registered on the British political Richter scale, and those who had played a prominent role at LSE or Essex University were regarded with enormous suspicion by the Labour Party. The lack of organizational continuity on the French or Italian left excludes any obvious crossovers in experience. The legacy of 1968 provides an uncertain aid in the battle of ideas on the centre left. Clinton and Blair owe much of their success to the way in which they have been able to construct platforms combining rights and responsibilities.[12] This is a formula which the '68ers', whose formative experience was almost exclusively about the assertion of rights, will find hard to emulate with conviction.

## Notes

1. Rob Burns and Wilfried van der Will, *Protest and Democracy in West Germany. Extra-Parliamentary Opposition and the Democratic Agenda* (London, 1988).
2. Some things did change, however. The relationship with the trade unions, although still close, was more distant than in Weimar. The women's movement, which had been a force in the Weimar SPD, failed to really get off the ground within the early post-war SPD. Why this was the case remains a fruitful area for research.
3. See Hartmut Soell, *Fritz Erler – Eine Politische Biographie* (Bonn, 1976), vol. 2, pp. 900–16.
4. Kurt Shell, 'Extra-parliamentary Opposition in Post-War Germany', *Comparative Politics* (1970), pp. 670–1.
5. See Eva Kolinsky, 'Democracy and Opposition in West Germany: Rearmament and Nuclear Weapons in the Fifties', *Contemporary German Studies*, 1 (1985), pp. 17–38.
6. See Shell, (*op. cit.*, p. 676).
7. Cited in K.H. Schonauer, *Die ungeliebten Kinder der Mutter/SPD. Die Geschichte der JUSOS von der Braven Parteijugend zur Innerparteilichen Opposition* (Bonn, 1982), p. 120.
8. See Willy Brandt in *Deutscher Bundestag. Protokoll der Verhandlungen, 30 Mai 1968*, pp. 9625–31.
9. Cited in Schonauer, *Die ungeliebten Kinder der Mutter/SPD*, p. 121.
10. Gert Börnsen, *Innerparteiliche Opposition (Jungsozialisten und SPD)* (Hamburg, 1969), p. 33.
11. *Ibid.*, p. 68.
12. See Anthony Giddens, *The Third Way. The Renewal of Social Democracy* (Cambridge, 1998).

# Wilfried van der Will: Publications

1999     'German Studies' in John Sandford (ed.), *Encyclopedia of German Studies*, London, 1999.

1998     *The Cambridge Companion to Modern German Culture* (edited with Eva Kolinsky), Cambridge, 1998.

'In Search of German Culture. An Introduction' (with Eva Kolinsky), in *The Cambridge Companion to Modern German Culture*, Cambridge, 1998, pp. 1–19.

'The Functions of *Volkskultur*, Mass Culture and Alternative Culture', in *The Cambridge Companion to Modern German Culture*, pp. 153–71.

1997     'From the 1940s to the 1990s: The Critical Intelligentsia's Changing Role in the Political Culture of the Federal Republic', *Debatte. Review of Contemporary German Affairs*, 5, 1 (1997), pp. 25–48.

1995     'Die Bedeutung der britischen Reedukationspolitik für die Entwicklung der politischen Kultur in Deutschland' in *Aus der Geschichte lernen?* Vorträge einer Ringvorlesung der Christian-Albrechts Universität zu Kiel, Kiel, 1995, pp. 123–43

'Culture and the Organisation of National Socialist Ideology 1933–1945', in Rob Burns (ed.), *German Cultural Studies*, Oxford/New York, 1995, pp. 101–45.

'The Federal Republic 1968 to 1990: From the Industrial Society to the Cultural Society' (with Rob Burns), in *German Cultural Studies*, 1995, pp. 257–323.

1994     'Aspects of the Neo-Picaresque in 20th-Century German Literature', in T. Dadson, R. Oakley and P. Odber de Baubeta (eds), *New Frontiers in Hispanic and Luso-Brazilian Scholarship*, Lampeter, 1994, pp. 481–500.

'The Embattled Intellectual', in Michael Butler (ed.), *The Narrative Fiction of Heinrich Böll*, Cambridge, 1994, pp. 21–48.

'Fürsorgliche Belagerung: The Citizen and the Surveillance State', in *The Narrative Fiction of Heinrich Böll*, pp. 219–38.

1993     'Nietzsche and Postmodernism', in K. Ansell-Pearson and H. Caygill (eds), *The Fate of the New Nietzsche*, Aldershot/Brookfield/Hong Kong/Sidney/Avebury, 1993, pp. 43–54.

'The Changing Responses to the Provocations of German Society. An Interview with Martin Walser conducted by Wilfried van der Will and Rob Burns', *Debatte. Review of Contemporary German Affairs*, 1, 1 (1993), pp. 47–64.

'Angst vor Deutschland? A Review of Recent Literature on the German Question' (with Rob Burns), *Debatte. Review of Contemporary German Affairs*, 1, 1 (1993), pp. 135–53.

1991     'E.Y. Meyer: The Construction of History through Literature', in Michael Butler and Malcolm Pender (eds), *Rejection and Emancipation. Writing in*

*German-speaking Switzerland 1945–1991*, New York/Oxford, 1991, pp. 141–55.

1990    *The Nazification of Art. Art, Design, Music, Architecture and Film in the Third Reich* (edited with Brandon Taylor), Winchester, 1990.
'Aesthetics and National Socialism', in *The Nazification of Art*, pp. 1–13.
'The Body and the Body Politic as Symptom and Metaphor in the Transition of German Culture to National Socialism', in *The Nazification of Art*, pp. 14–52.

1989    'The Republic of Letters and the State. Permutations of "Geist" and "Macht" in the Federal Republic Since the Early 1970s', in Keith Bullivant (ed.), *After the Death of Literature*, Oxford/New York/Munich, 1989, pp. 3–35.
'Nietzsche in America. Fashion and Fascination', *History of European Ideas*, vol. 11, 1989, pp. 1015–23.

1988    *Protest and Democracy in West Germany. Extra-Parliamentary Opposition and the Democratic Agenda* (with Rob Burns), London, 1988.

1987    'Approaches to Reality Through Narrative Perspectives in Uwe Johnson's Prose', in Keith Bullivant (ed.), *The Modern German Novel*, Leamington Spa/Hamburg/New York, 1987, pp. 171–95.
'Some Observations on the Language of Advertising in West Germany', in Eva Kolinsky (ed.), *The German Language Between Yesterday and Tomorrow*, Birmingham, 1987, pp. 29–37.

1986    'Die literarische Intelligenz und der Staat' in Hans-Joachim Althof *et al.* (eds), *Subjektivität – Innerlichkeit – Abkehr vom Politischen? Tendenzen der deutschsprachigen Literatur der 70er Jahre* (DAAD Dokumentationen und Materialien, no. 6), Bonn, 1986, pp. 1–18.
'The German Literary Intelligentsia and the Anti-Authoritarian Student Movement', *Contemporary German Studies* (Occasional Papers, no. 2), Glasgow, 1986, pp. 34–53.
'Arbeiterdichtung' (with Rob Burns); 'Arbeiterkultur'; 'Arbeiter-sängerbünde'; 'Arbeitersprechchor'; 'Arbeitertheater', in T. Meyer *et al.* (eds), *Lexikon des Sozialismus*, Cologne, 1986, pp. 48–9; 49–50; 51; 55–6; 56.

1985    'The Politics of Cultural Struggle: Intellectuals and the Labour Movement', in Anthony Phelan (ed.), *The Weimar Dilemma. Intellectuals in the Weimar Republic*, Manchester, 1985, pp. 162–201.

1984    'Kulturelles Leben in der Arbeiterbewegung' (with Rob Burns), in T. Meyer *et al.* (eds), *Lern- und Arbeitsbuch deutsche Arbeiterbewegung*, Bonn, 1984, pp. 317–36.
'The Nature of Dissidence in the GDR', in Ian Wallace (ed.), *The GDR in the 1980s* (GDR Monitor Special Series, no. 4), Dundee, 1984, pp. 31–44.

1983    'Ernst Bloch'; 'Else Lasker-Schüler'; 'Friedrich Nietzsche'; 'Hans Reichenbach'; 'Robert Walser'; 'Stefan Zweig', in A. Bullock and R.B. Woodings (eds), *The Fontana Bibliographical Companion to Modern Thought*, London/Oxford, 1983, pp. 77; 426; 555–6; 634; 799; 846.

1982    *Arbeiterkulturbewegung in der Weimarer Republik. Historisch-theoretische Analyse der kulturellen Bestrebungen der sozialdemokratisch organisierten Arbeiterschaft* (with Rob Burns), Berlin/Frankfurt am Main/Vienna, 1982.

*Arbeiterkulturbewegung in der Weimarer Republik. Texte – Dokumente – Bilder* (edited with Rob Burns), Berlin/Frankfurt am Main/Vienna, 1982.

'Johann Gottlob Fichte'; 'Friedrich Wilhelm Joseph Schelling'; 'Arthur Schopenhauer', in J. Wintle (ed.), *Makers of Nineteenth-Century Culture*, London, 1982, pp. 211–12; 552–4; 553–6.

1981    'Robert Musil', in J. Wintle (ed.), *Makers of Modern Culture*, London, 1981, pp. 374–5.

1980    'Working-Class Organisation and the Importance of Cultural Struggle' (with Rob Burns), *Capital and Class*, 10 (1980), pp. 161–74.

1979    'German Through Reading: Hitler's Era. An Invitation to admire Hitler in the Classroom?', *Searchlight*, 43 (1979), pp. 10–11.

1978    'Methoden und Forschungsprojekte im Bereich Literatursoziologie und Medienwissenschaft in Großbritannien. Eine kritische Darstellung des Centre for Contemporary Cultural Studies in Birmingham und des Centre for Mass Communication Research in Leicester', *Jahrbuch für internationale Germanistik*, Bern, 1978, pp. 27–45.

1976    'Ideology in Literary Analysis', in *The Study of German in England*, Bonn (DAAD), 1976, pp. 1–25.

1975    (ed.) *Workers and Writers*, Proceedings of the Conference on Present-Day Working-Class Literature in Britain and West Germany, Birmingham, 1975.

'Contemporary Working-Class Literature in West Germany and Britain', in Wilfried van der Will (ed.), *Workers and Writers*, Birmingham, 1975, pp. 1–18.

1973    'Deutsche sozialkritische Literatur an einer britischen Universität', *Neue Volkskunst*, 97 (1973), pp. 7–9.

1969    *Der deutsche Roman und die Wohlstandsgesellschaft* (German version of *The German Novel and the Affluent Society*, reworked and enlarged by Wilfried van der Will), Stuttgart, 1969.

'The Language Laboratory in Advanced Language Teaching: Gimmick or Challenge?', in *Innovations and Experiments in University Teaching Methods. A Report of the Proceedings of the Third Conference Organised by the University Teaching Methods Research Unit*, London, 1969, pp. 65–73.

'Name, Semeion, Energeia: Notes on the Permutations of Language Theories', in Siegbert Prawer *et al.* (eds), *Essays in German Language, Culture and Society*, London, 1969, pp. 211–30.

1968    *The German Novel and the Affluent Society* (with R. Hinton Thomas), Manchester, 1968.

1967    *Pikaro heute. Metamorphosen des Schelms bei Thomas Mann, Döblin, Brecht, Grass*, Stuttgart, 1967.

'Die Position des Intellektuellen in der deutschen Gesellschaft', in *Mitteilungen der Vereinigung ehemaliger Abiturienten des Gymnasiums Geldern*, 1967, pp. 19–25.

1966    'The Language Laboratory in Advanced Language Learning', *Modern Languages*, 47, 2 (1966), pp. 56–9.

1962    *Voraussetzungen und Möglichkeiten einer Symbolsprache im Werk Gerhart Hauptmanns*, Cologne, 1962.

# Tabula Gratulatoria

David Adshead
*University of Birmingham*

Nick Baker
*University of Birmingham*

Benedikt S. Benedikz
*University of Birmingham*

Elizabeth Boa
*University of Nottingham*

James T. Boulton
*University of Birmingham*

John Breuilly
*University of Birmingham*

Keith Bullivant
*University of Florida*

Rob Burns
*University of Warwick*

Michael Butler
*University of Birmingham*

Michael Caesar
*University of Birmingham*

Jon Clarke
*University of Southampton*

Paul Cooke
*University of Wales, Aberystwyth*

Máire Davies
*University of London*

Bill Dodd
*University of Birmingham*

Manfred Durzak
*University of Osnabrück*

Robert Evans
*University of Birmingham*

Frank Finlay
*University of Leeds*

Caroline Gay
*University of Birmingham*

Jonathan Grix
*University of Birmingham*

Hans J. Hahn
*Oxford Brookes University*

David Hill
*University of Birmingham*

Rodney H. Hilton
*University of Birmingham*

Robert Halsall
*Robert Gordon University*

Nigel Harris
*University of Birmingham*

David Holmes
*University of Oxford*

Charlie Jeffery
*University of Birmingham*

Martin Kane
*University of Kent at Canterbury*

John Klapper
*University of Birmingham*

Eva Kolinsky
*University of Wolverhampton*

Robert Leach
*University of Birmingham*

Johanna Liddle
*Birmingham City Council*

Hugh McLeod
*University of Birmingham*

Moray McGowan
*Trinity College Dublin*

Michael Minden
*University of Cambridge*

Günter Minnerup
*University of Birmingham*

Wolfgang Müller-Funk
*University of Birmingham*

John Osborne
*University of Warwick*

William E. Paterson
*University of Birmingham*

Malcolm Pender
*University of Strathclyde*

Michael Perraudin
*University of Sheffield*

Leon Pompa
*Edinburgh*

Siegbert and Helga Prawer
*University of Oxford*

T. J. Reed
*University of Oxford*

J. H. Reid
*University of Nottingham*

Nigel Reeves
*University of Aston*

Jens Röhrkasten
*University of Birmingham*

Margaret Rogers
*University of Surrey*

John Sandford
*University of Reading*

Richard Sheppard
*University of Oxford*

Robert Smith
*University of Birmingham*

Ronald Speirs
*University of Birmingham*

Bernard Standring
*University of Birmingham*

E. Stones
*University of Birmingham*

Erika Swales
*University of Cambridge*

Martin Swales
*University of London*

Dennis Tate
*University of Bath*

Brandon Taylor
*University of Southampton*

Werner Ustorf
*University of Birmingham*

Martin Watson
*De Montfort University*

Gordon C. Wells
*Coventry University*

**Chris Wickham**
*University of Birmingham*

**Philip Wiener**
*University of Birmingham*

**Ruth Whittle**
*University of Birmingham*

**Dennis Wood**
*University of Birmingham*

**George Edwards Library**
*University of Surrey*

**Main Library**
*University of Birmingham*

**The Library**
*Institute of Germanic Studies*
*University of London*